HOAX HUNTERS™

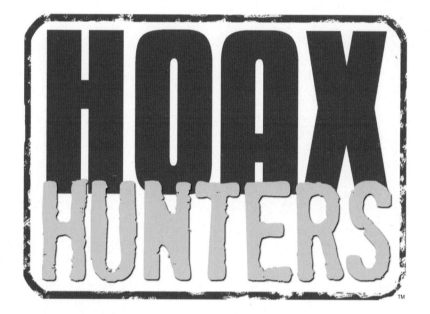

HOAX HUNTERS

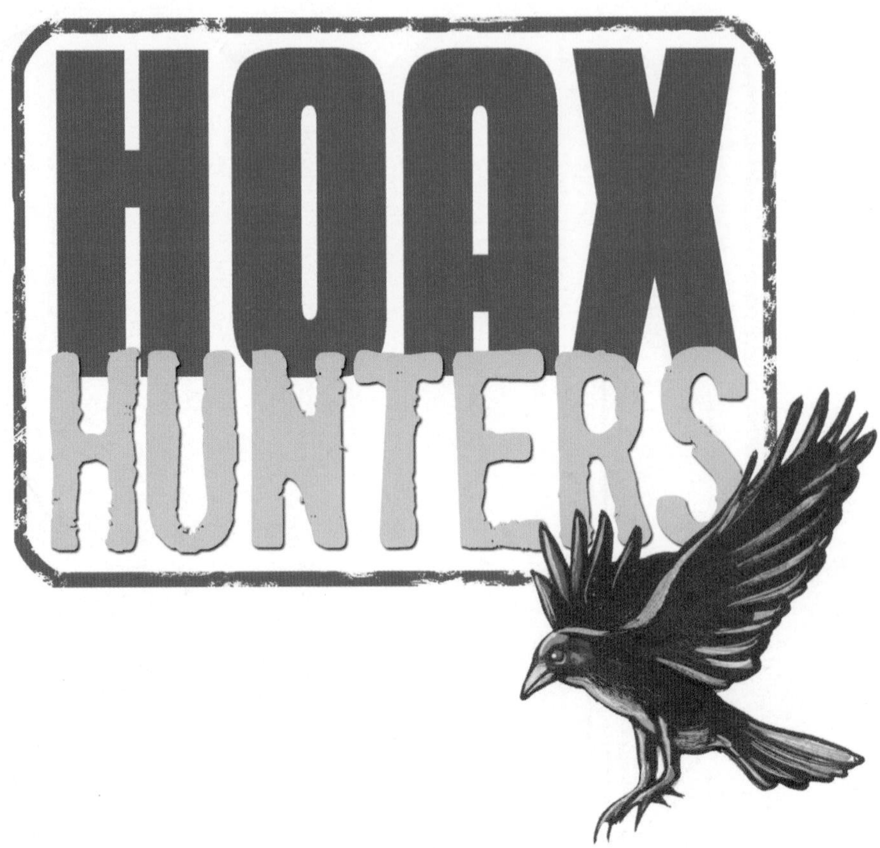

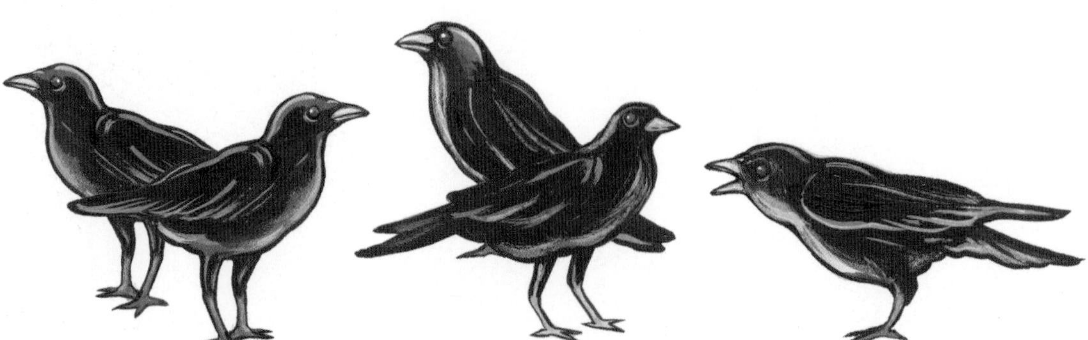

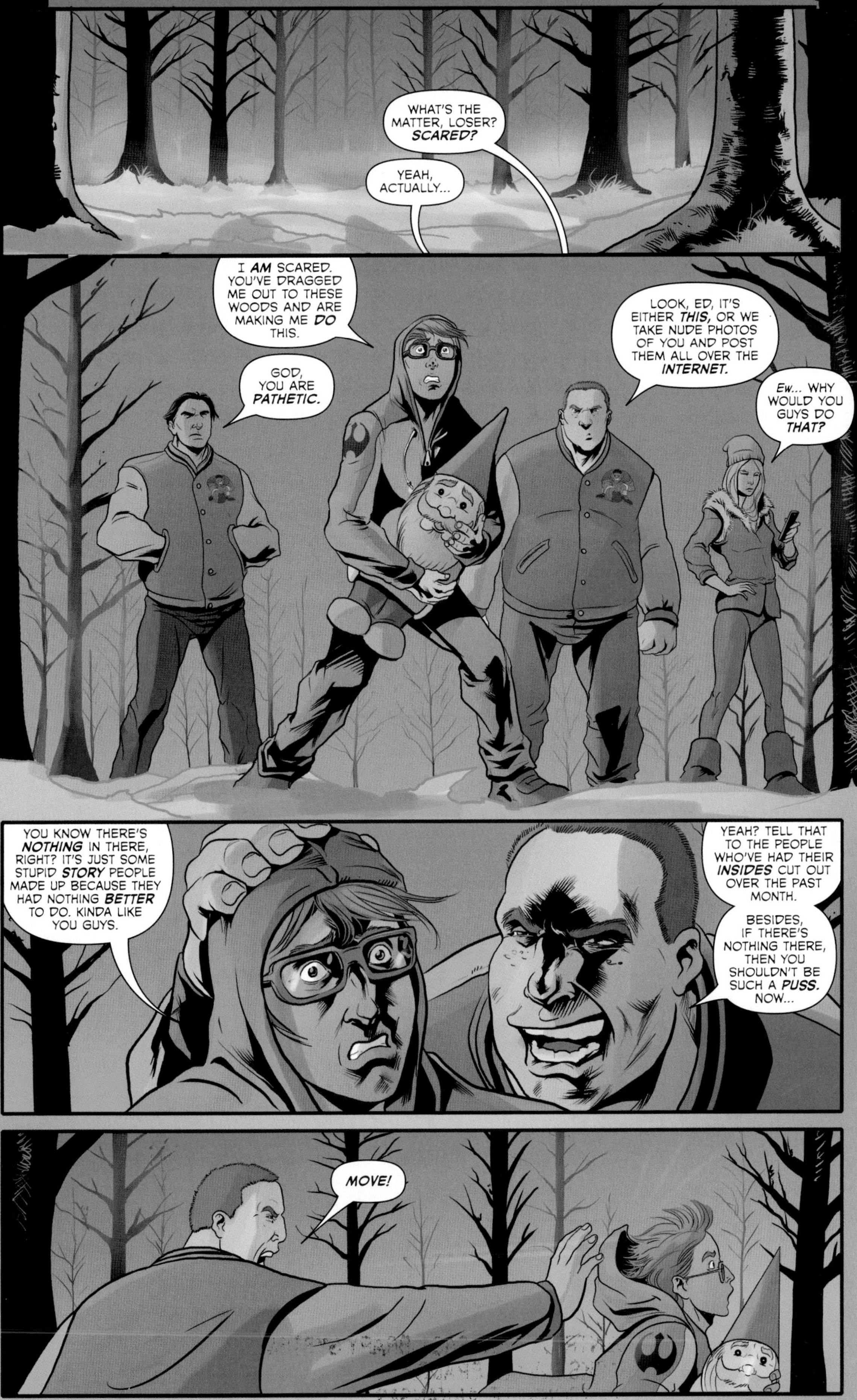
WHAT'S THE MATTER, LOSER? SCARED?
YEAH, ACTUALLY...
I AM SCARED. YOU'VE DRAGGED ME OUT TO THESE WOODS AND ARE MAKING ME DO THIS.
GOD, YOU ARE PATHETIC.
LOOK, ED, IT'S EITHER THIS, OR WE TAKE NUDE PHOTOS OF YOU AND POST THEM ALL OVER THE INTERNET.
Ew... WHY WOULD YOU GUYS DO THAT?
YOU KNOW THERE'S NOTHING IN THERE, RIGHT? IT'S JUST SOME STUPID STORY PEOPLE MADE UP BECAUSE THEY HAD NOTHING BETTER TO DO. KINDA LIKE YOU GUYS.
YEAH? TELL THAT TO THE PEOPLE WHO'VE HAD THEIR INSIDES CUT OUT OVER THE PAST MONTH.
BESIDES, IF THERE'S NOTHING THERE, THEN YOU SHOULDN'T BE SUCH A PUSS. NOW...
MOVE!

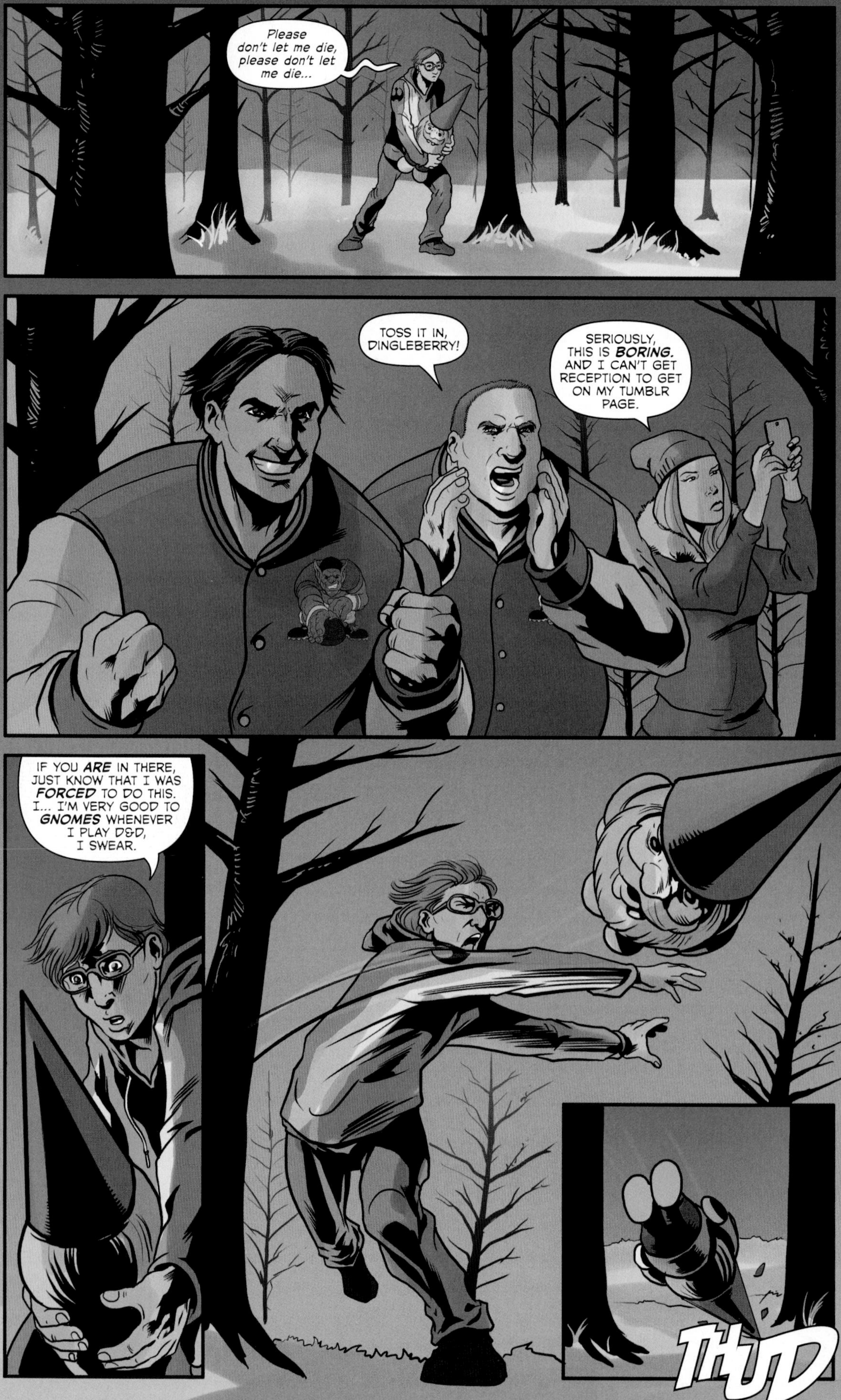
Please don't let me die, please don't let me die...
TOSS IT IN, DINGLEBERRY!
SERIOUSLY, THIS IS BORING. AND I CAN'T GET RECEPTION TO GET ON MY TUMBLR PAGE.
IF YOU ARE IN THERE, JUST KNOW THAT I WAS FORCED TO DO THIS. I... I'M VERY GOOD TO GNOMES WHENEVER I PLAY D&D, I SWEAR.
THUD

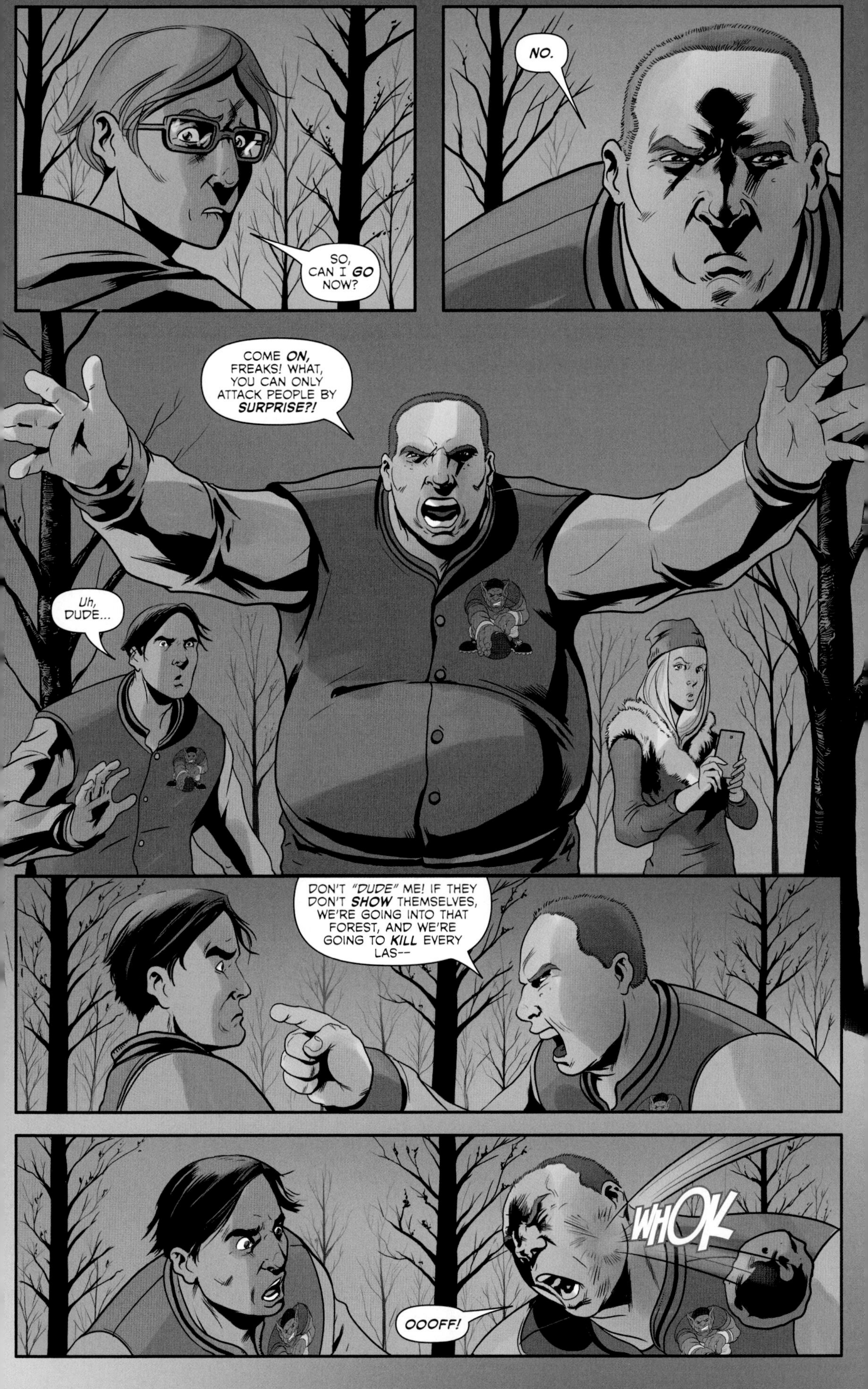
SO, CAN I GO NOW?
NO.
COME ON, FREAKS! WHAT, YOU CAN ONLY ATTACK PEOPLE BY SURPRISE?!
Uh, DUDE...
DON'T "DUDE" ME! IF THEY DON'T SHOW THEMSELVES, WE'RE GOING INTO THAT FOREST, AND WE'RE GOING TO KILL EVERY LAS--
WHOK
OOOFF!

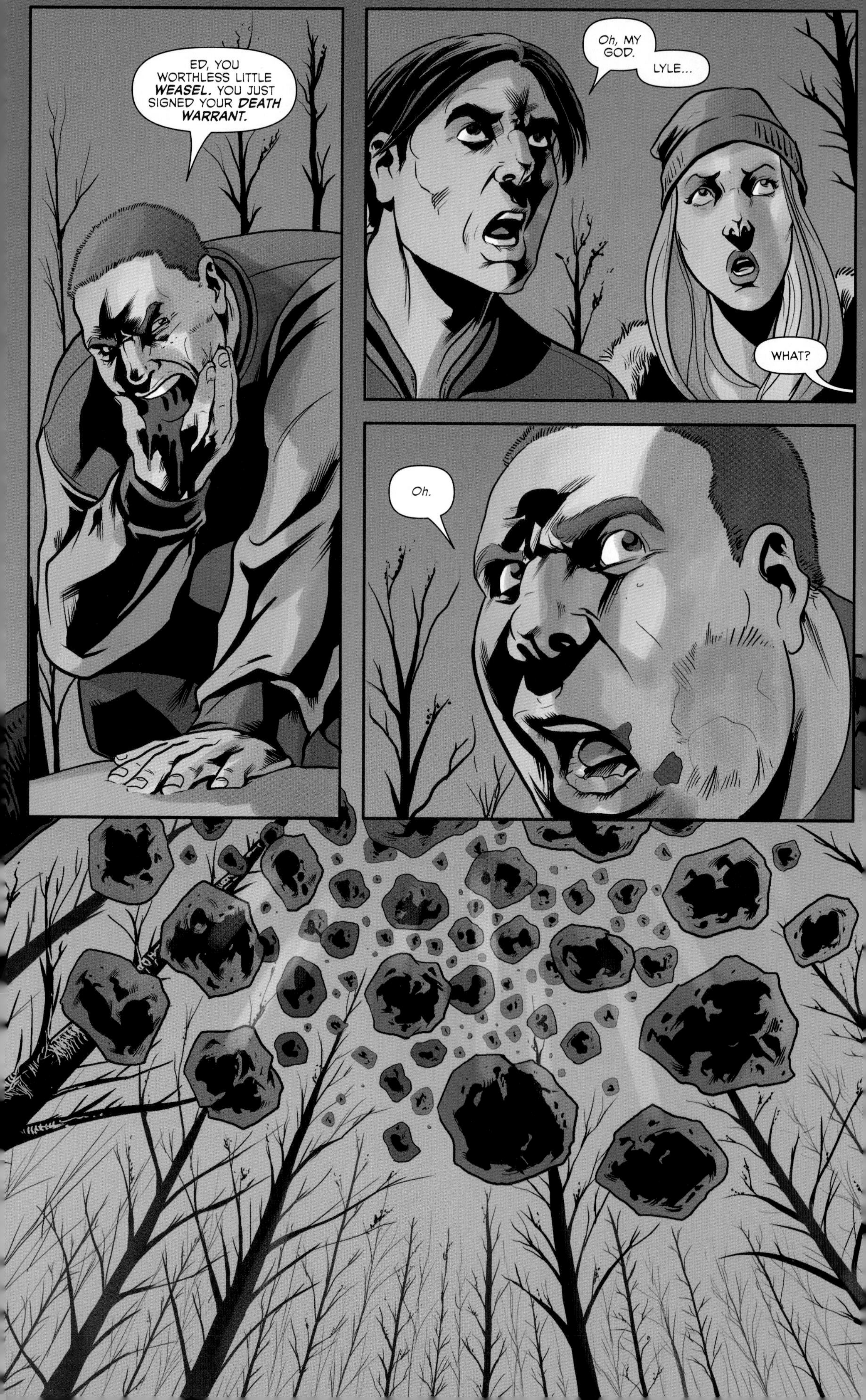
ED, YOU WORTHLESS LITTLE WEASEL. YOU JUST SIGNED YOUR DEATH WARRANT.
Oh, MY GOD.
LYLE...
WHAT?
Oh.

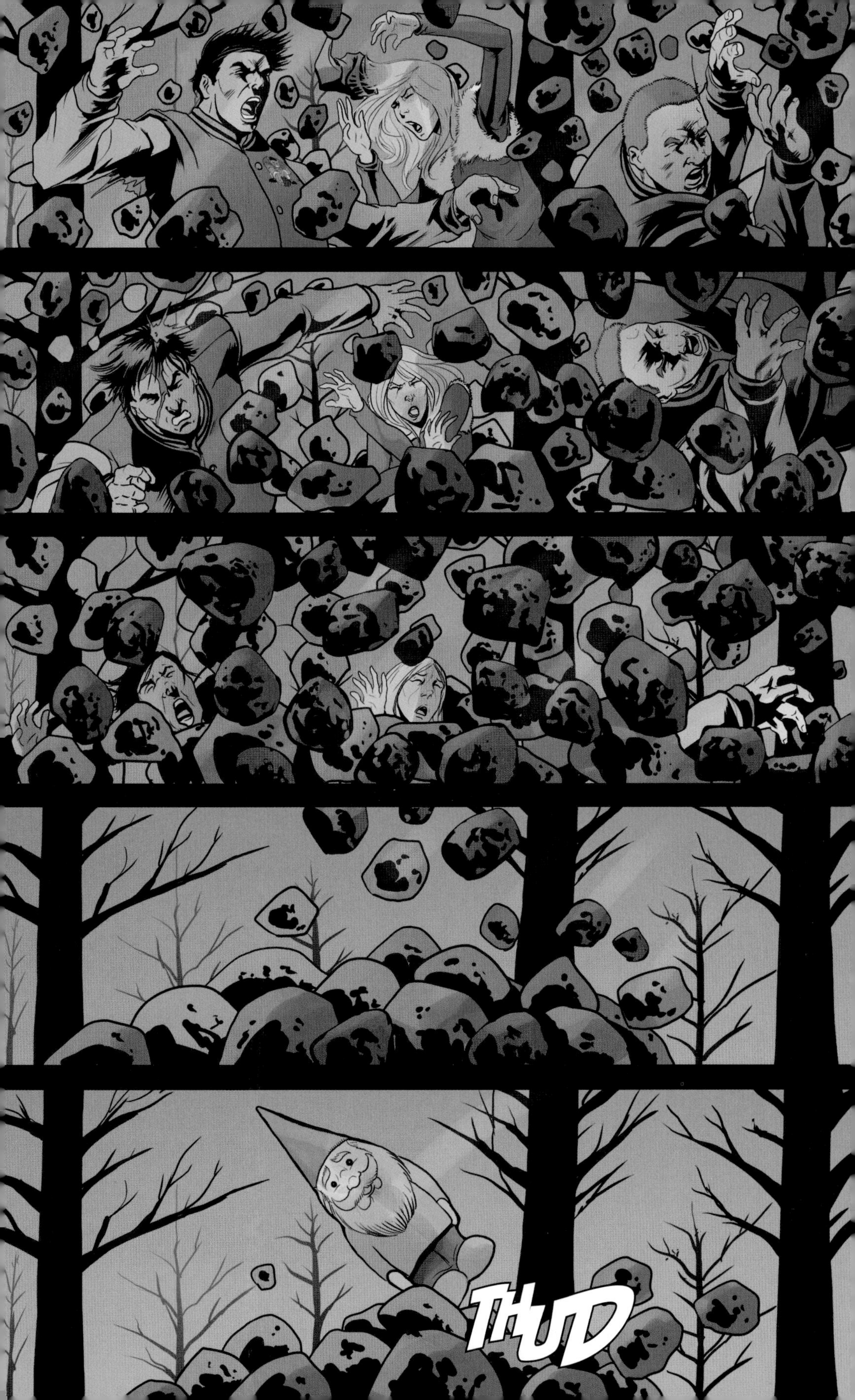
THUD

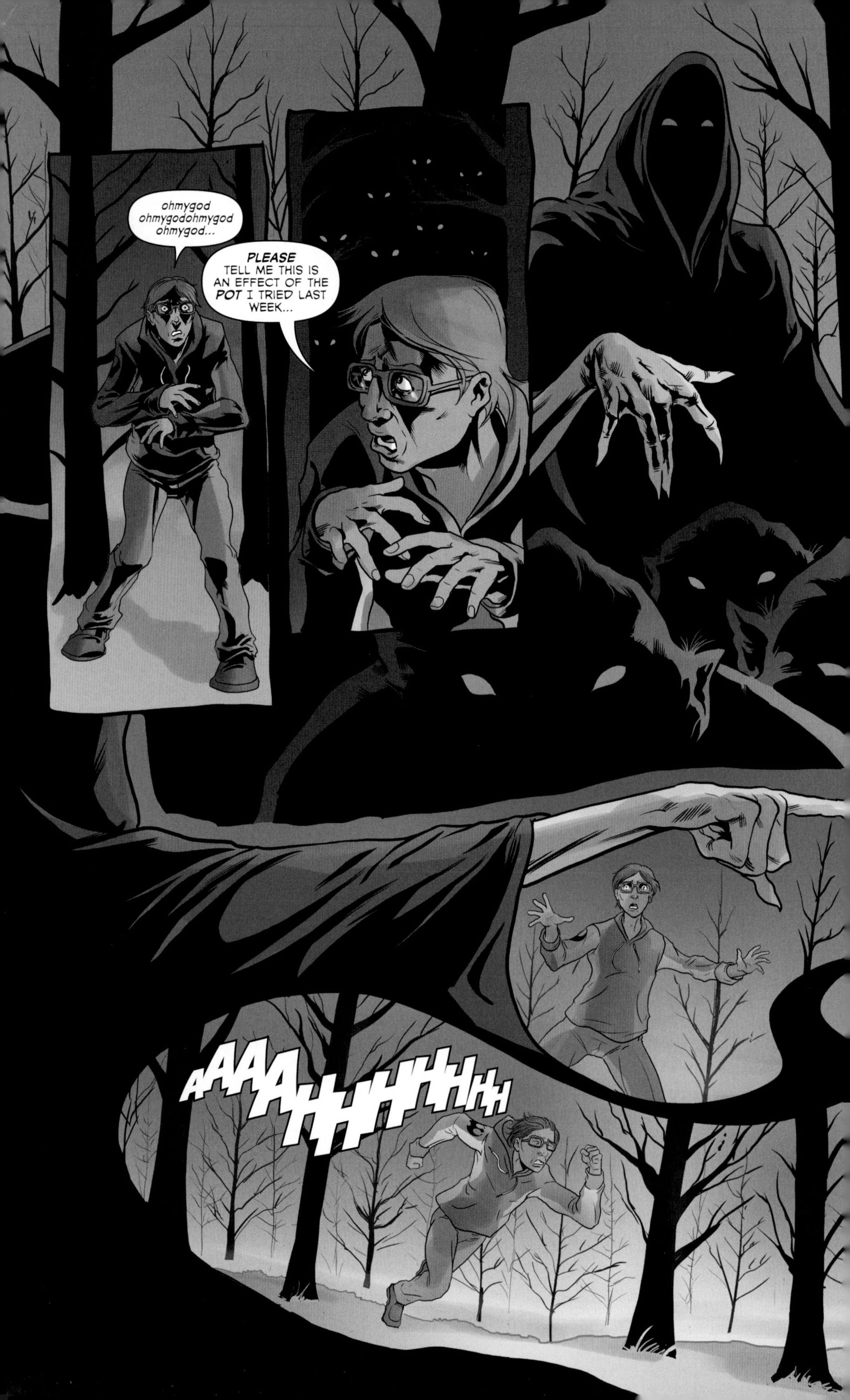
ohmygod
ohmygodohmygod
ohmygod...
PLEASE TELL ME THIS IS AN EFFECT OF THE POT I TRIED LAST WEEK...
AAAAHHHHHHHH

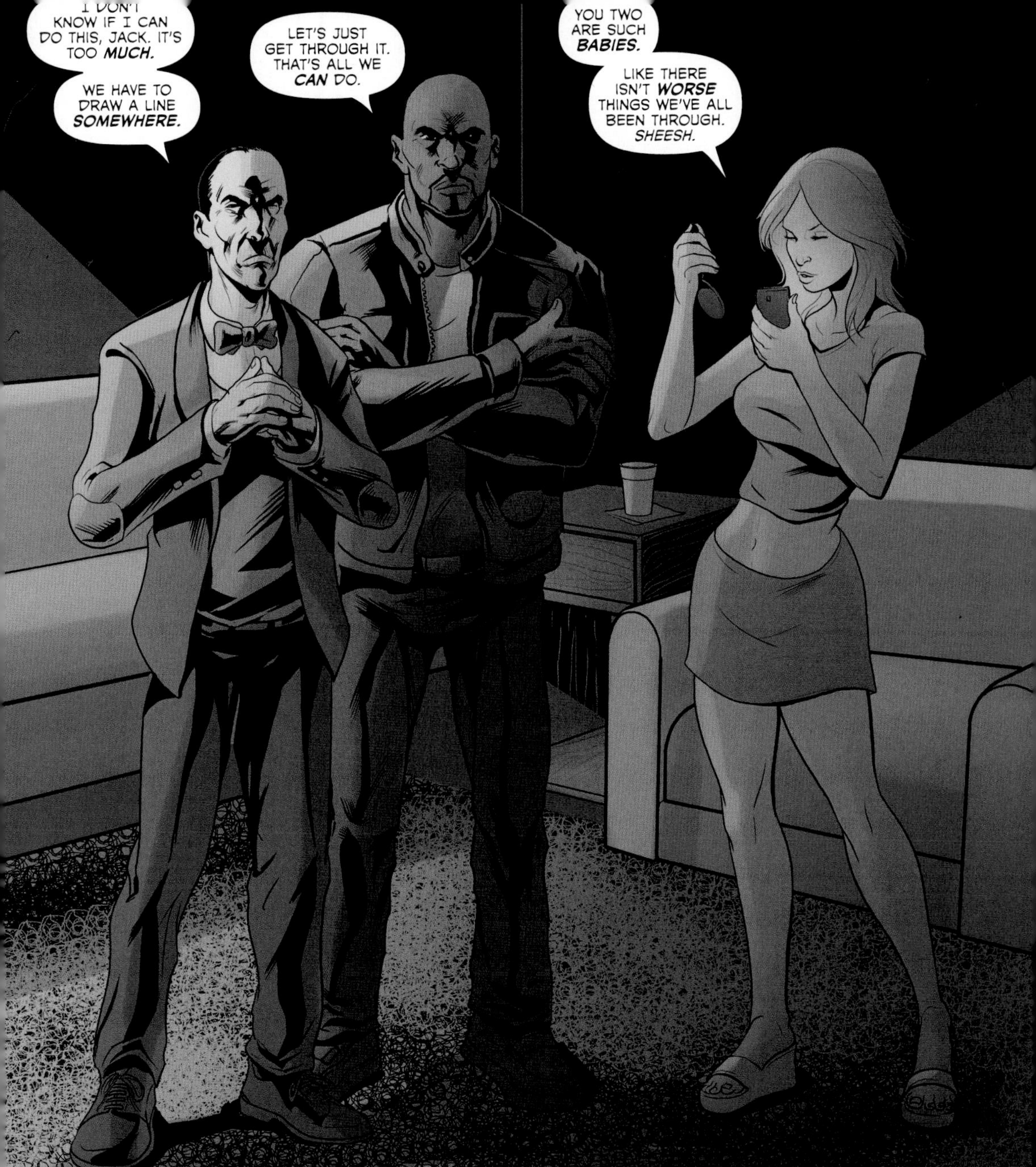
I DON'T KNOW IF I CAN DO THIS, JACK. IT'S TOO **MUCH.**
WE HAVE TO DRAW A LINE **SOMEWHERE.**
LET'S JUST GET THROUGH IT. THAT'S ALL WE **CAN** DO.
YOU TWO ARE SUCH **BABIES.**
LIKE THERE ISN'T **WORSE** THINGS WE'VE ALL BEEN THROUGH. *SHEESH.*

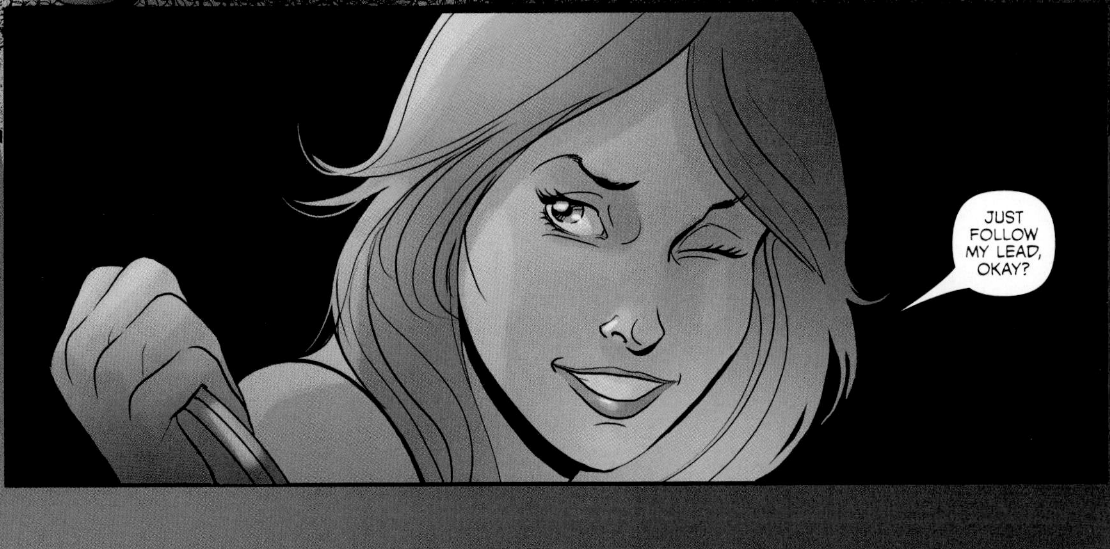
JUST FOLLOW MY LEAD, OKAY?

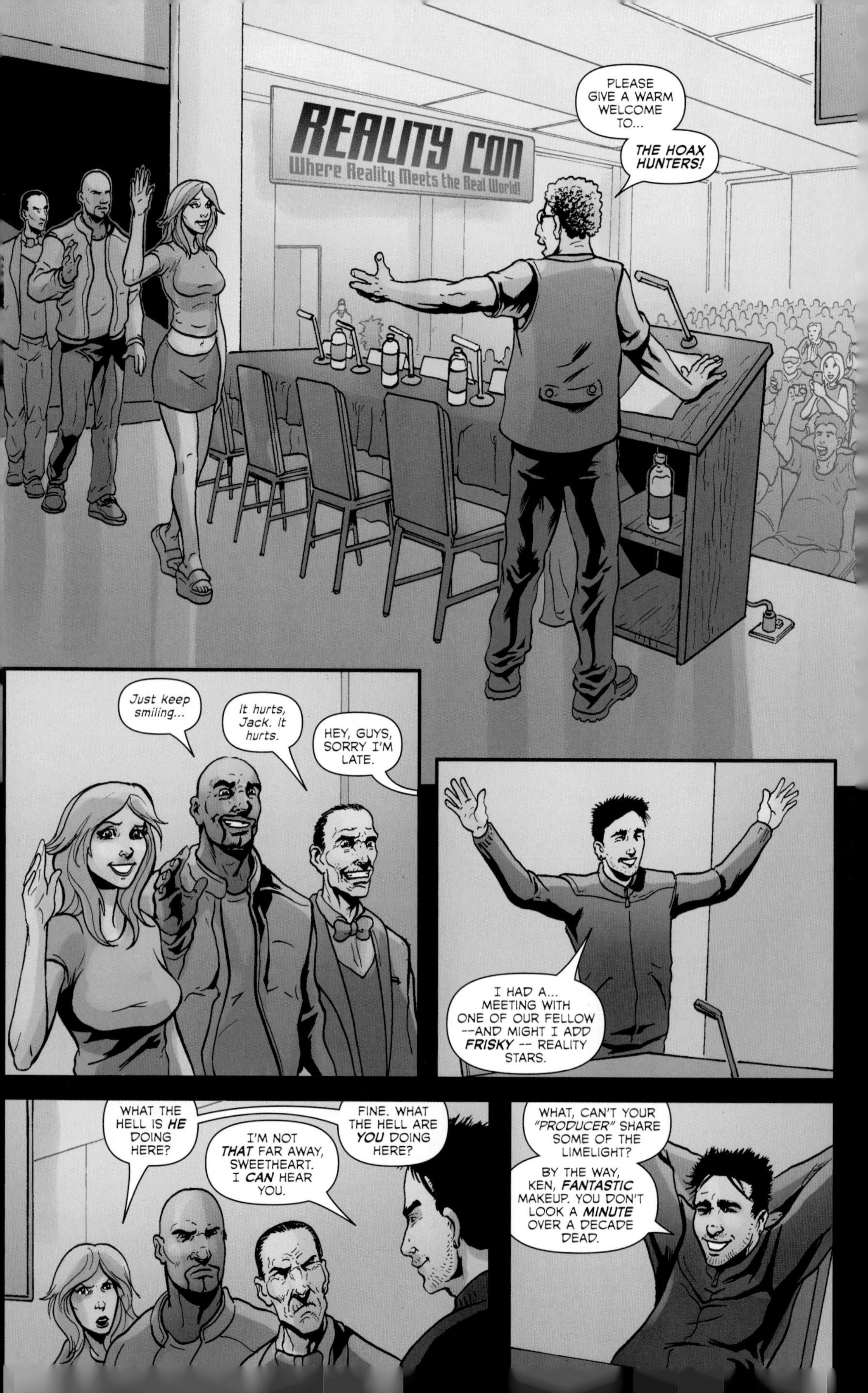
REALITY CON
Where Reality Meets the Real World!
PLEASE GIVE A WARM WELCOME TO...
THE HOAX HUNTERS!
Just keep smiling...
It hurts, Jack. It hurts.
HEY, GUYS, SORRY I'M LATE.
I HAD A... MEETING WITH ONE OF OUR FELLOW --AND MIGHT I ADD FRISKY -- REALITY STARS.
WHAT THE HELL IS HE DOING HERE?
FINE. WHAT THE HELL ARE YOU DOING HERE?
I'M NOT THAT FAR AWAY, SWEETHEART. I CAN HEAR YOU.
WHAT, CAN'T YOUR "PRODUCER" SHARE SOME OF THE LIMELIGHT?
BY THE WAY, KEN, FANTASTIC MAKEUP. YOU DON'T LOOK A MINUTE OVER A DECADE DEAD.

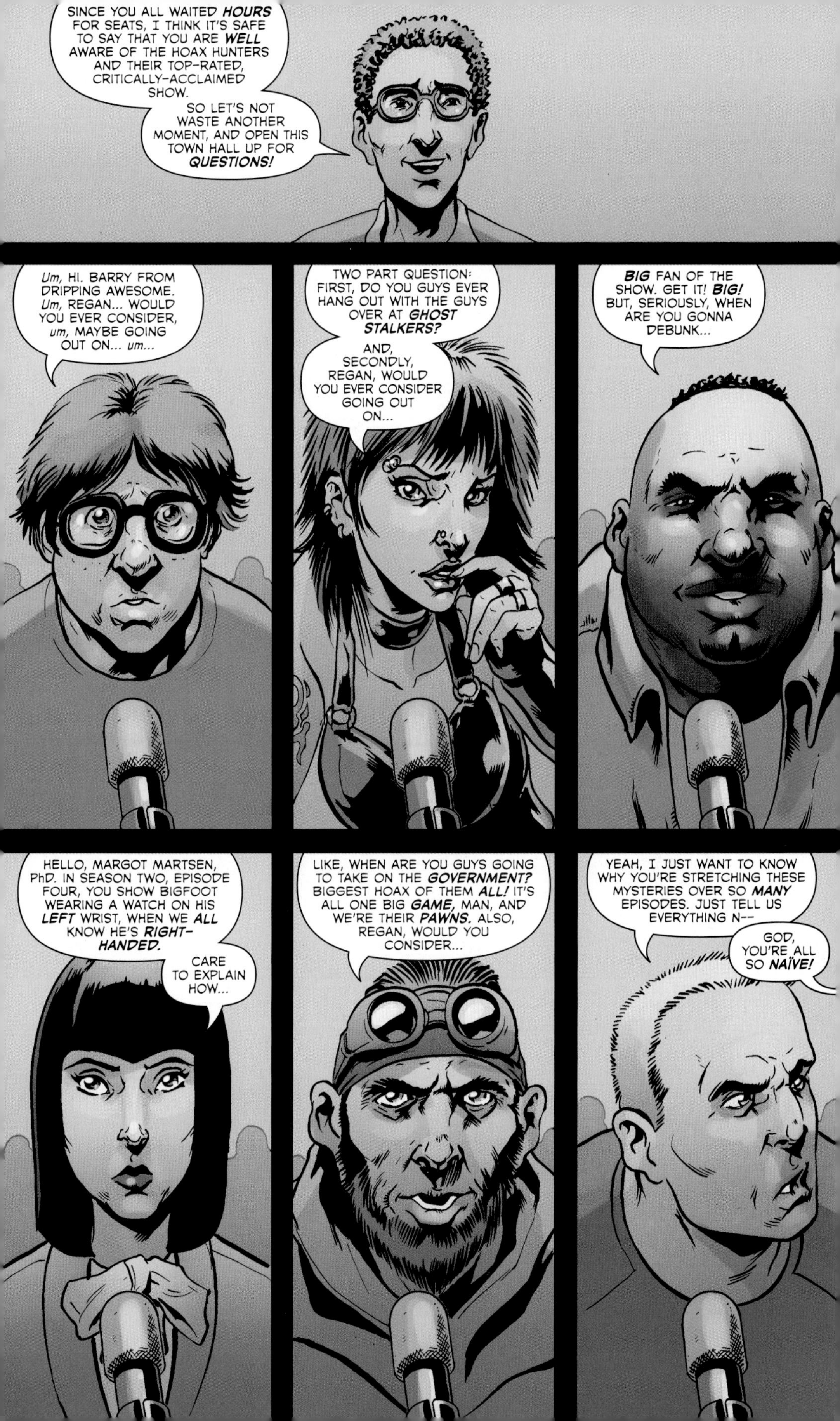
SINCE YOU ALL WAITED **HOURS** FOR SEATS, I THINK IT'S SAFE TO SAY THAT YOU ARE **WELL** AWARE OF THE HOAX HUNTERS AND THEIR TOP-RATED, CRITICALLY-ACCLAIMED SHOW.
SO LET'S NOT WASTE ANOTHER MOMENT, AND OPEN THIS TOWN HALL UP FOR ***QUESTIONS!***
Um, HI. BARRY FROM DRIPPING AWESOME. *Um*, REGAN... WOULD YOU EVER CONSIDER, *um*, MAYBE GOING OUT ON... *um*...
TWO PART QUESTION: FIRST, DO YOU GUYS EVER HANG OUT WITH THE GUYS OVER AT ***GHOST STALKERS?***
AND, SECONDLY, REGAN, WOULD YOU EVER CONSIDER GOING OUT ON...
BIG FAN OF THE SHOW. GET IT! ***BIG!*** BUT, SERIOUSLY, WHEN ARE YOU GONNA DEBUNK...
HELLO, MARGOT MARTSEN, PhD. IN SEASON TWO, EPISODE FOUR, YOU SHOW BIGFOOT WEARING A WATCH ON HIS ***LEFT*** WRIST, WHEN WE ***ALL*** KNOW HE'S ***RIGHT-HANDED.***
CARE TO EXPLAIN HOW...
LIKE, WHEN ARE YOU GUYS GOING TO TAKE ON THE ***GOVERNMENT?*** BIGGEST HOAX OF THEM ***ALL!*** IT'S ALL ONE BIG ***GAME,*** MAN, AND WE'RE THEIR ***PAWNS.*** ALSO, REGAN, WOULD YOU CONSIDER...
YEAH, I JUST WANT TO KNOW WHY YOU'RE STRETCHING THESE MYSTERIES OVER SO ***MANY*** EPISODES. JUST TELL US EVERYTHING N--
GOD, YOU'RE ALL SO ***NAÏVE!***

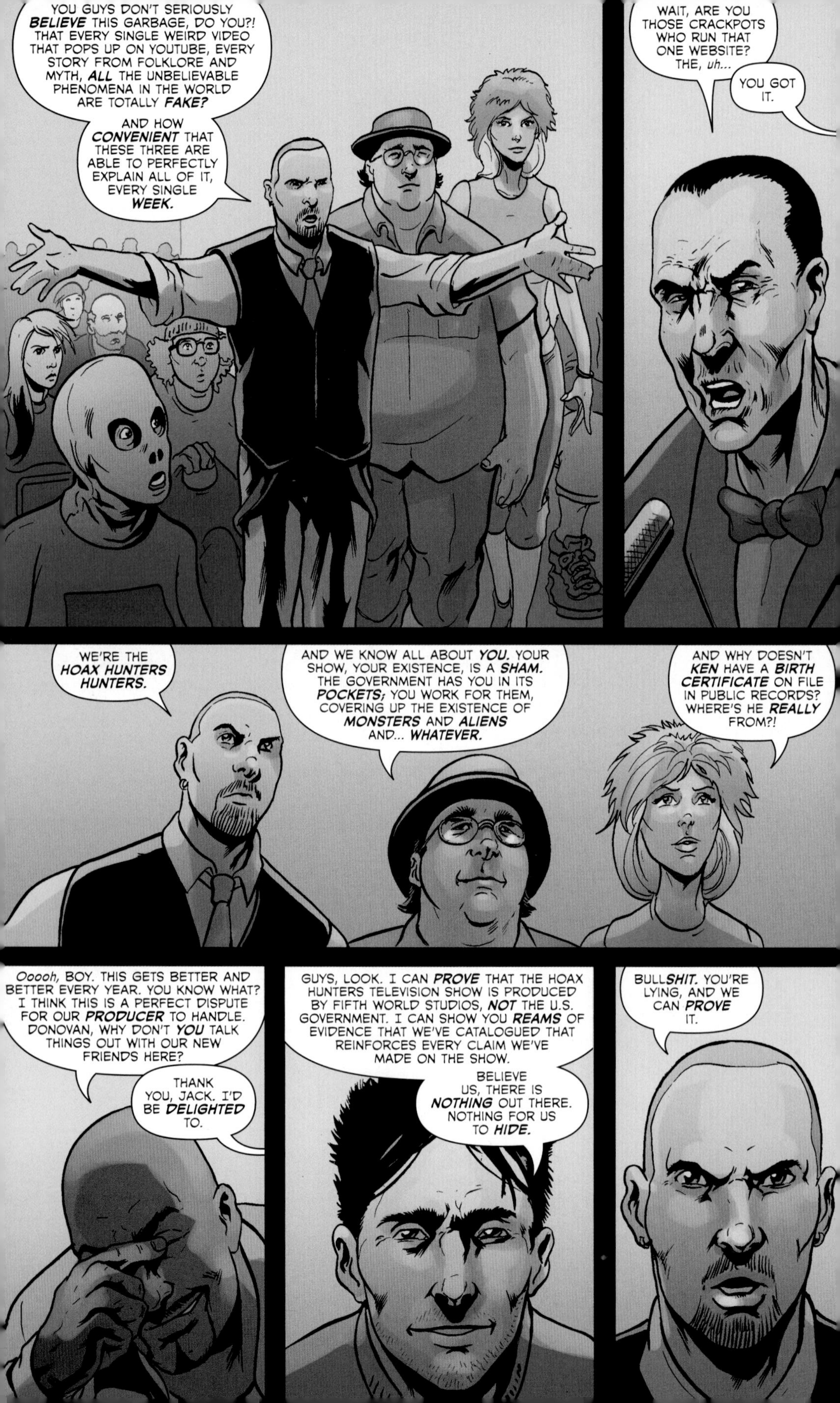

YOU GUYS DON'T SERIOUSLY **BELIEVE** THIS GARBAGE, DO YOU?! THAT EVERY SINGLE WEIRD VIDEO THAT POPS UP ON YOUTUBE, EVERY STORY FROM FOLKLORE AND MYTH, **ALL** THE UNBELIEVABLE PHENOMENA IN THE WORLD ARE TOTALLY **FAKE?**
AND HOW **CONVENIENT** THAT THESE THREE ARE ABLE TO PERFECTLY EXPLAIN ALL OF IT, EVERY SINGLE **WEEK.**
WAIT, ARE YOU THOSE CRACKPOTS WHO RUN THAT ONE WEBSITE? THE, *uh...*
YOU GOT IT.
WE'RE THE **HOAX HUNTERS HUNTERS.**
AND WE KNOW ALL ABOUT **YOU.** YOUR SHOW, YOUR EXISTENCE, IS A **SHAM.** THE GOVERNMENT HAS YOU IN ITS **POCKETS;** YOU WORK FOR THEM, COVERING UP THE EXISTENCE OF **MONSTERS** AND **ALIENS** AND... **WHATEVER.**
AND WHY DOESN'T **KEN** HAVE A **BIRTH CERTIFICATE** ON FILE IN PUBLIC RECORDS? WHERE'S HE **REALLY** FROM?!
Ooooh, BOY. THIS GETS BETTER AND BETTER EVERY YEAR. YOU KNOW WHAT? I THINK THIS IS A PERFECT DISPUTE FOR OUR **PRODUCER** TO HANDLE. DONOVAN, WHY DON'T **YOU** TALK THINGS OUT WITH OUR NEW FRIENDS HERE?
THANK YOU, JACK. I'D BE **DELIGHTED** TO.
GUYS, LOOK. I CAN **PROVE** THAT THE HOAX HUNTERS TELEVISION SHOW IS PRODUCED BY FIFTH WORLD STUDIOS, **NOT** THE U.S. GOVERNMENT. I CAN SHOW YOU **REAMS** OF EVIDENCE THAT WE'VE CATALOGUED THAT REINFORCES EVERY CLAIM WE'VE MADE ON THE SHOW.
BELIEVE US, THERE IS **NOTHING** OUT THERE. NOTHING FOR US TO **HIDE.**
BULL**SHIT.** YOU'RE LYING, AND WE CAN **PROVE** IT.

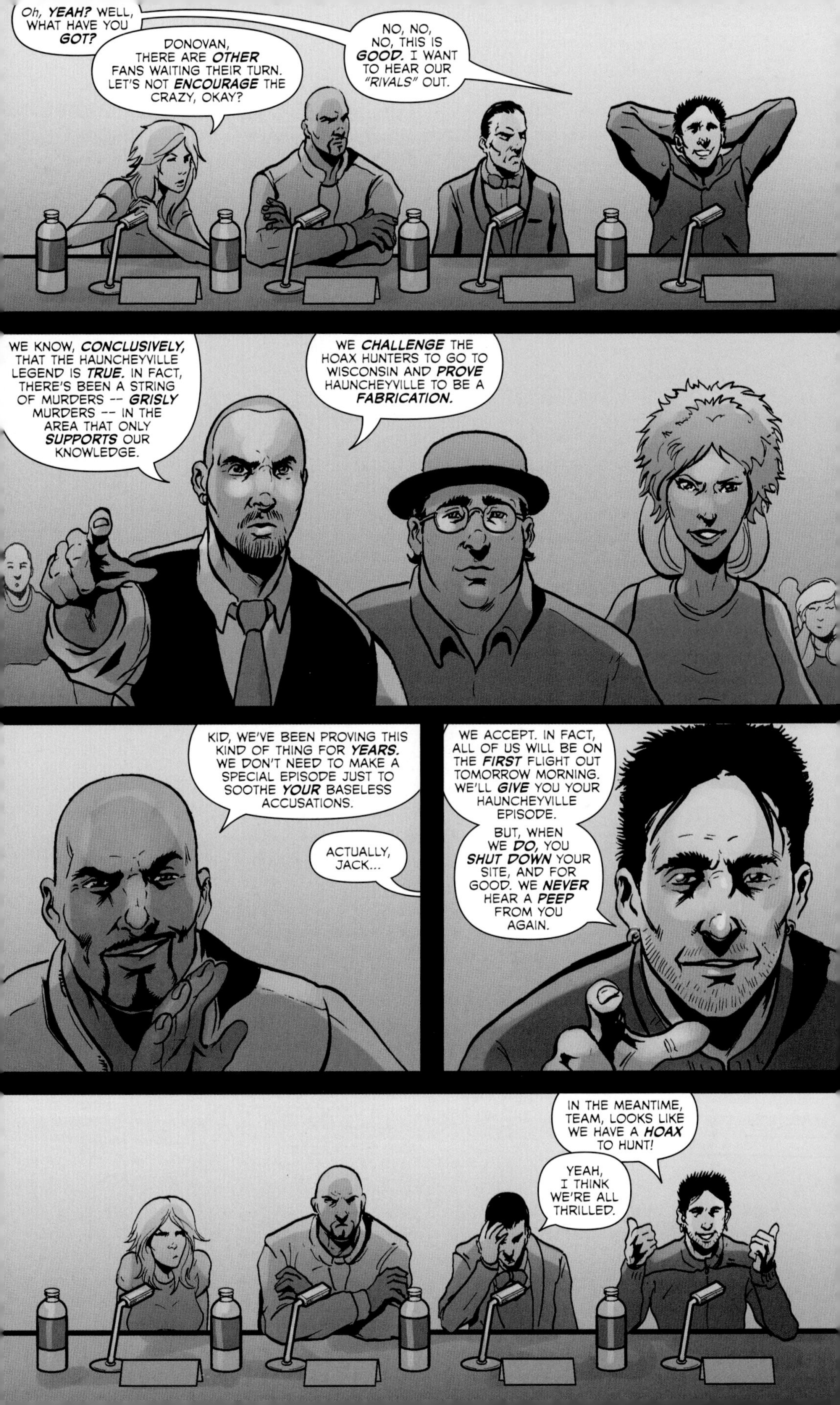

Oh, YEAH? WELL, WHAT HAVE YOU GOT?
DONOVAN, THERE ARE OTHER FANS WAITING THEIR TURN. LET'S NOT ENCOURAGE THE CRAZY, OKAY?
NO, NO, NO, THIS IS GOOD. I WANT TO HEAR OUR "RIVALS" OUT.
WE KNOW, CONCLUSIVELY, THAT THE HAUNCHEYVILLE LEGEND IS TRUE. IN FACT, THERE'S BEEN A STRING OF MURDERS -- GRISLY MURDERS -- IN THE AREA THAT ONLY SUPPORTS OUR KNOWLEDGE.
WE CHALLENGE THE HOAX HUNTERS TO GO TO WISCONSIN AND PROVE HAUNCHEYVILLE TO BE A FABRICATION.
KID, WE'VE BEEN PROVING THIS KIND OF THING FOR YEARS. WE DON'T NEED TO MAKE A SPECIAL EPISODE JUST TO SOOTHE YOUR BASELESS ACCUSATIONS.
ACTUALLY, JACK...
WE ACCEPT. IN FACT, ALL OF US WILL BE ON THE FIRST FLIGHT OUT TOMORROW MORNING. WE'LL GIVE YOU YOUR HAUNCHEYVILLE EPISODE.
BUT, WHEN WE DO, YOU SHUT DOWN YOUR SITE, AND FOR GOOD. WE NEVER HEAR A PEEP FROM YOU AGAIN.
IN THE MEANTIME, TEAM, LOOKS LIKE WE HAVE A HOAX TO HUNT!
YEAH, I THINK WE'RE ALL THRILLED.

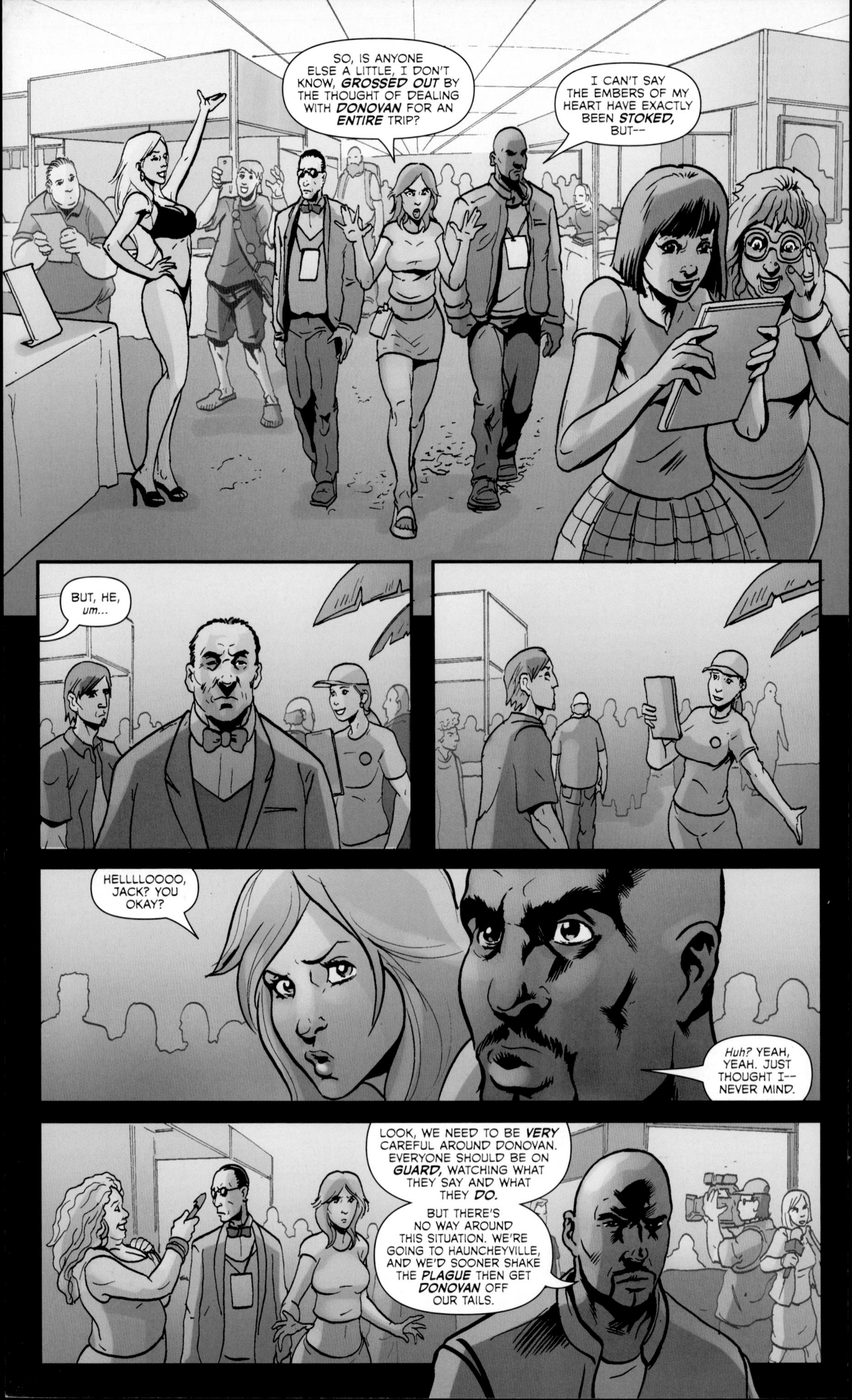
SO, IS ANYONE ELSE A LITTLE, I DON'T KNOW, GROSSED OUT BY THE THOUGHT OF DEALING WITH DONOVAN FOR AN ENTIRE TRIP?
I CAN'T SAY THE EMBERS OF MY HEART HAVE EXACTLY BEEN STOKED, BUT--
BUT, HE, um...
HELLLLOOOO, JACK? YOU OKAY?
Huh? YEAH, YEAH. JUST THOUGHT I-- NEVER MIND.
LOOK, WE NEED TO BE VERY CAREFUL AROUND DONOVAN. EVERYONE SHOULD BE ON GUARD, WATCHING WHAT THEY SAY AND WHAT THEY DO.
BUT THERE'S NO WAY AROUND THIS SITUATION. WE'RE GOING TO HAUNCHEYVILLE, AND WE'D SOONER SHAKE THE PLAGUE THEN GET DONOVAN OFF OUR TAILS.

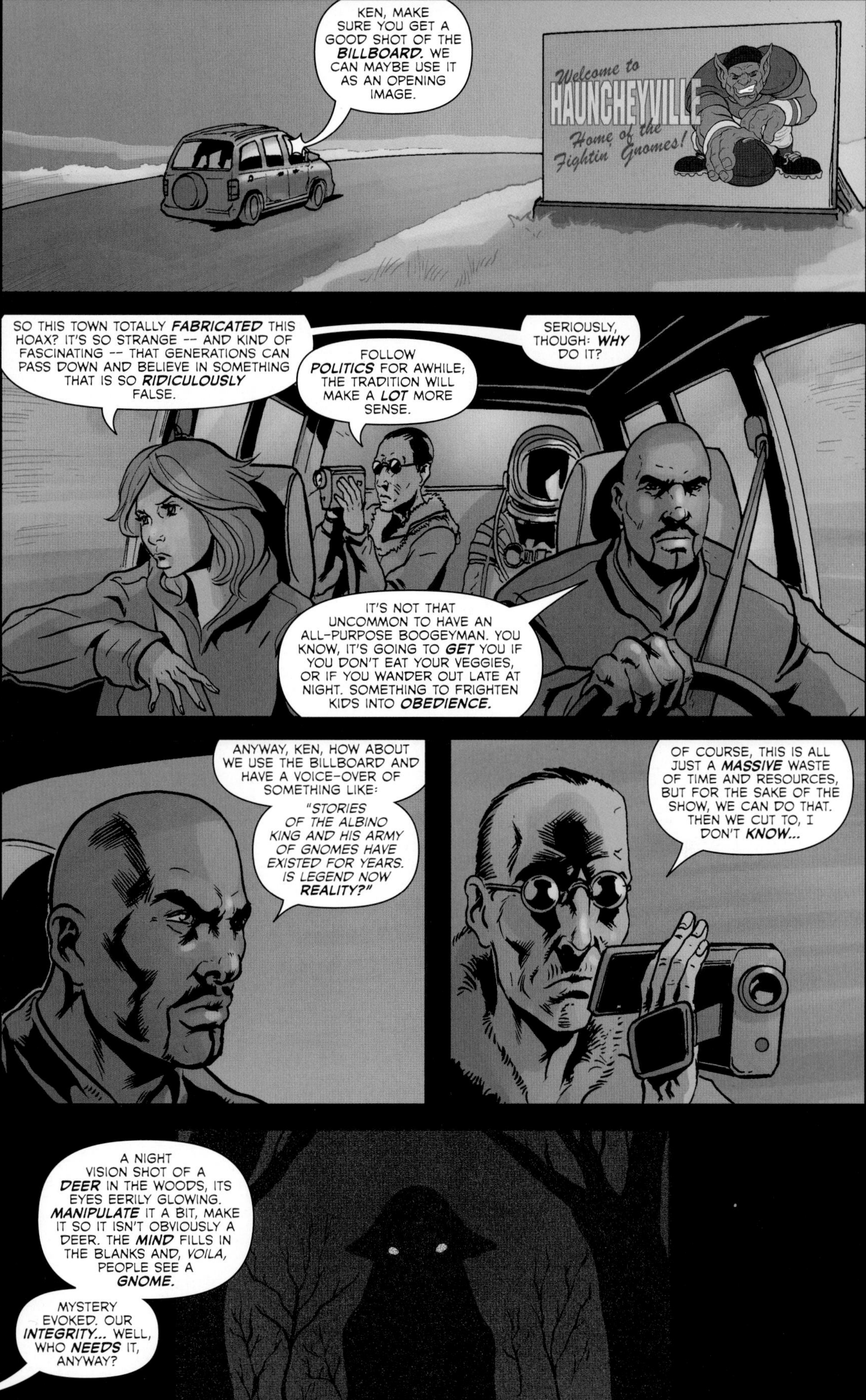
KEN, MAKE SURE YOU GET A GOOD SHOT OF THE BILLBOARD. WE CAN MAYBE USE IT AS AN OPENING IMAGE.
Welcome to HAUNCHEYVILLE Home of the Fightin' Gnomes!
SO THIS TOWN TOTALLY FABRICATED THIS HOAX? IT'S SO STRANGE -- AND KIND OF FASCINATING -- THAT GENERATIONS CAN PASS DOWN AND BELIEVE IN SOMETHING THAT IS SO RIDICULOUSLY FALSE.
SERIOUSLY, THOUGH: WHY DO IT?
FOLLOW POLITICS FOR AWHILE; THE TRADITION WILL MAKE A LOT MORE SENSE.
IT'S NOT THAT UNCOMMON TO HAVE AN ALL-PURPOSE BOOGEYMAN. YOU KNOW, IT'S GOING TO GET YOU IF YOU DON'T EAT YOUR VEGGIES, OR IF YOU WANDER OUT LATE AT NIGHT. SOMETHING TO FRIGHTEN KIDS INTO OBEDIENCE.
ANYWAY, KEN, HOW ABOUT WE USE THE BILLBOARD AND HAVE A VOICE-OVER OF SOMETHING LIKE: "STORIES OF THE ALBINO KING AND HIS ARMY OF GNOMES HAVE EXISTED FOR YEARS. IS LEGEND NOW REALITY?"
OF COURSE, THIS IS ALL JUST A MASSIVE WASTE OF TIME AND RESOURCES, BUT FOR THE SAKE OF THE SHOW, WE CAN DO THAT. THEN WE CUT TO, I DON'T KNOW...
A NIGHT VISION SHOT OF A DEER IN THE WOODS, ITS EYES EERILY GLOWING. MANIPULATE IT A BIT, MAKE IT SO IT ISN'T OBVIOUSLY A DEER. THE MIND FILLS IN THE BLANKS AND, VOILA, PEOPLE SEE A GNOME.
MYSTERY EVOKED. OUR INTEGRITY... WELL, WHO NEEDS IT, ANYWAY?

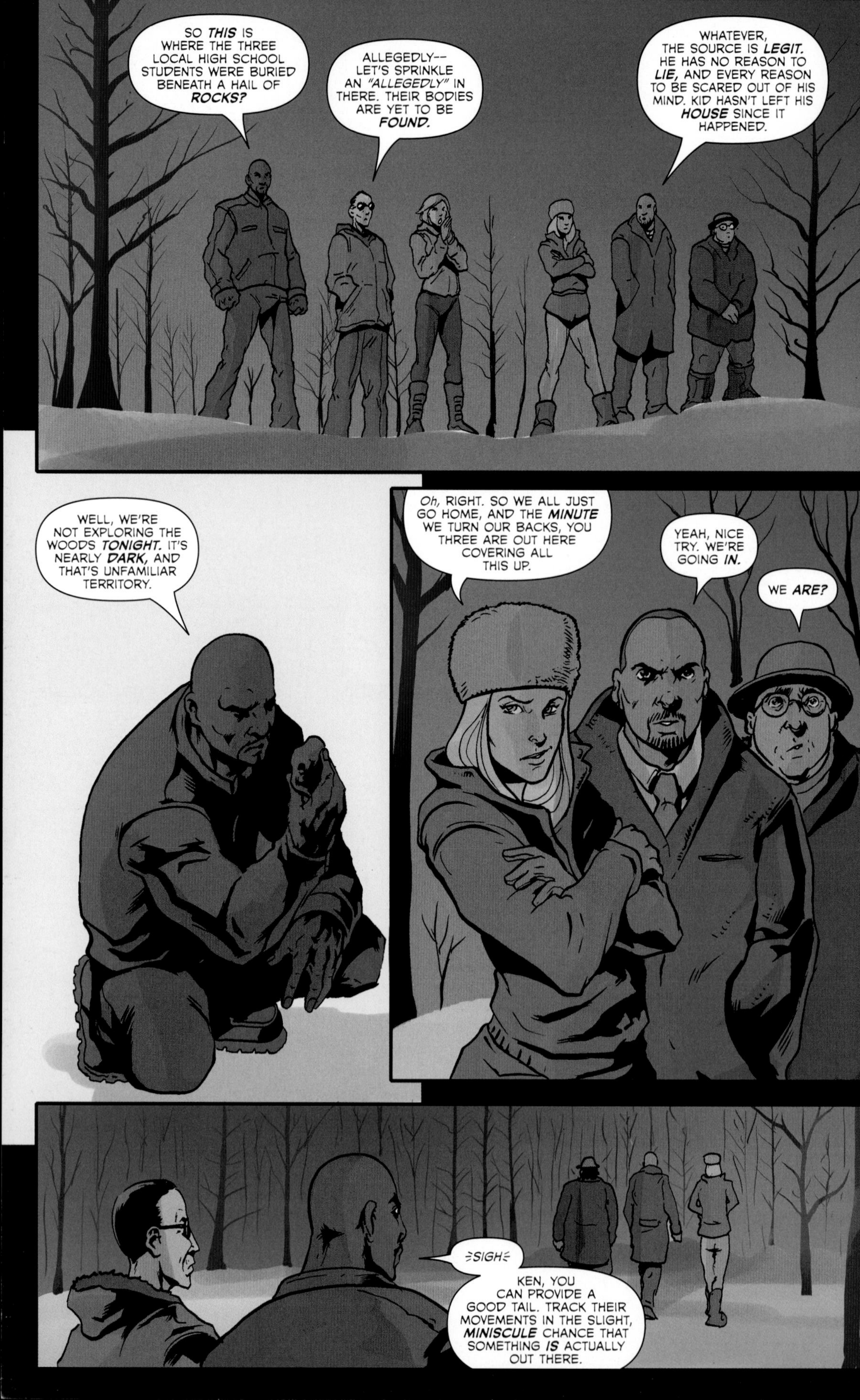
SO THIS IS WHERE THE THREE LOCAL HIGH SCHOOL STUDENTS WERE BURIED BENEATH A HAIL OF ROCKS?
ALLEGEDLY-- LET'S SPRINKLE AN "ALLEGEDLY" IN THERE. THEIR BODIES ARE YET TO BE FOUND.
WHATEVER, THE SOURCE IS LEGIT. HE HAS NO REASON TO LIE, AND EVERY REASON TO BE SCARED OUT OF HIS MIND. KID HASN'T LEFT HIS HOUSE SINCE IT HAPPENED.
WELL, WE'RE NOT EXPLORING THE WOODS TONIGHT. IT'S NEARLY DARK, AND THAT'S UNFAMILIAR TERRITORY.
Oh, RIGHT. SO WE ALL JUST GO HOME, AND THE MINUTE WE TURN OUR BACKS, YOU THREE ARE OUT HERE COVERING ALL THIS UP.
YEAH, NICE TRY. WE'RE GOING IN.
WE ARE?
=SIGH=
KEN, YOU CAN PROVIDE A GOOD TAIL. TRACK THEIR MOVEMENTS IN THE SLIGHT, MINISCULE CHANCE THAT SOMETHING IS ACTUALLY OUT THERE.

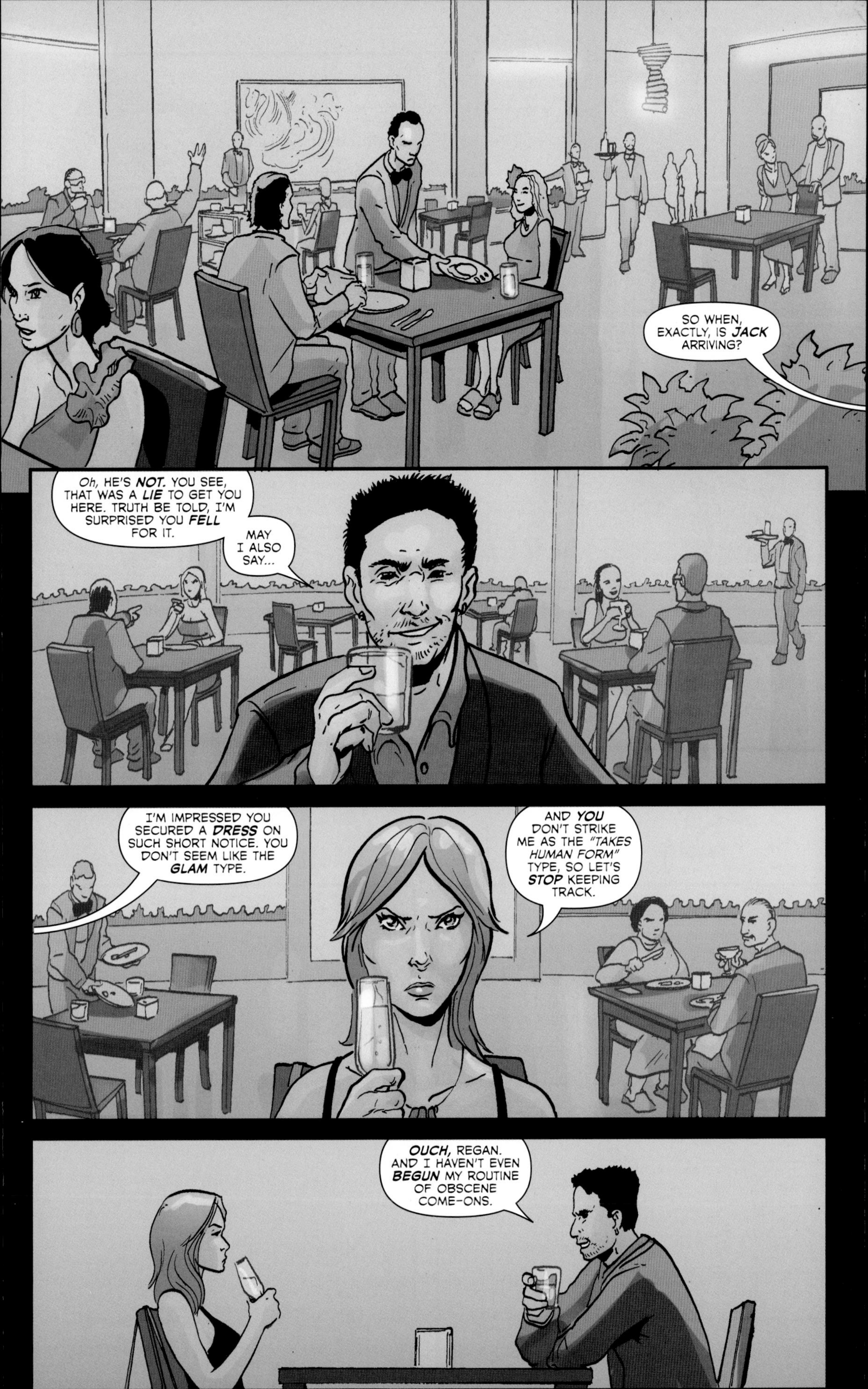
SO WHEN, EXACTLY, IS JACK ARRIVING?
Oh, HE'S NOT. YOU SEE, THAT WAS A LIE TO GET YOU HERE. TRUTH BE TOLD, I'M SURPRISED YOU FELL FOR IT.
MAY I ALSO SAY...
I'M IMPRESSED YOU SECURED A DRESS ON SUCH SHORT NOTICE. YOU DON'T SEEM LIKE THE GLAM TYPE.
AND YOU DON'T STRIKE ME AS THE "TAKES HUMAN FORM" TYPE, SO LET'S STOP KEEPING TRACK.
OUCH, REGAN. AND I HAVEN'T EVEN BEGUN MY ROUTINE OF OBSCENE COME-ONS.

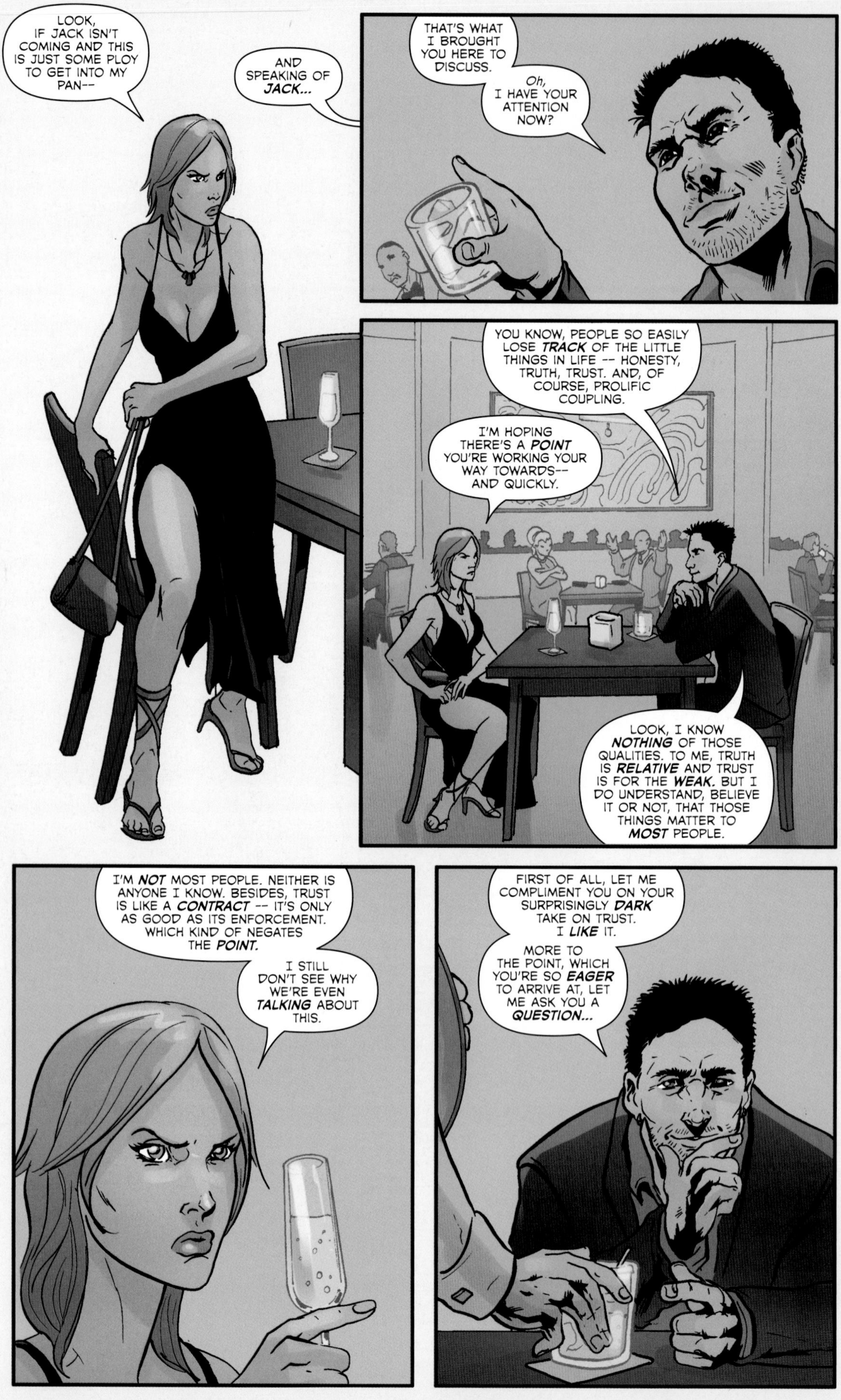
LOOK, IF JACK ISN'T COMING AND THIS IS JUST SOME PLOY TO GET INTO MY PAN--
AND SPEAKING OF ***JACK...***
THAT'S WHAT I BROUGHT YOU HERE TO DISCUSS.
Oh, I HAVE YOUR ATTENTION NOW?
YOU KNOW, PEOPLE SO EASILY LOSE ***TRACK*** OF THE LITTLE THINGS IN LIFE -- HONESTY, TRUTH, TRUST. AND, OF COURSE, PROLIFIC COUPLING.
I'M HOPING THERE'S A ***POINT*** YOU'RE WORKING YOUR WAY TOWARDS-- AND QUICKLY.
LOOK, I KNOW ***NOTHING*** OF THOSE QUALITIES. TO ME, TRUTH IS ***RELATIVE*** AND TRUST IS FOR THE ***WEAK.*** BUT I DO UNDERSTAND, BELIEVE IT OR NOT, THAT THOSE THINGS MATTER TO ***MOST*** PEOPLE.
I'M ***NOT*** MOST PEOPLE. NEITHER IS ANYONE I KNOW. BESIDES, TRUST IS LIKE A ***CONTRACT*** -- IT'S ONLY AS GOOD AS ITS ENFORCEMENT. WHICH KIND OF NEGATES THE ***POINT.***
I STILL DON'T SEE WHY WE'RE EVEN ***TALKING*** ABOUT THIS.
FIRST OF ALL, LET ME COMPLIMENT YOU ON YOUR SURPRISINGLY ***DARK*** TAKE ON TRUST. I ***LIKE*** IT.
MORE TO THE POINT, WHICH YOU'RE SO ***EAGER*** TO ARRIVE AT, LET ME ASK YOU A ***QUESTION...***

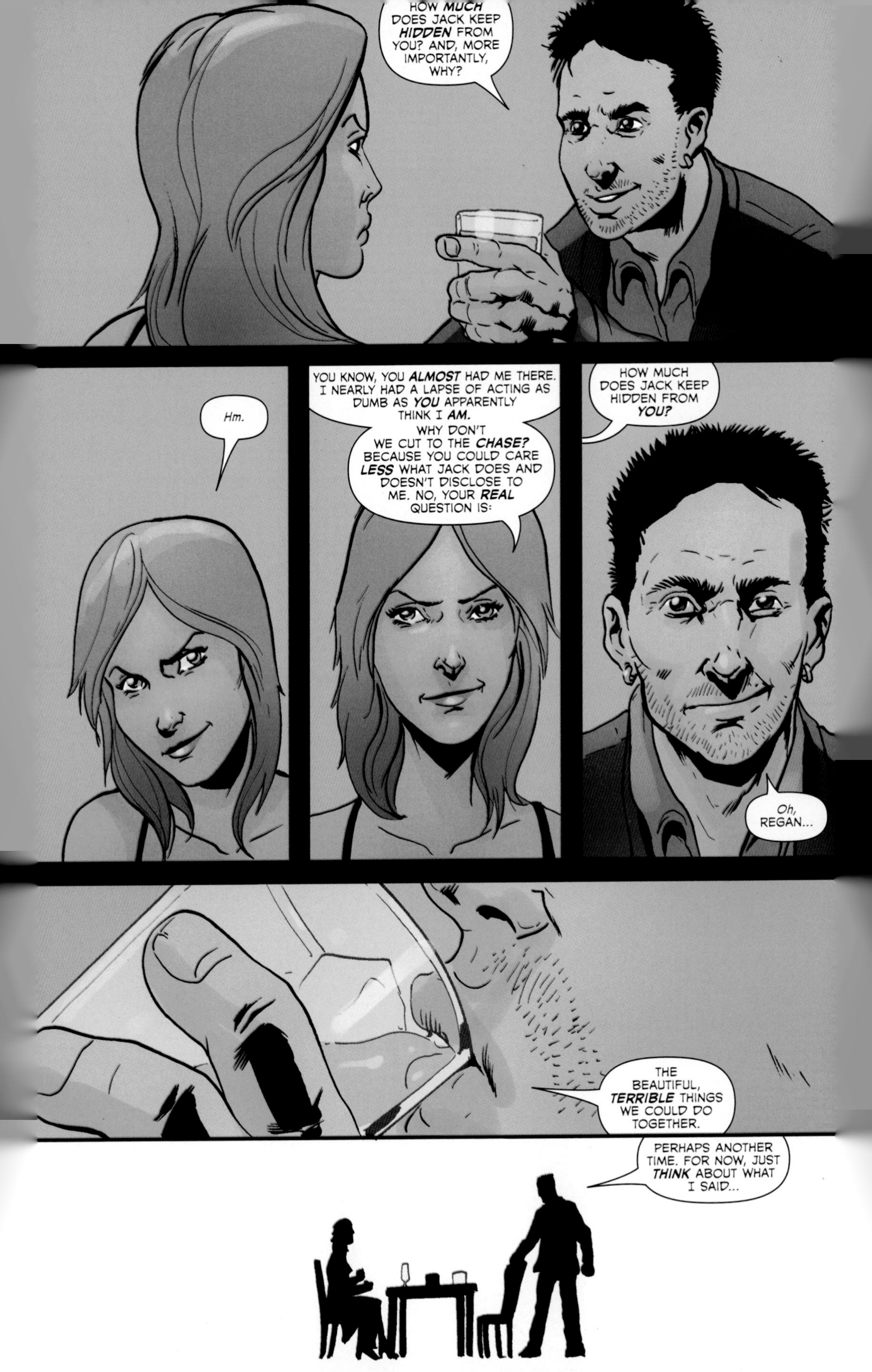
HOW MUCH DOES JACK KEEP HIDDEN FROM YOU? AND, MORE IMPORTANTLY, WHY?
Hm.
YOU KNOW, YOU ALMOST HAD ME THERE. I NEARLY HAD A LAPSE OF ACTING AS DUMB AS YOU APPARENTLY THINK I AM.
WHY DON'T WE CUT TO THE CHASE? BECAUSE YOU COULD CARE LESS WHAT JACK DOES AND DOESN'T DISCLOSE TO ME. NO, YOUR REAL QUESTION IS:
HOW MUCH DOES JACK KEEP HIDDEN FROM YOU?
Oh, REGAN...
THE BEAUTIFUL, TERRIBLE THINGS WE COULD DO TOGETHER.
PERHAPS ANOTHER TIME. FOR NOW, JUST THINK ABOUT WHAT I SAID...

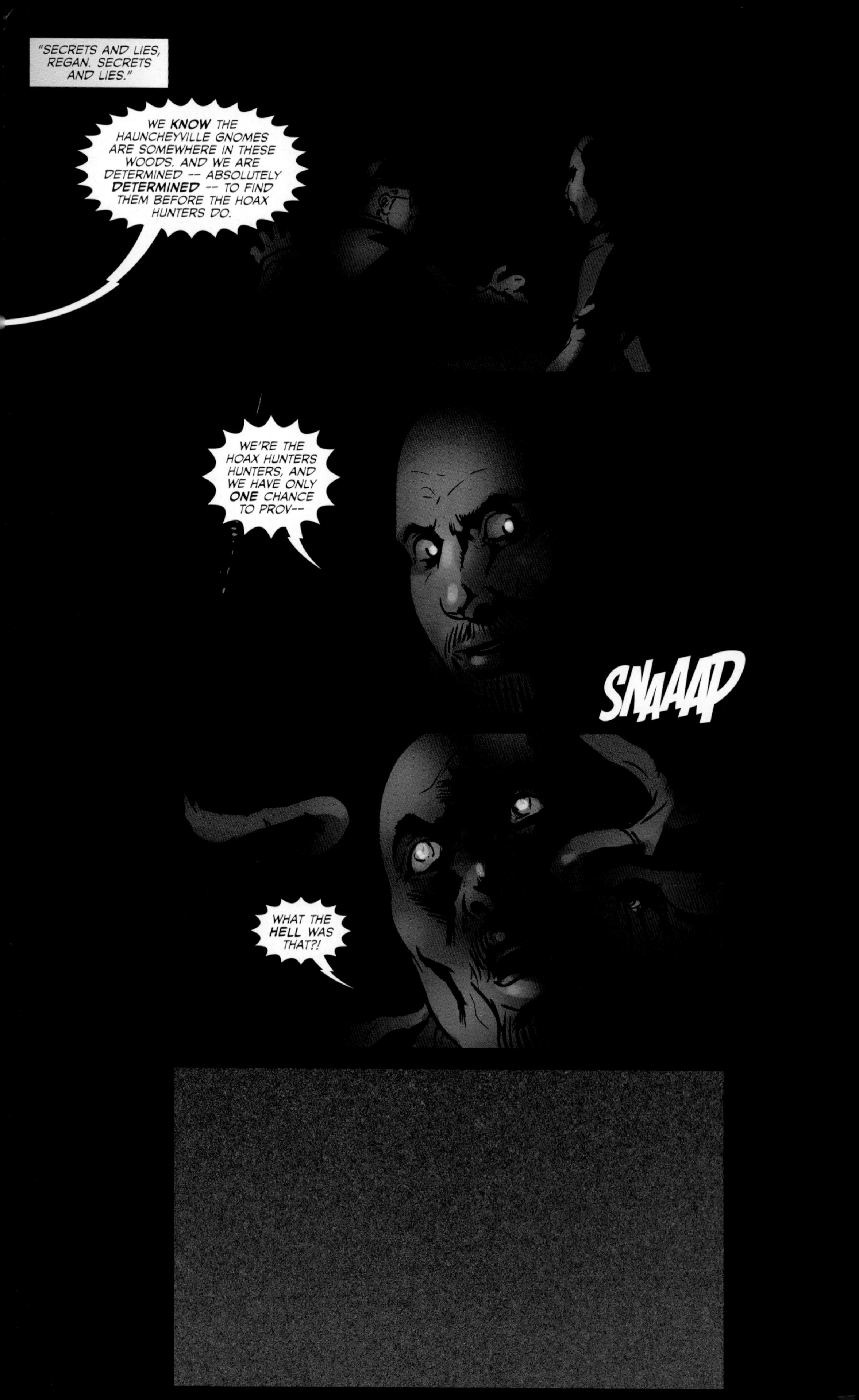
"SECRETS AND LIES, REGAN. SECRETS AND LIES."
WE **KNOW** THE HAUNCHEYVILLE GNOMES ARE SOMEWHERE IN THESE WOODS. AND WE ARE DETERMINED -- ABSOLUTELY **DETERMINED** -- TO FIND THEM BEFORE THE HOAX HUNTERS DO.
WE'RE THE HOAX HUNTERS HUNTERS, AND WE HAVE ONLY **ONE** CHANCE TO PROV--
SNAAAP
WHAT THE **HELL** WAS THAT?!

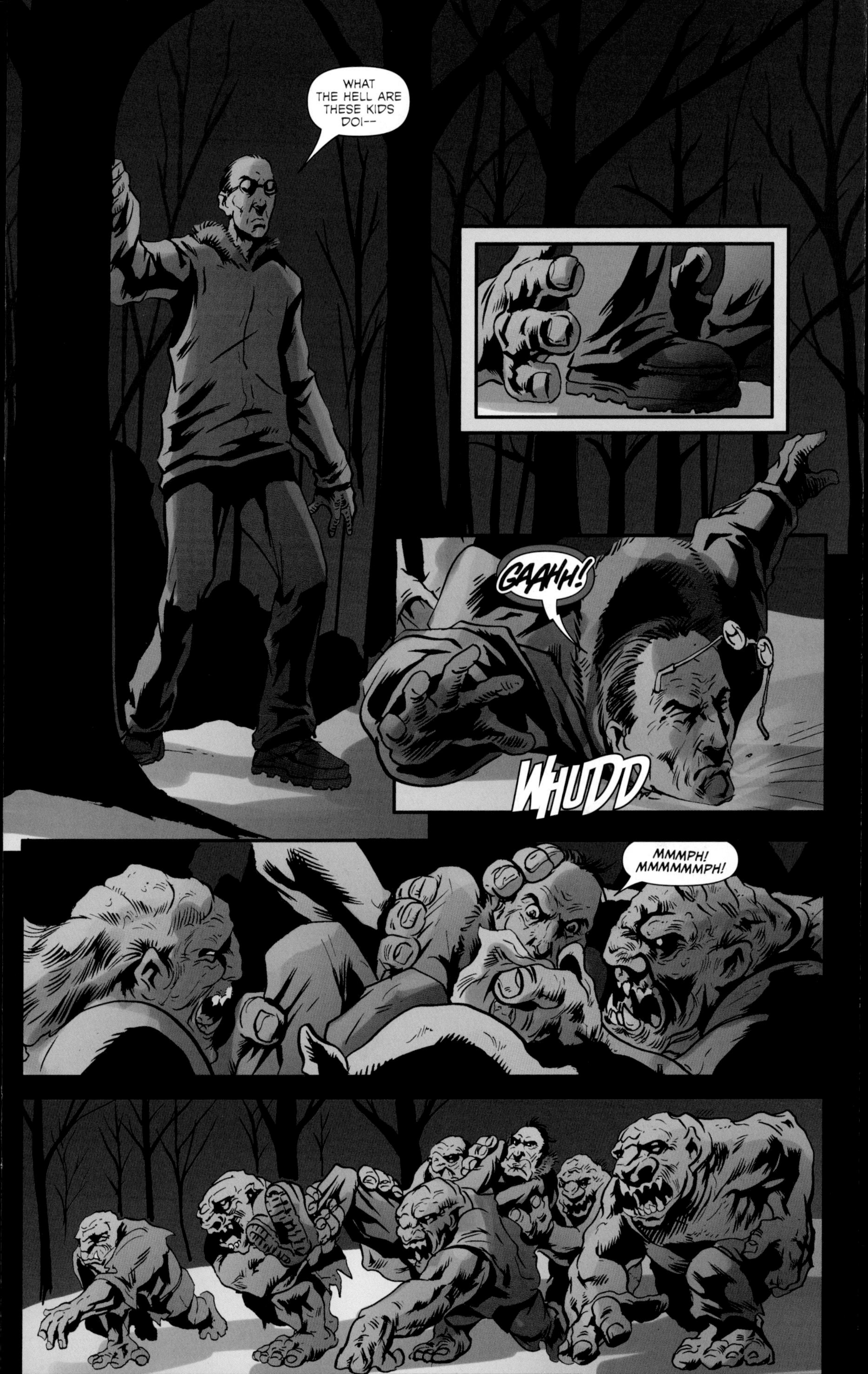
WHAT THE HELL ARE THESE KIDS DOI--
GAAHH!
WHUDD
MMMPH! MMMMMMPH!

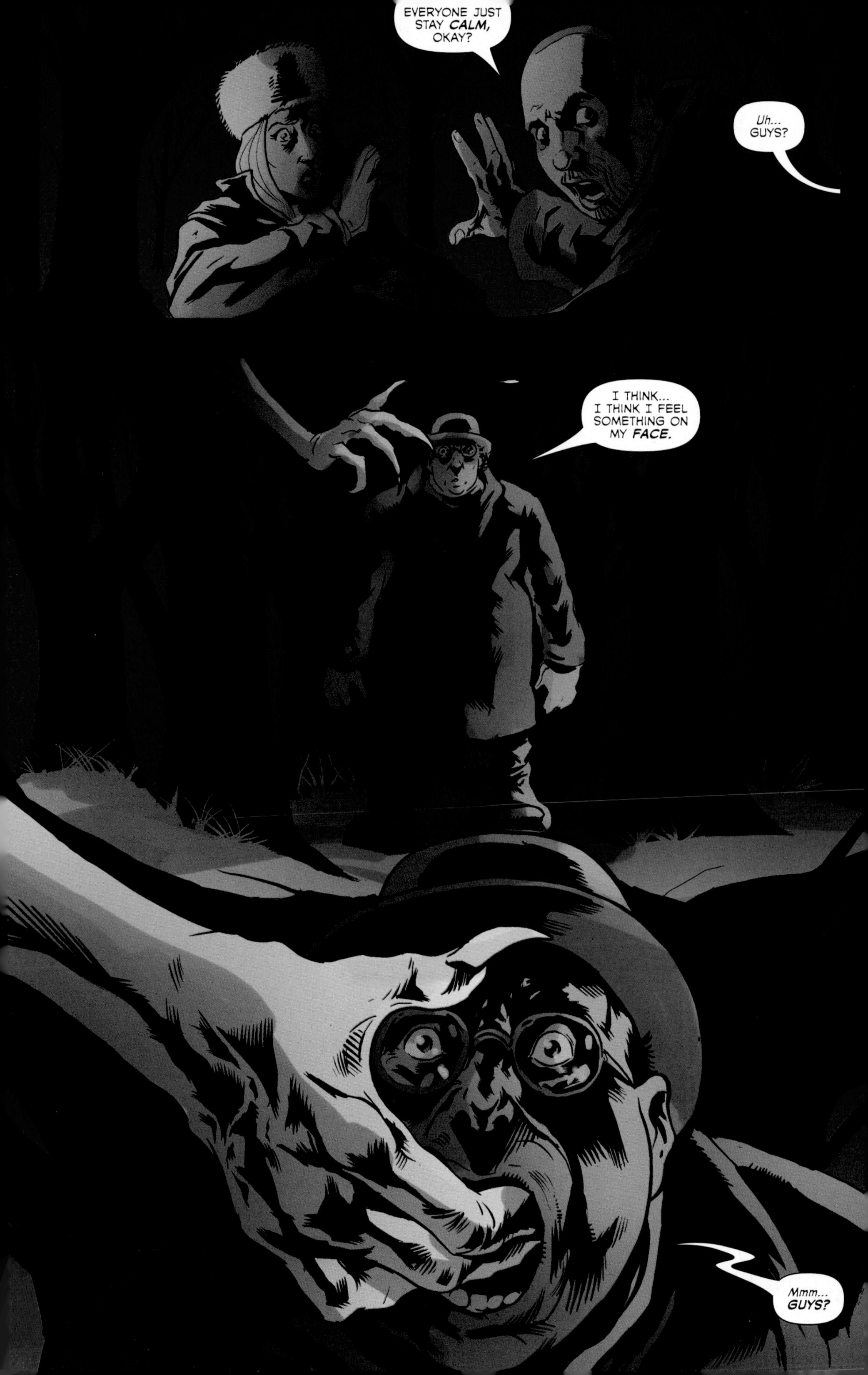
EVERYONE JUST STAY *CALM,* OKAY?
Uh... GUYS?
I THINK... I THINK I FEEL SOMETHING ON MY ***FACE.***
Mmm... ***GUYS?***

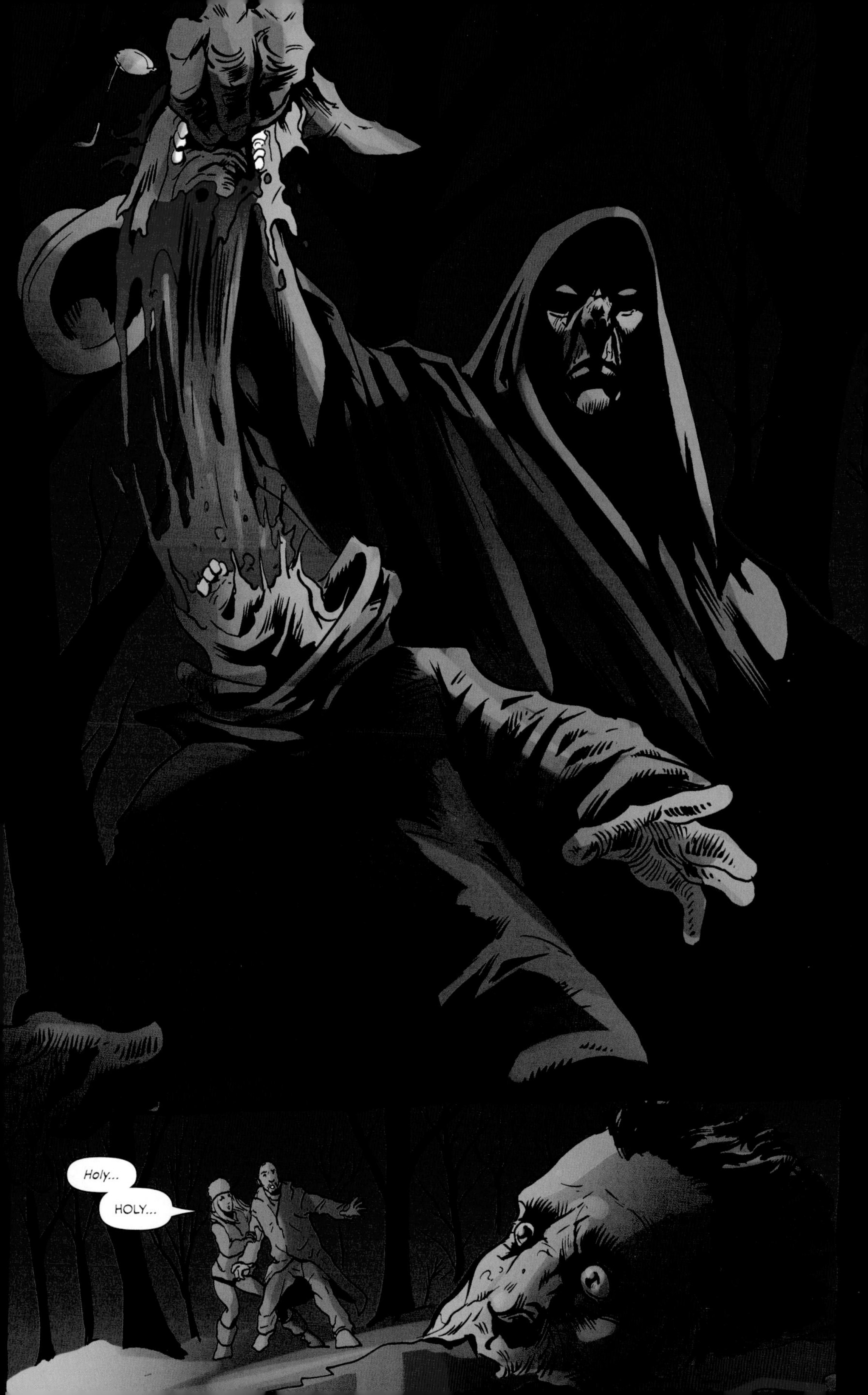
Holy...
HOLY...

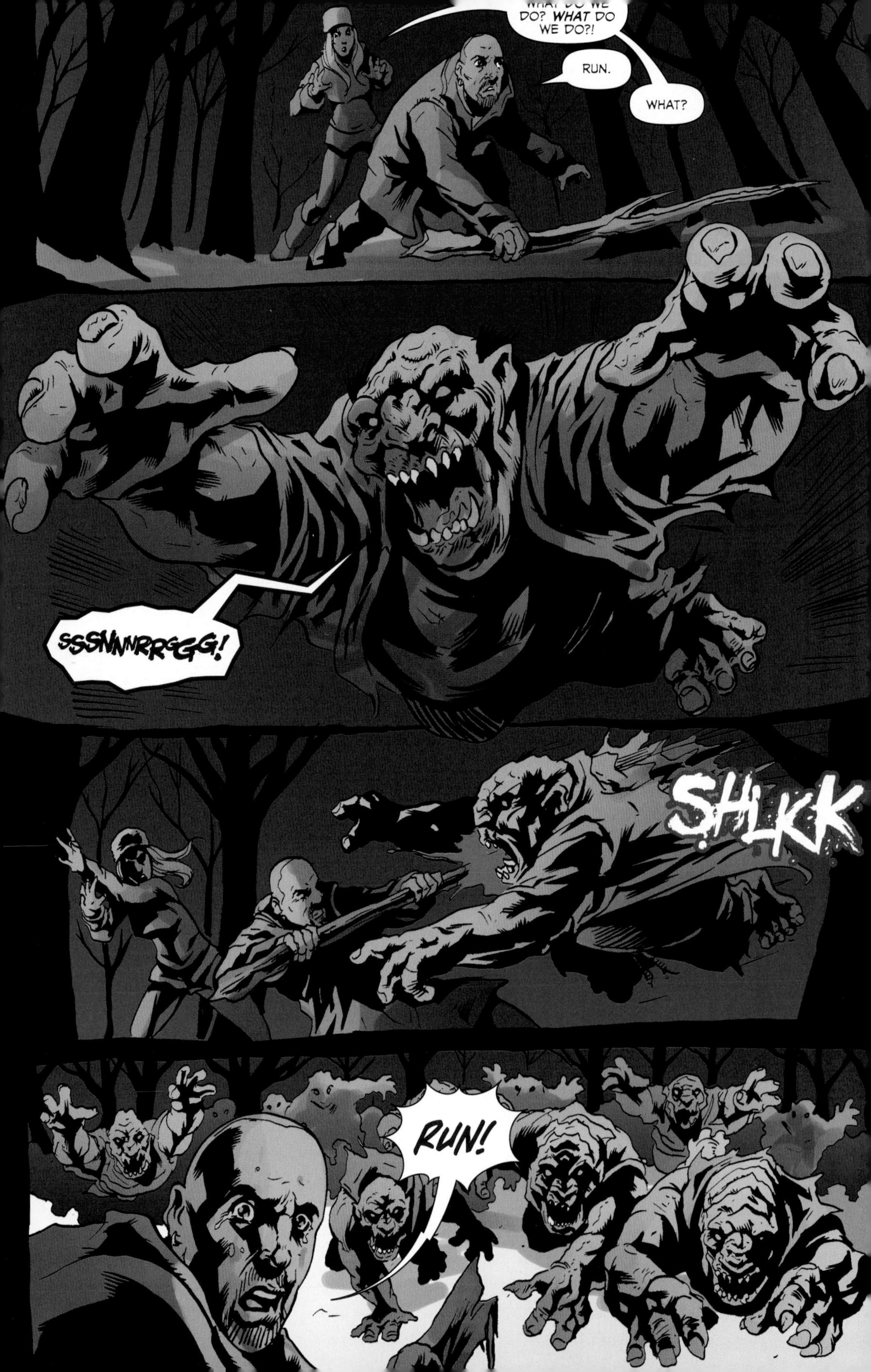
WHAT DO WE DO? WHAT DO WE DO?!
RUN.
WHAT?
SSSNNNRRGGG!
SHLKK
RUN!

HOAX HUNTERS

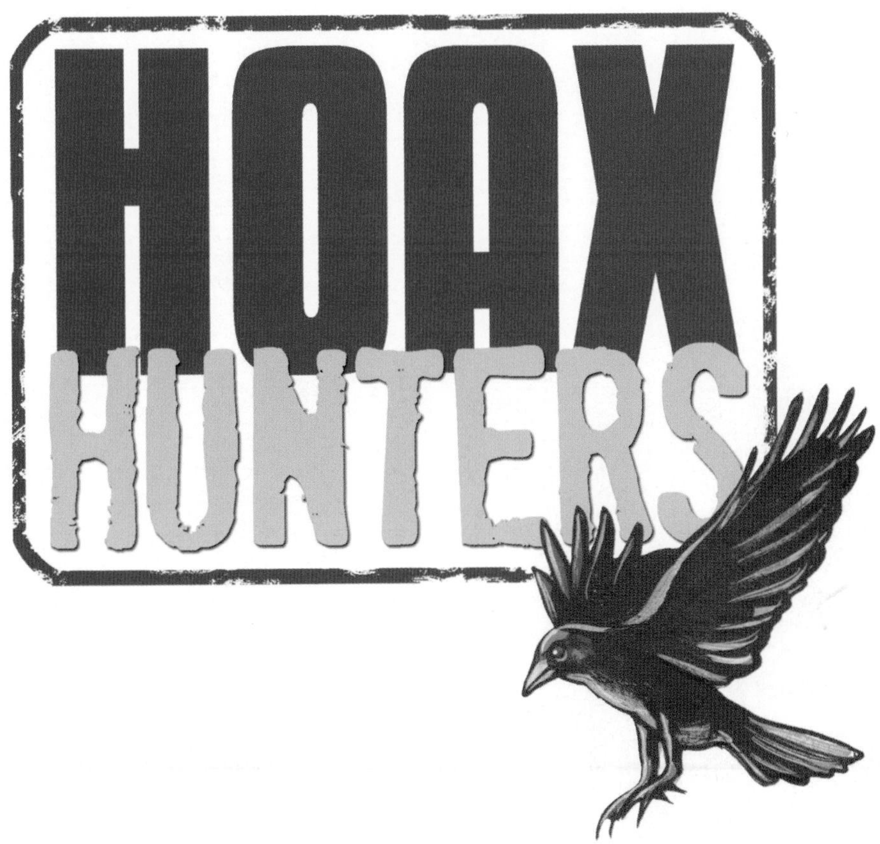

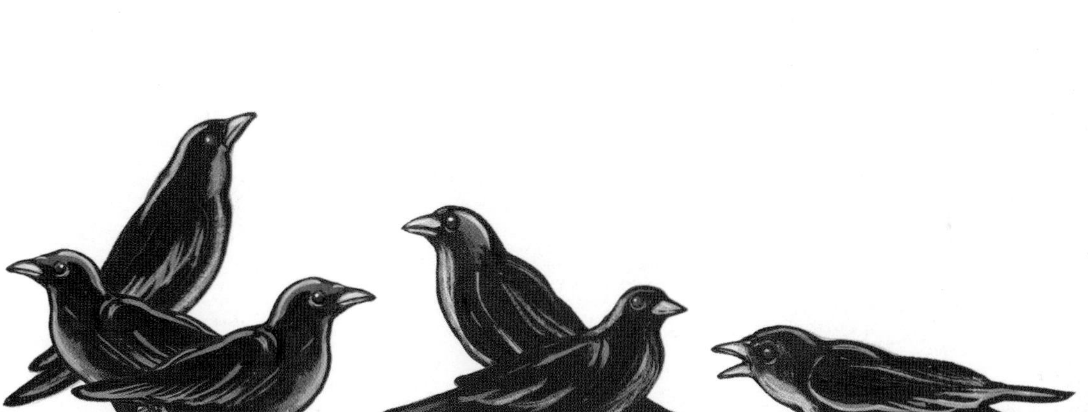

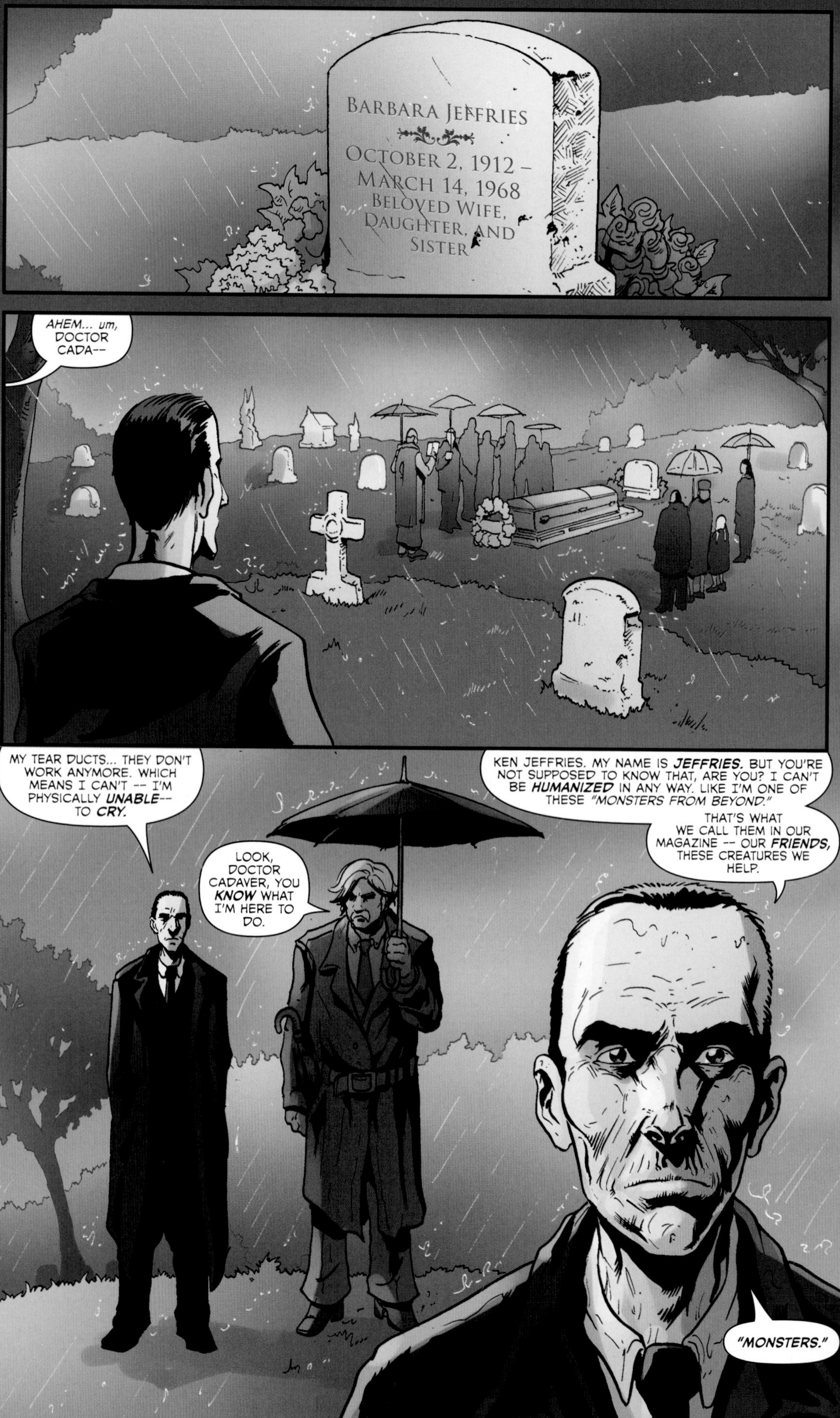
BARBARA JEFFRIES
OCTOBER 2, 1912 – MARCH 14, 1968
BELOVED WIFE, DAUGHTER, AND SISTER
AHEM... um, DOCTOR CADA--
MY TEAR DUCTS... THEY DON'T WORK ANYMORE. WHICH MEANS I CAN'T -- I'M PHYSICALLY UNABLE-- TO CRY.
LOOK, DOCTOR CADAVER, YOU KNOW WHAT I'M HERE TO DO.
KEN JEFFRIES. MY NAME IS JEFFRIES. BUT YOU'RE NOT SUPPOSED TO KNOW THAT, ARE YOU? I CAN'T BE HUMANIZED IN ANY WAY. LIKE I'M ONE OF THESE "MONSTERS FROM BEYOND."
THAT'S WHAT WE CALL THEM IN OUR MAGAZINE -- OUR FRIENDS, THESE CREATURES WE HELP.
"MONSTERS."

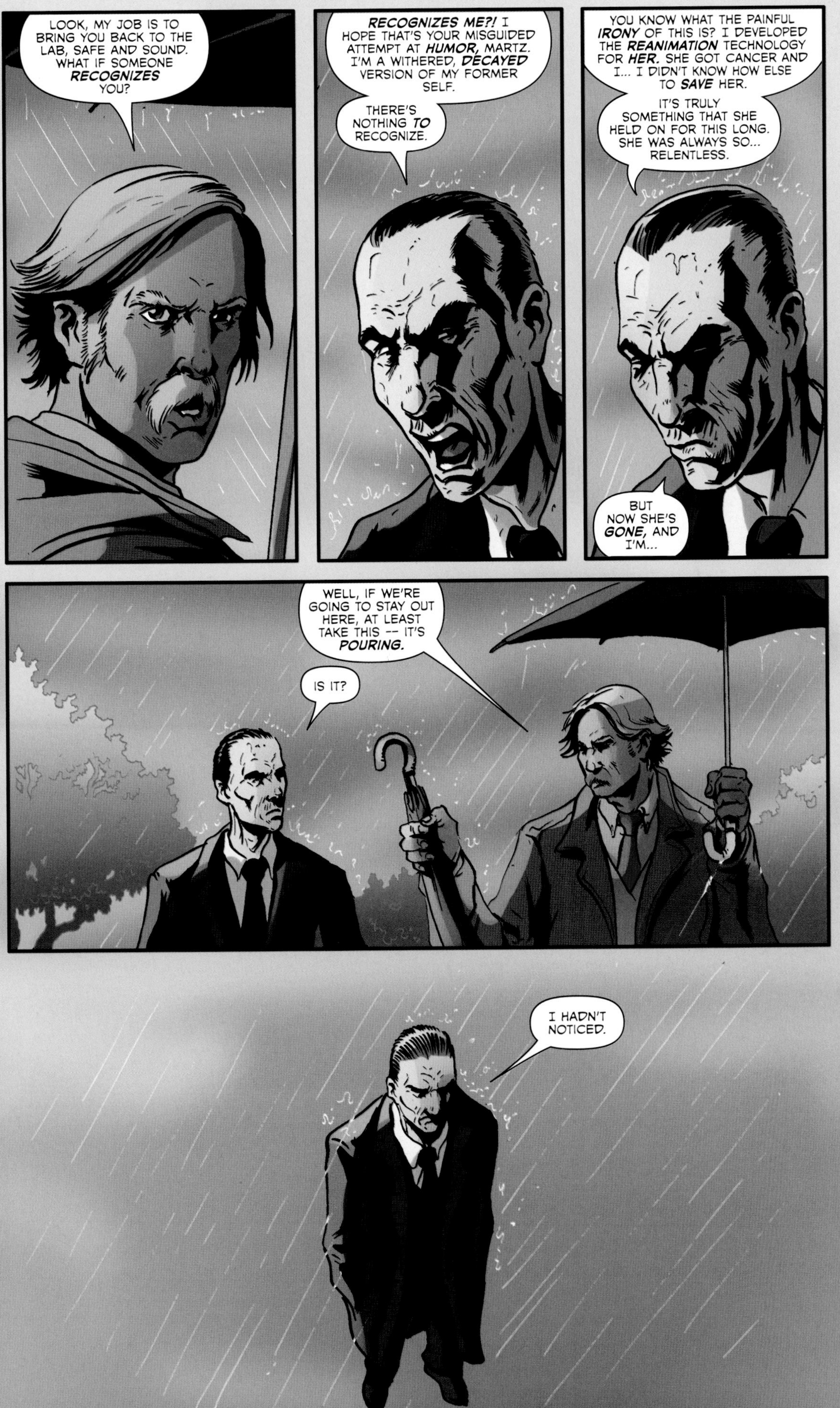
LOOK, MY JOB IS TO BRING YOU BACK TO THE LAB, SAFE AND SOUND. WHAT IF SOMEONE RECOGNIZES YOU?
RECOGNIZES ME?! I HOPE THAT'S YOUR MISGUIDED ATTEMPT AT HUMOR, MARTZ. I'M A WITHERED, DECAYED VERSION OF MY FORMER SELF.
THERE'S NOTHING TO RECOGNIZE.
YOU KNOW WHAT THE PAINFUL IRONY OF THIS IS? I DEVELOPED THE REANIMATION TECHNOLOGY FOR HER. SHE GOT CANCER AND I... I DIDN'T KNOW HOW ELSE TO SAVE HER.
IT'S TRULY SOMETHING THAT SHE HELD ON FOR THIS LONG. SHE WAS ALWAYS SO... RELENTLESS.
BUT NOW SHE'S GONE, AND I'M...
WELL, IF WE'RE GOING TO STAY OUT HERE, AT LEAST TAKE THIS -- IT'S POURING.
IS IT?
I HADN'T NOTICED.

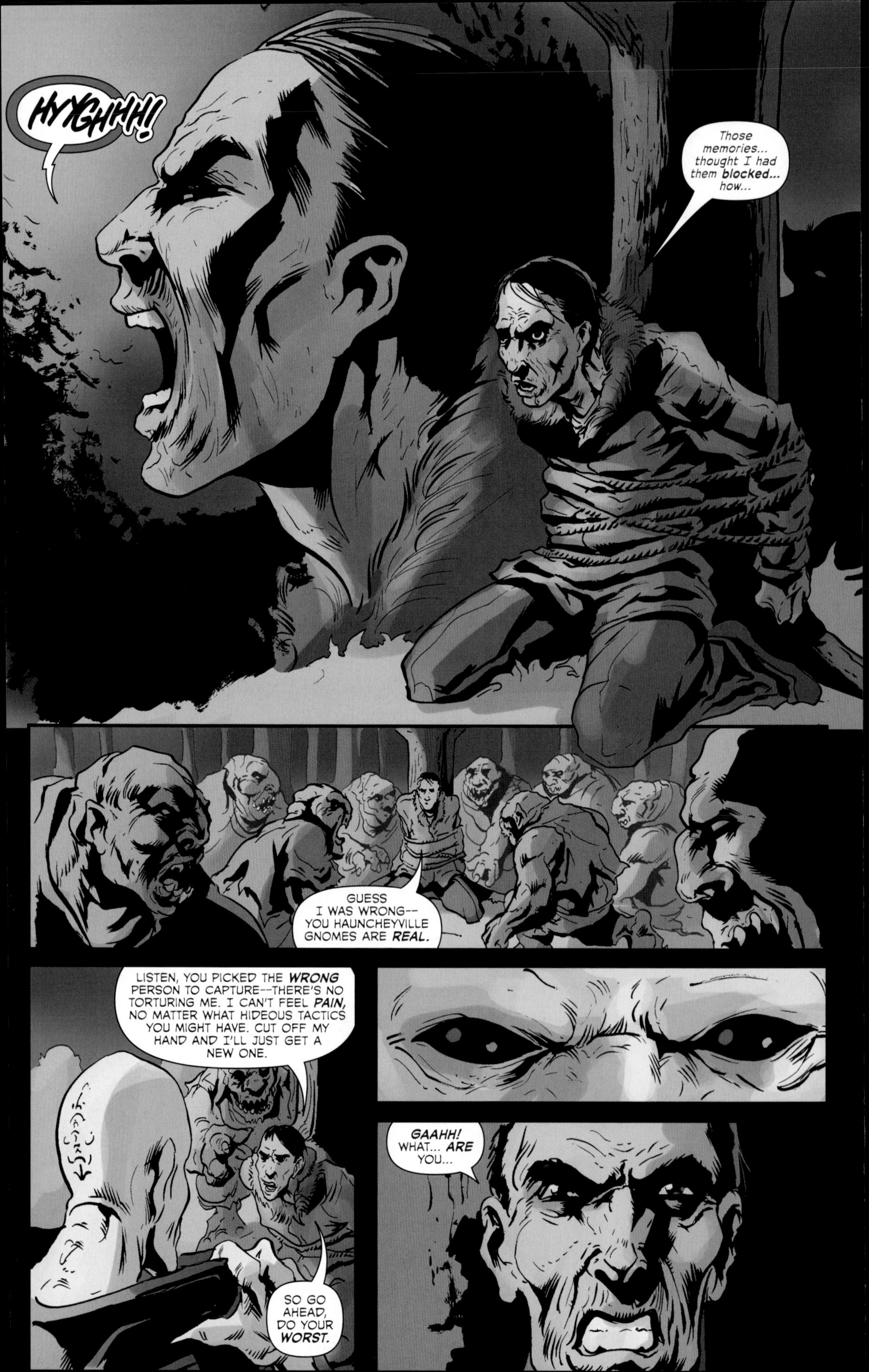
HYXGHHH!
Those memories... thought I had them blocked... how...
GUESS I WAS WRONG-- YOU HAUNCHEYVILLE GNOMES ARE REAL.
LISTEN, YOU PICKED THE WRONG PERSON TO CAPTURE--THERE'S NO TORTURING ME. I CAN'T FEEL PAIN, NO MATTER WHAT HIDEOUS TACTICS YOU MIGHT HAVE. CUT OFF MY HAND AND I'LL JUST GET A NEW ONE.
SO GO AHEAD, DO YOUR WORST.
GAAHH! WHAT... ARE YOU...

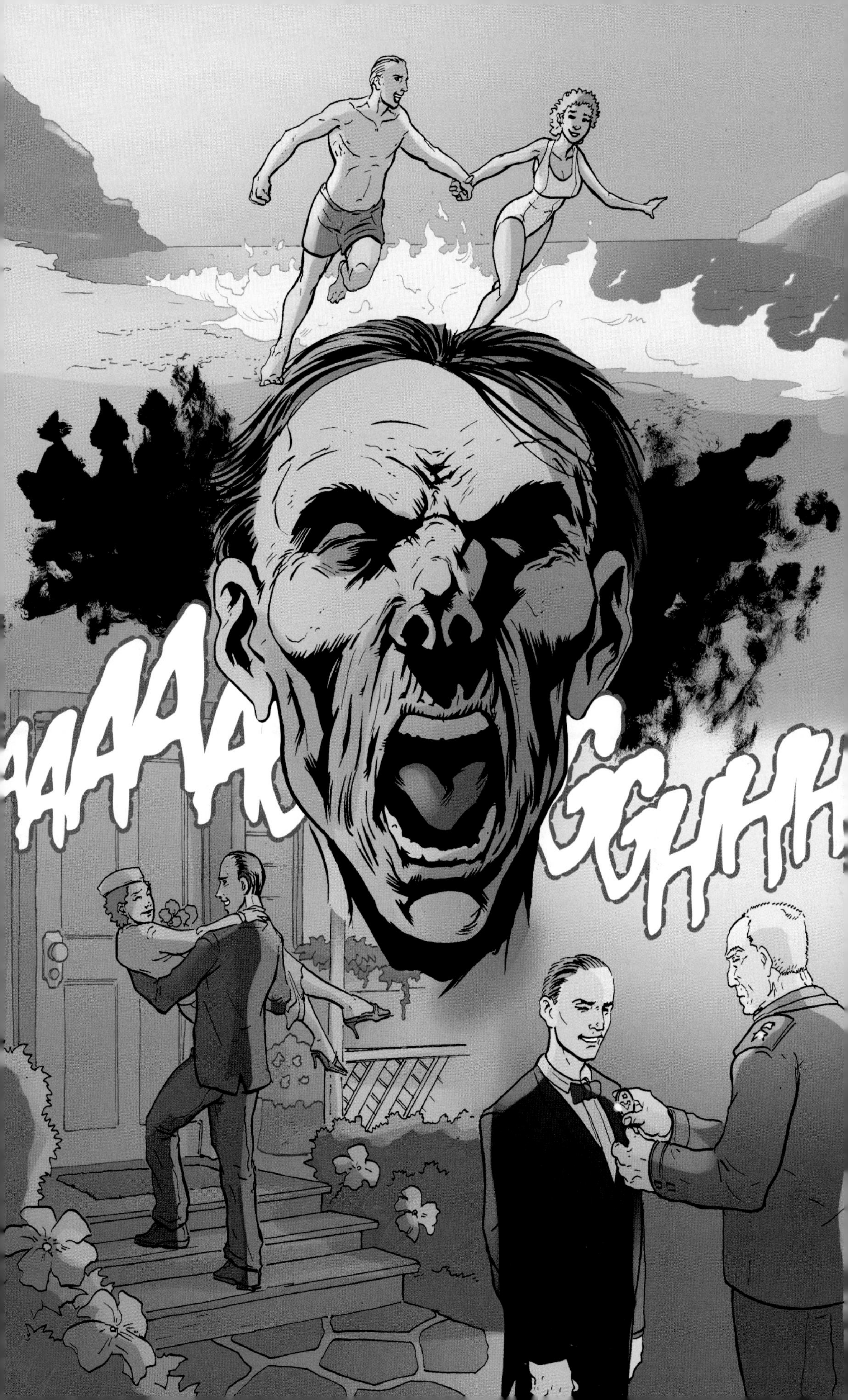

AAAAA
GHHH

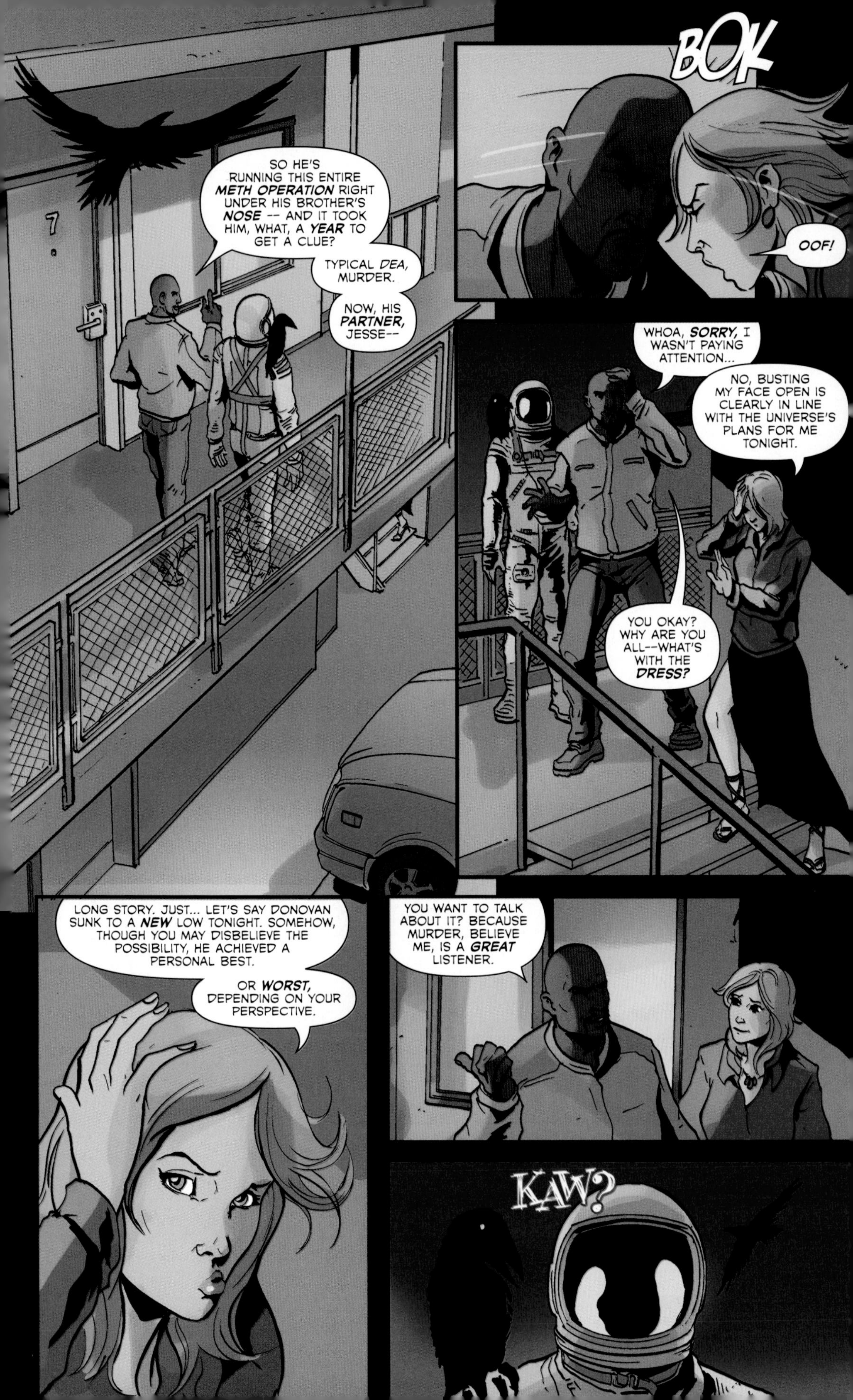
SO HE'S RUNNING THIS ENTIRE METH OPERATION RIGHT UNDER HIS BROTHER'S NOSE -- AND IT TOOK HIM, WHAT, A YEAR TO GET A CLUE?
TYPICAL DEA, MURDER.
NOW, HIS PARTNER, JESSE--
BOK
OOF!
WHOA, SORRY, I WASN'T PAYING ATTENTION...
NO, BUSTING MY FACE OPEN IS CLEARLY IN LINE WITH THE UNIVERSE'S PLANS FOR ME TONIGHT.
YOU OKAY? WHY ARE YOU ALL--WHAT'S WITH THE DRESS?
LONG STORY. JUST... LET'S SAY DONOVAN SUNK TO A NEW LOW TONIGHT. SOMEHOW, THOUGH YOU MAY DISBELIEVE THE POSSIBILITY, HE ACHIEVED A PERSONAL BEST.
OR WORST, DEPENDING ON YOUR PERSPECTIVE.
YOU WANT TO TALK ABOUT IT? BECAUSE MURDER, BELIEVE ME, IS A GREAT LISTENER.
KAW?

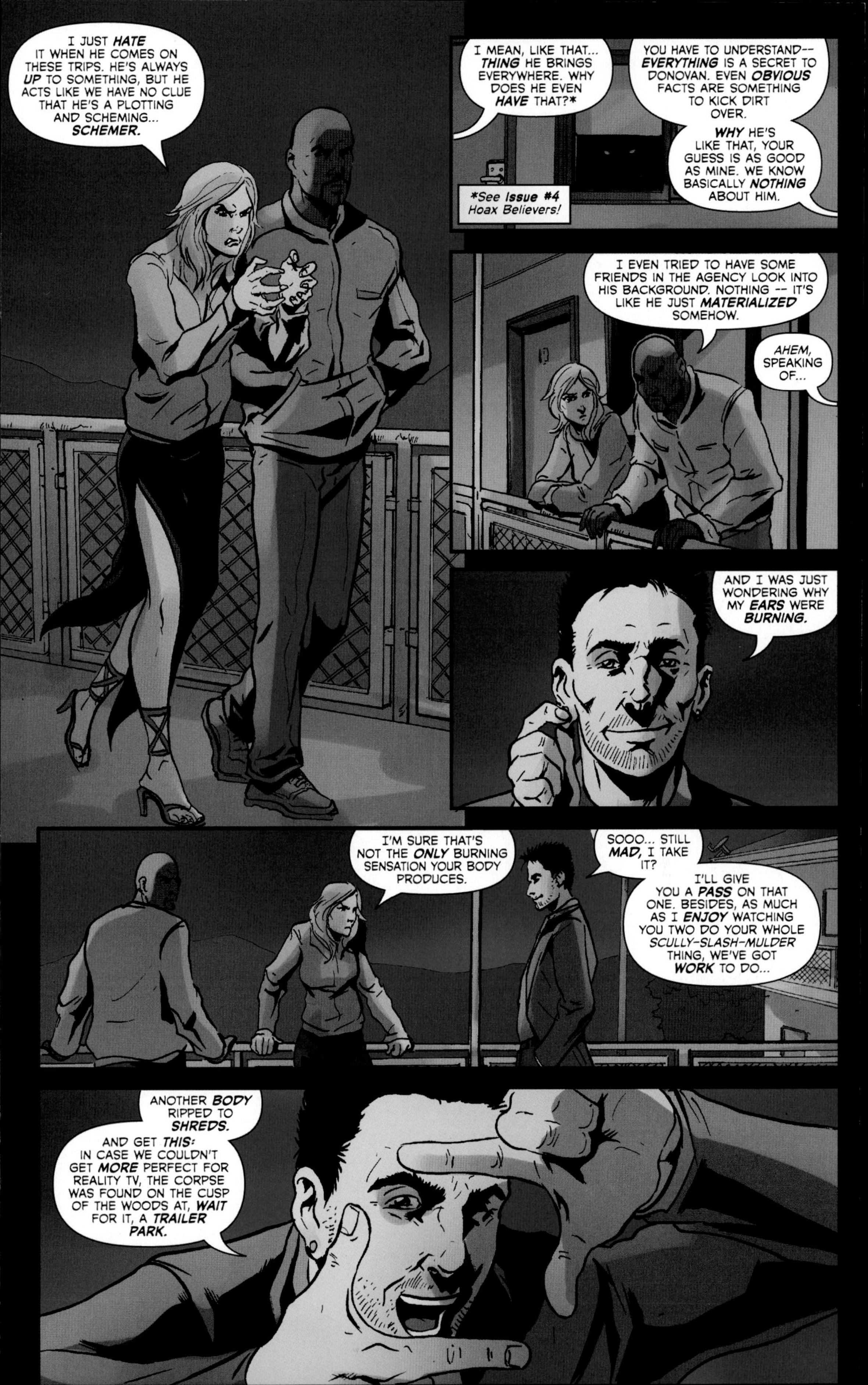
I JUST **HATE** IT WHEN HE COMES ON THESE TRIPS. HE'S ALWAYS **UP** TO SOMETHING, BUT HE ACTS LIKE WE HAVE NO CLUE THAT HE'S A PLOTTING AND SCHEMING... **SCHEMER.**
I MEAN, LIKE THAT... **THING** HE BRINGS EVERYWHERE. WHY DOES HE EVEN **HAVE** THAT?*
*See **Issue #4** Hoax Believers!
YOU HAVE TO UNDERSTAND-- **EVERYTHING** IS A SECRET TO DONOVAN. EVEN **OBVIOUS** FACTS ARE SOMETHING TO KICK DIRT OVER.
WHY HE'S LIKE THAT, YOUR GUESS IS AS GOOD AS MINE. WE KNOW BASICALLY **NOTHING** ABOUT HIM.
I EVEN TRIED TO HAVE SOME FRIENDS IN THE AGENCY LOOK INTO HIS BACKGROUND. NOTHING -- IT'S LIKE HE JUST **MATERIALIZED** SOMEHOW.
AHEM, SPEAKING OF...
AND I WAS JUST WONDERING WHY MY **EARS** WERE **BURNING.**
I'M SURE THAT'S NOT THE **ONLY** BURNING SENSATION YOUR BODY PRODUCES.
SOOO... STILL **MAD**, I TAKE IT?
I'LL GIVE YOU A **PASS** ON THAT ONE. BESIDES, AS MUCH AS I **ENJOY** WATCHING YOU TWO DO YOUR WHOLE *SCULLY-SLASH-MULDER* THING, WE'VE GOT **WORK** TO DO...
ANOTHER **BODY** RIPPED TO **SHREDS.**
AND GET **THIS:** IN CASE WE COULDN'T GET **MORE** PERFECT FOR REALITY TV, THE CORPSE WAS FOUND ON THE CUSP OF THE WOODS AT, **WAIT** FOR IT, A **TRAILER PARK.**

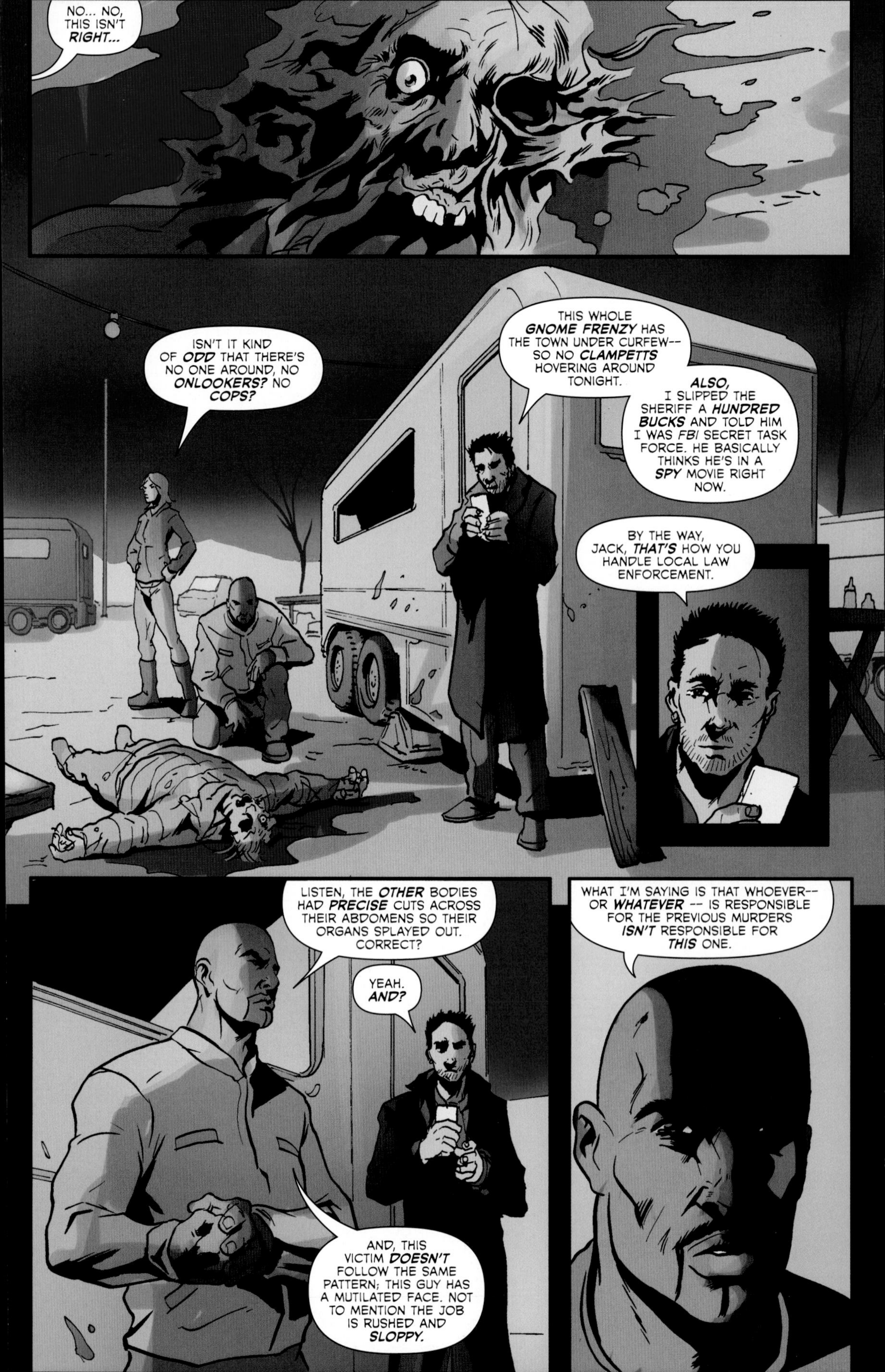
NO... NO, THIS ISN'T RIGHT...
ISN'T IT KIND OF ODD THAT THERE'S NO ONE AROUND, NO ONLOOKERS? NO COPS?
THIS WHOLE GNOME FRENZY HAS THE TOWN UNDER CURFEW-- SO NO CLAMPETTS HOVERING AROUND TONIGHT.
ALSO, I SLIPPED THE SHERIFF A HUNDRED BUCKS AND TOLD HIM I WAS FBI SECRET TASK FORCE. HE BASICALLY THINKS HE'S IN A SPY MOVIE RIGHT NOW.
BY THE WAY, JACK, THAT'S HOW YOU HANDLE LOCAL LAW ENFORCEMENT.
LISTEN, THE OTHER BODIES HAD PRECISE CUTS ACROSS THEIR ABDOMENS SO THEIR ORGANS SPLAYED OUT. CORRECT?
YEAH. AND?
AND, THIS VICTIM DOESN'T FOLLOW THE SAME PATTERN; THIS GUY HAS A MUTILATED FACE. NOT TO MENTION THE JOB IS RUSHED AND SLOPPY.
WHAT I'M SAYING IS THAT WHOEVER-- OR WHATEVER -- IS RESPONSIBLE FOR THE PREVIOUS MURDERS ISN'T RESPONSIBLE FOR THIS ONE.

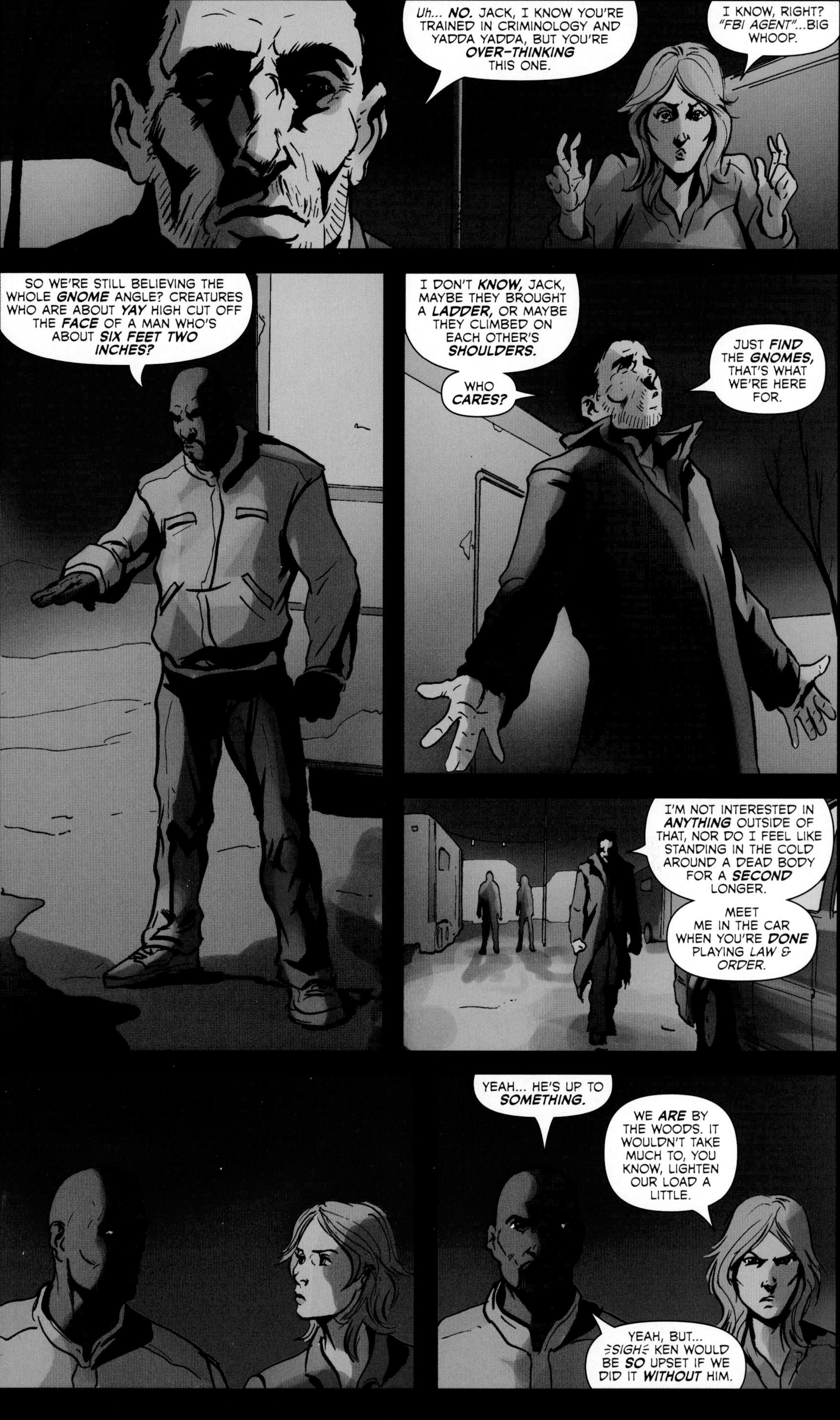
Uh... NO. JACK, I KNOW YOU'RE TRAINED IN CRIMINOLOGY AND YADDA YADDA, BUT YOU'RE OVER-THINKING THIS ONE.
I KNOW, RIGHT? "FBI AGENT"...BIG WHOOP.
SO WE'RE STILL BELIEVING THE WHOLE GNOME ANGLE? CREATURES WHO ARE ABOUT YAY HIGH CUT OFF THE FACE OF A MAN WHO'S ABOUT SIX FEET TWO INCHES?
I DON'T KNOW, JACK, MAYBE THEY BROUGHT A LADDER, OR MAYBE THEY CLIMBED ON EACH OTHER'S SHOULDERS.
WHO CARES?
JUST FIND THE GNOMES, THAT'S WHAT WE'RE HERE FOR.
I'M NOT INTERESTED IN ANYTHING OUTSIDE OF THAT, NOR DO I FEEL LIKE STANDING IN THE COLD AROUND A DEAD BODY FOR A SECOND LONGER.
MEET ME IN THE CAR WHEN YOU'RE DONE PLAYING LAW & ORDER.
YEAH... HE'S UP TO SOMETHING.
WE ARE BY THE WOODS. IT WOULDN'T TAKE MUCH TO, YOU KNOW, LIGHTEN OUR LOAD A LITTLE.
YEAH, BUT... SIGH KEN WOULD BE SO UPSET IF WE DID IT WITHOUT HIM.

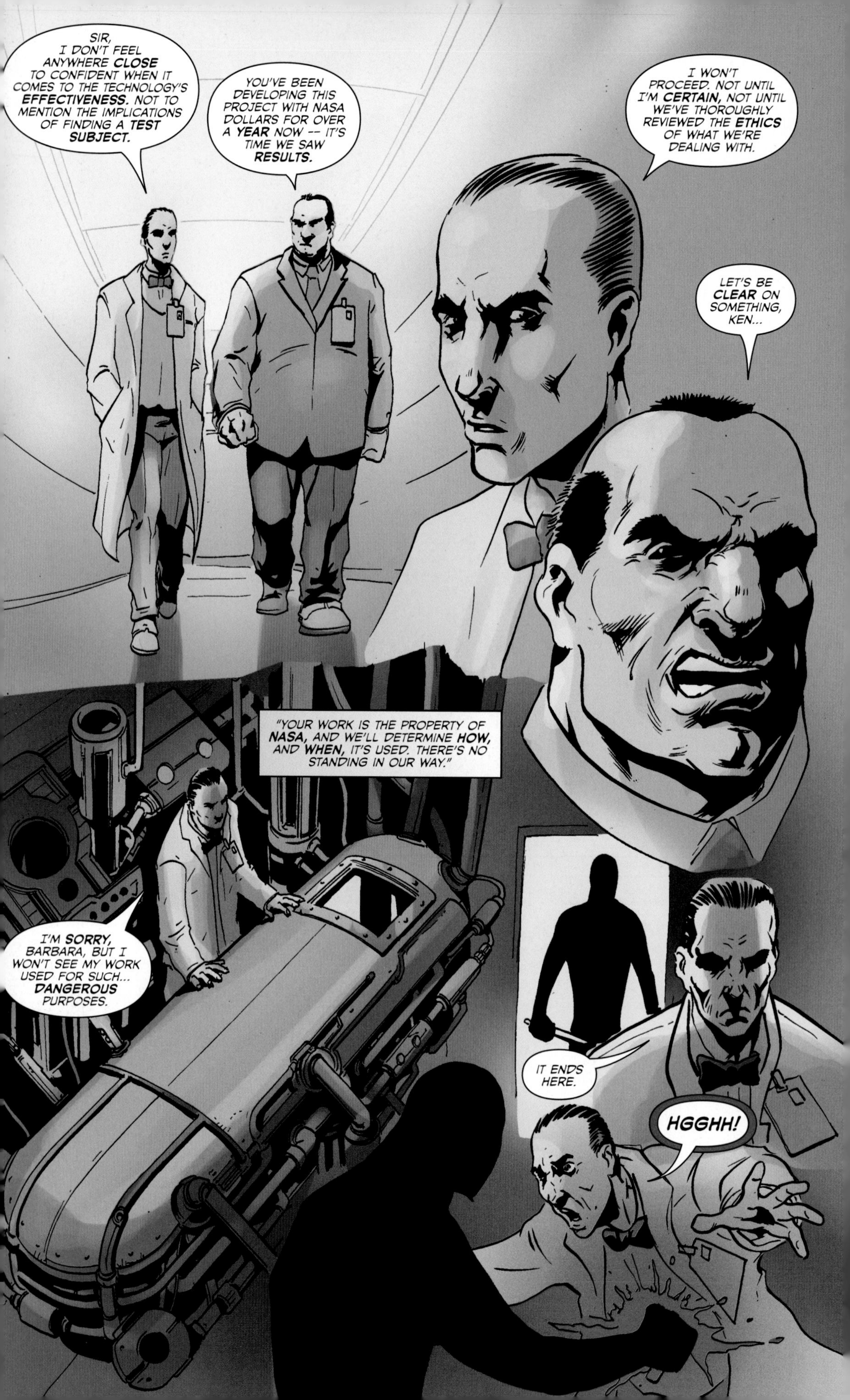
SIR, I DON'T FEEL ANYWHERE CLOSE TO CONFIDENT WHEN IT COMES TO THE TECHNOLOGY'S EFFECTIVENESS. NOT TO MENTION THE IMPLICATIONS OF FINDING A TEST SUBJECT.
YOU'VE BEEN DEVELOPING THIS PROJECT WITH NASA DOLLARS FOR OVER A YEAR NOW -- IT'S TIME WE SAW RESULTS.
I WON'T PROCEED. NOT UNTIL I'M CERTAIN, NOT UNTIL WE'VE THOROUGHLY REVIEWED THE ETHICS OF WHAT WE'RE DEALING WITH.
LET'S BE CLEAR ON SOMETHING, KEN...
"YOUR WORK IS THE PROPERTY OF NASA, AND WE'LL DETERMINE HOW, AND WHEN, IT'S USED. THERE'S NO STANDING IN OUR WAY."
I'M SORRY, BARBARA, BUT I WON'T SEE MY WORK USED FOR SUCH... DANGEROUS PURPOSES.
IT ENDS HERE.
HGGHH!

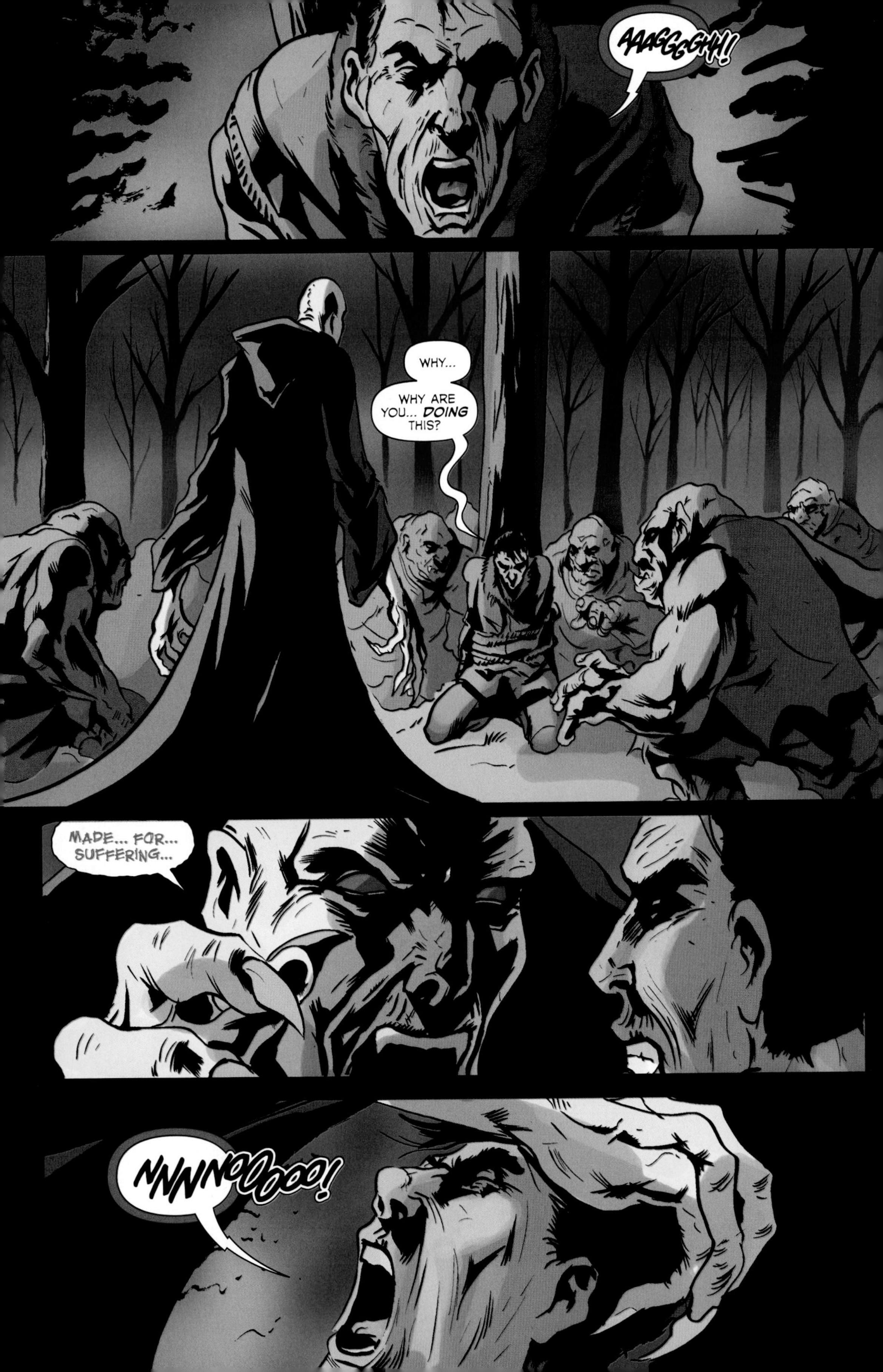
AAAGGGGHH!
WHY...
WHY ARE YOU... DOING THIS?
MADE... FOR... SUFFERING...
NNNNOOOooo!

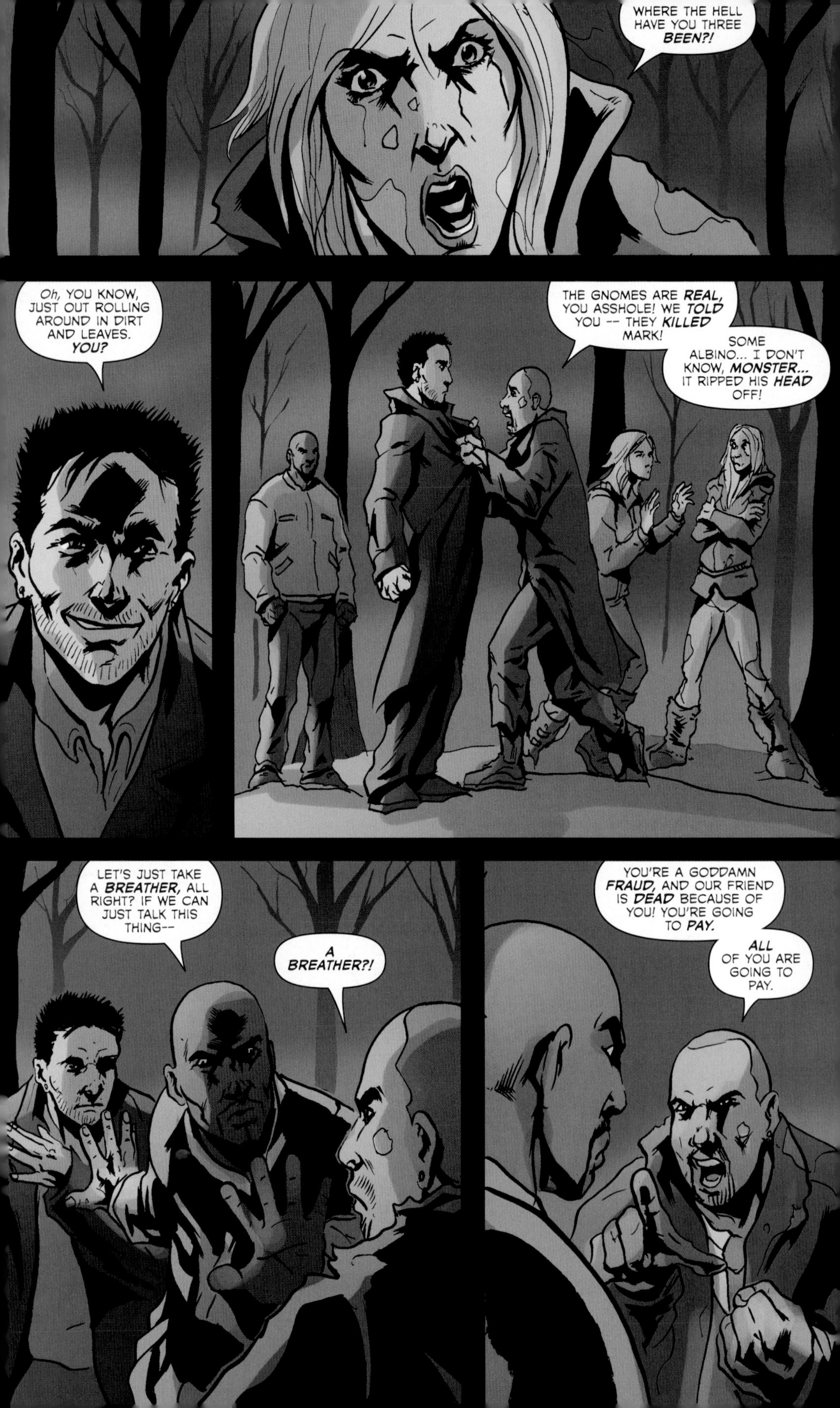
WHERE THE HELL HAVE YOU THREE *BEEN?!*
Oh, YOU KNOW, JUST OUT ROLLING AROUND IN DIRT AND LEAVES. *YOU?*
THE GNOMES ARE *REAL,* YOU ASSHOLE! WE *TOLD* YOU -- THEY *KILLED* MARK!
SOME ALBINO... I DON'T KNOW, *MONSTER...* IT RIPPED HIS *HEAD* OFF!
LET'S JUST TAKE A *BREATHER,* ALL RIGHT? IF WE CAN JUST TALK THIS THING--
A BREATHER?!
YOU'RE A GODDAMN *FRAUD,* AND OUR FRIEND IS *DEAD* BECAUSE OF YOU! YOU'RE GOING TO *PAY.*
ALL OF YOU ARE GOING TO PAY.

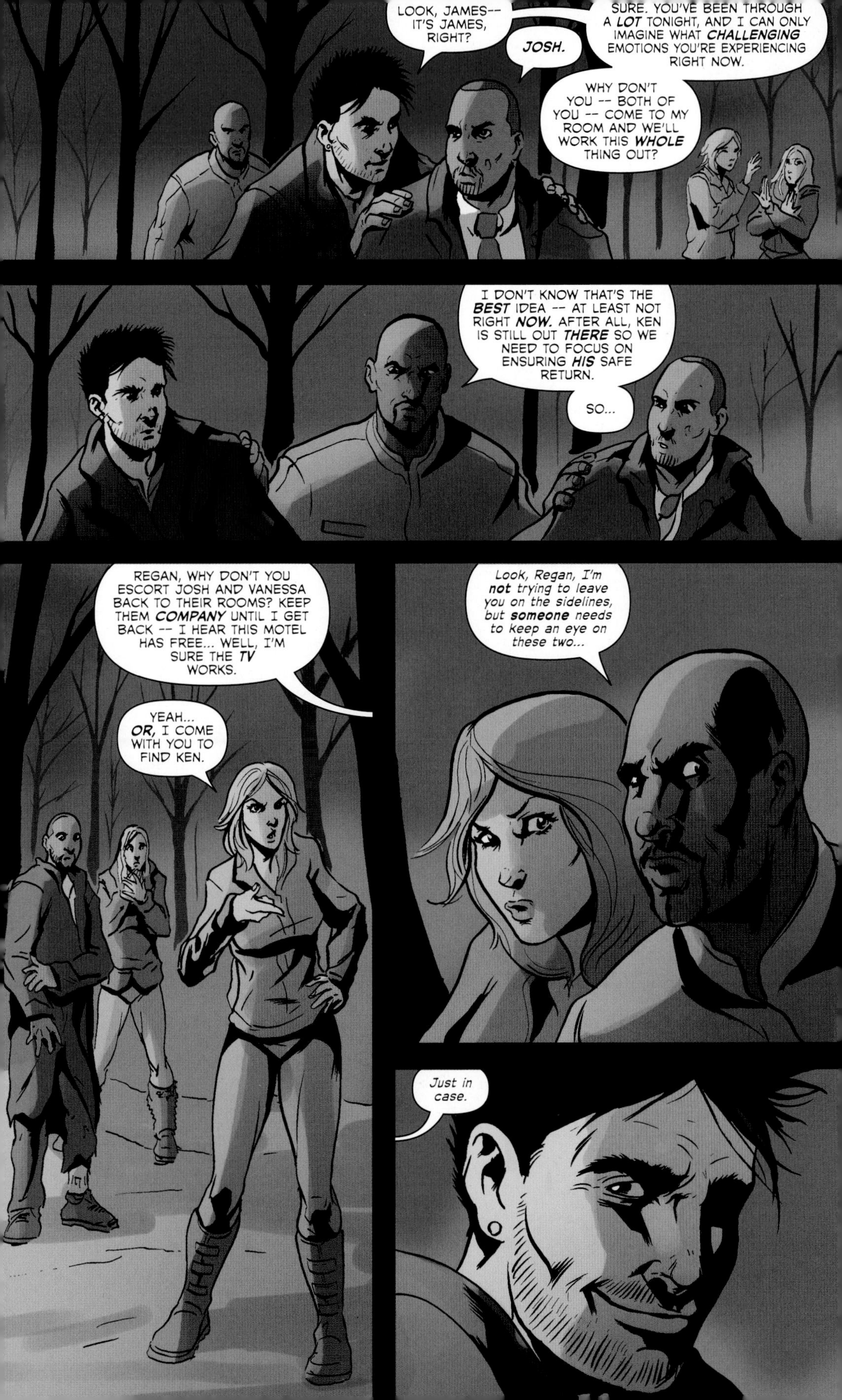
LOOK, JAMES-- IT'S JAMES, RIGHT?
JOSH.
SURE. YOU'VE BEEN THROUGH A LOT TONIGHT, AND I CAN ONLY IMAGINE WHAT CHALLENGING EMOTIONS YOU'RE EXPERIENCING RIGHT NOW.
WHY DON'T YOU -- BOTH OF YOU -- COME TO MY ROOM AND WE'LL WORK THIS WHOLE THING OUT?
I DON'T KNOW THAT'S THE BEST IDEA -- AT LEAST NOT RIGHT NOW. AFTER ALL, KEN IS STILL OUT THERE SO WE NEED TO FOCUS ON ENSURING HIS SAFE RETURN.
SO...
REGAN, WHY DON'T YOU ESCORT JOSH AND VANESSA BACK TO THEIR ROOMS? KEEP THEM COMPANY UNTIL I GET BACK -- I HEAR THIS MOTEL HAS FREE... WELL, I'M SURE THE TV WORKS.
YEAH... OR, I COME WITH YOU TO FIND KEN.
Look, Regan, I'm not trying to leave you on the sidelines, but someone needs to keep an eye on these two...
Just in case.

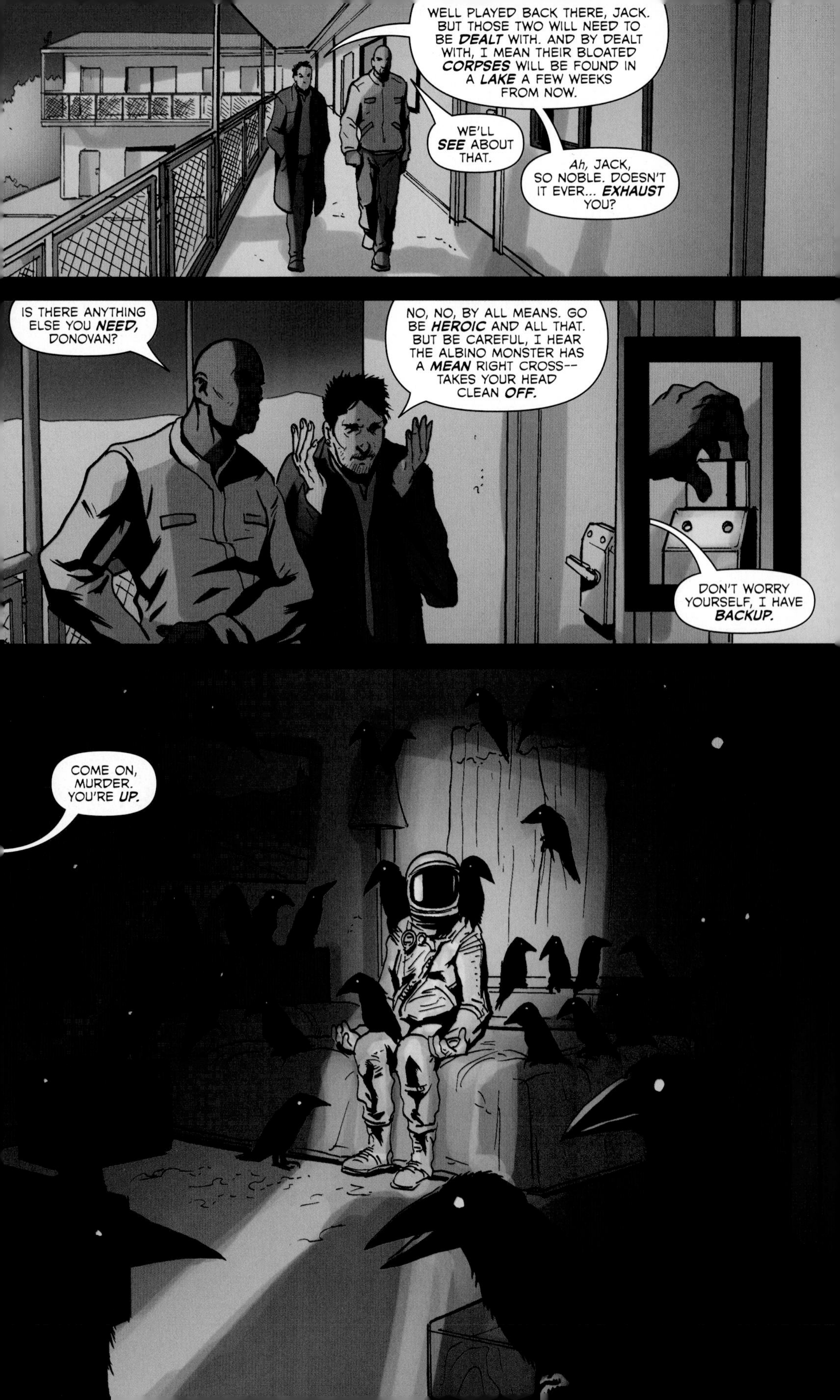
WELL PLAYED BACK THERE, JACK. BUT THOSE TWO WILL NEED TO BE DEALT WITH. AND BY DEALT WITH, I MEAN THEIR BLOATED CORPSES WILL BE FOUND IN A LAKE A FEW WEEKS FROM NOW.
WE'LL SEE ABOUT THAT.
Ah, JACK, SO NOBLE. DOESN'T IT EVER... EXHAUST YOU?
IS THERE ANYTHING ELSE YOU NEED, DONOVAN?
NO, NO, BY ALL MEANS. GO BE HEROIC AND ALL THAT. BUT BE CAREFUL, I HEAR THE ALBINO MONSTER HAS A MEAN RIGHT CROSS-- TAKES YOUR HEAD CLEAN OFF.
DON'T WORRY YOURSELF, I HAVE BACKUP.
COME ON, MURDER. YOU'RE UP.

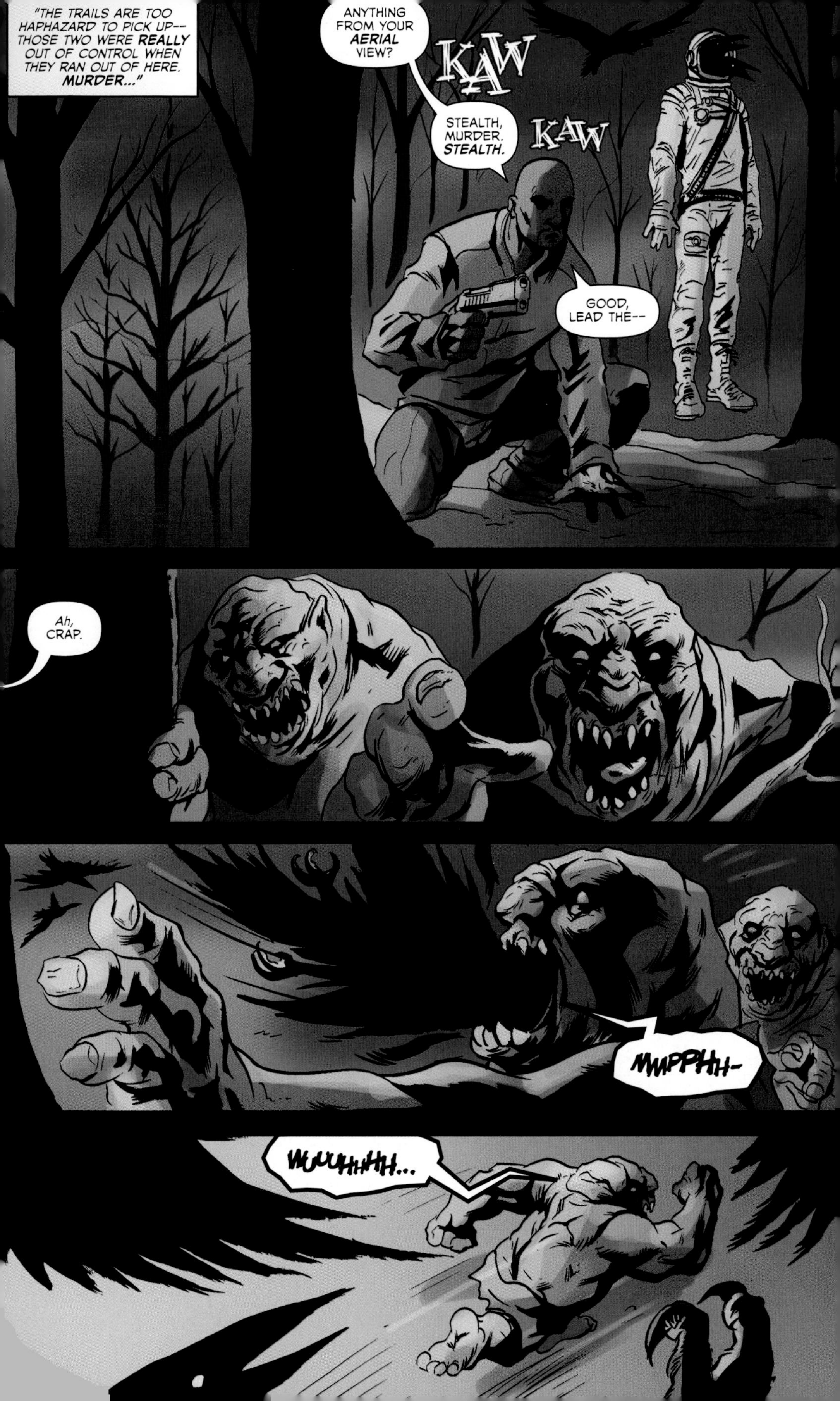
"THE TRAILS ARE TOO HAPHAZARD TO PICK UP-- THOSE TWO WERE REALLY OUT OF CONTROL WHEN THEY RAN OUT OF HERE. MURDER..."
ANYTHING FROM YOUR AERIAL VIEW?
KAW
KAW
STEALTH, MURDER. STEALTH.
GOOD, LEAD THE--
Ah, CRAP.
MMPPHH-
WUUUHHHH...

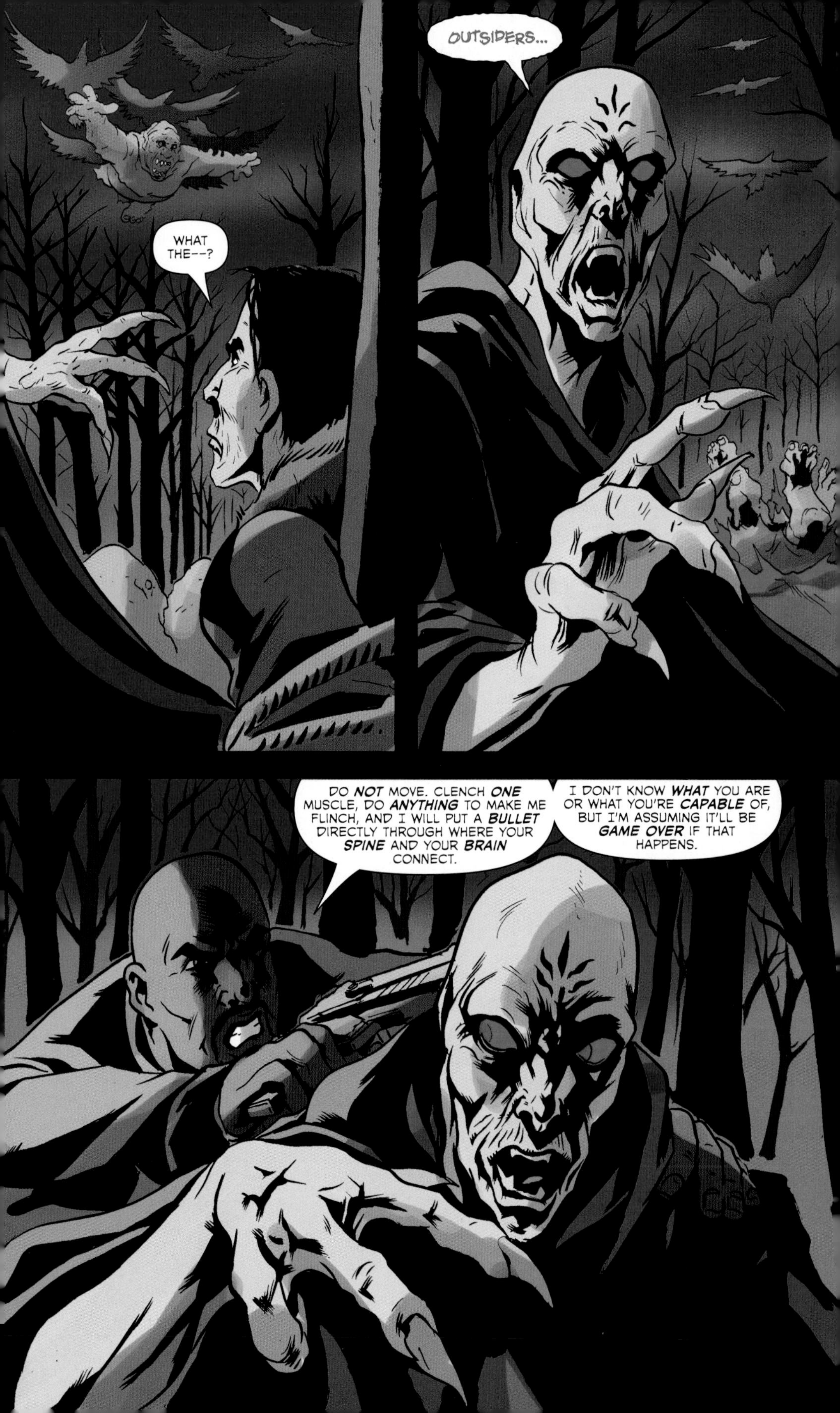
WHAT THE--?
OUTSIDERS...
DO NOT MOVE. CLENCH ONE MUSCLE, DO ANYTHING TO MAKE ME FLINCH, AND I WILL PUT A BULLET DIRECTLY THROUGH WHERE YOUR SPINE AND YOUR BRAIN CONNECT.
I DON'T KNOW WHAT YOU ARE OR WHAT YOU'RE CAPABLE OF, BUT I'M ASSUMING IT'LL BE GAME OVER IF THAT HAPPENS.

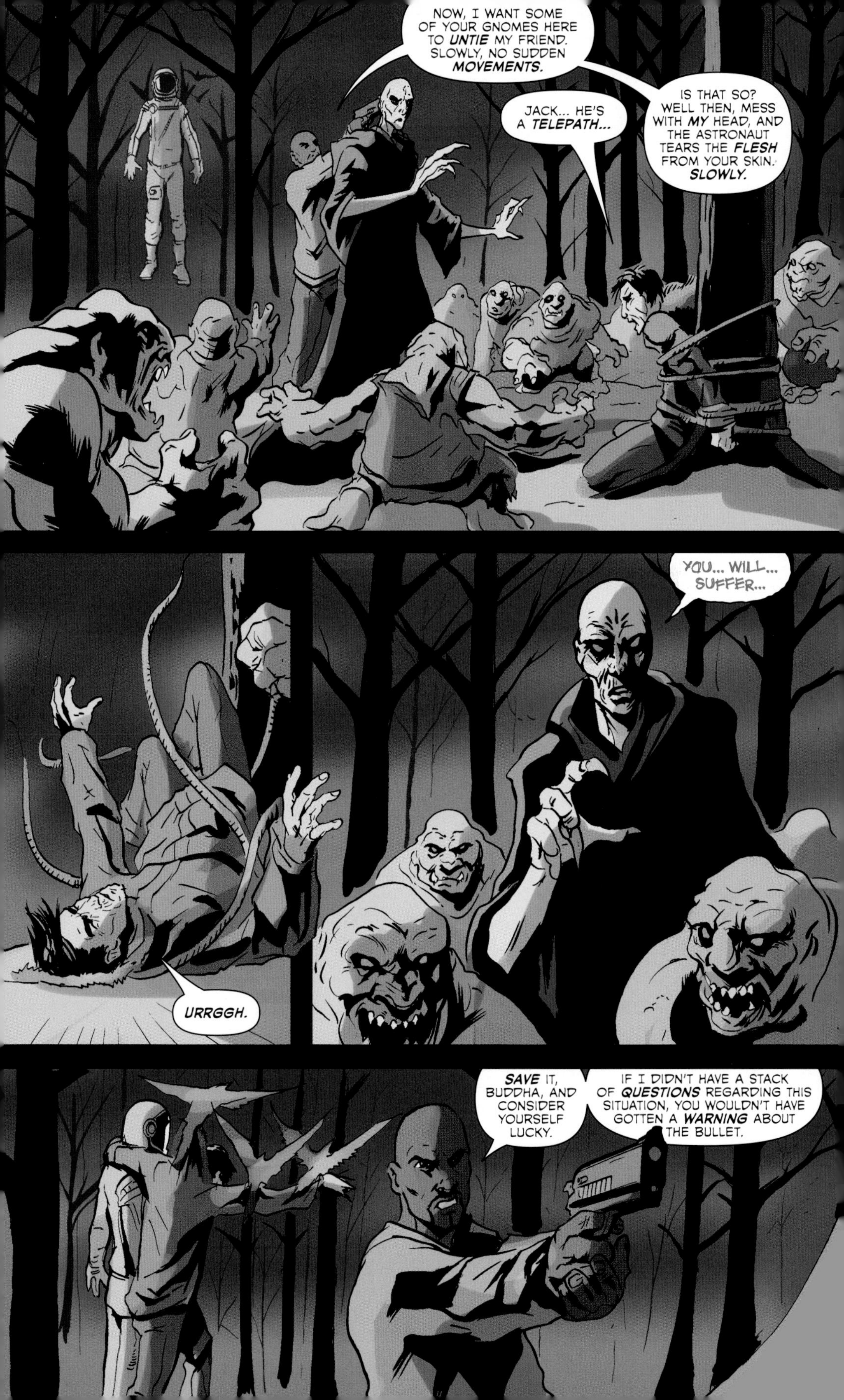
NOW, I WANT SOME OF YOUR GNOMES HERE TO UNTIE MY FRIEND. SLOWLY, NO SUDDEN MOVEMENTS.
JACK... HE'S A TELEPATH...
IS THAT SO? WELL THEN, MESS WITH MY HEAD, AND THE ASTRONAUT TEARS THE FLESH FROM YOUR SKIN. SLOWLY.
URRGGH.
YOU... WILL... SUFFER...
SAVE IT, BUDDHA, AND CONSIDER YOURSELF LUCKY.
IF I DIDN'T HAVE A STACK OF QUESTIONS REGARDING THIS SITUATION, YOU WOULDN'T HAVE GOTTEN A WARNING ABOUT THE BULLET.

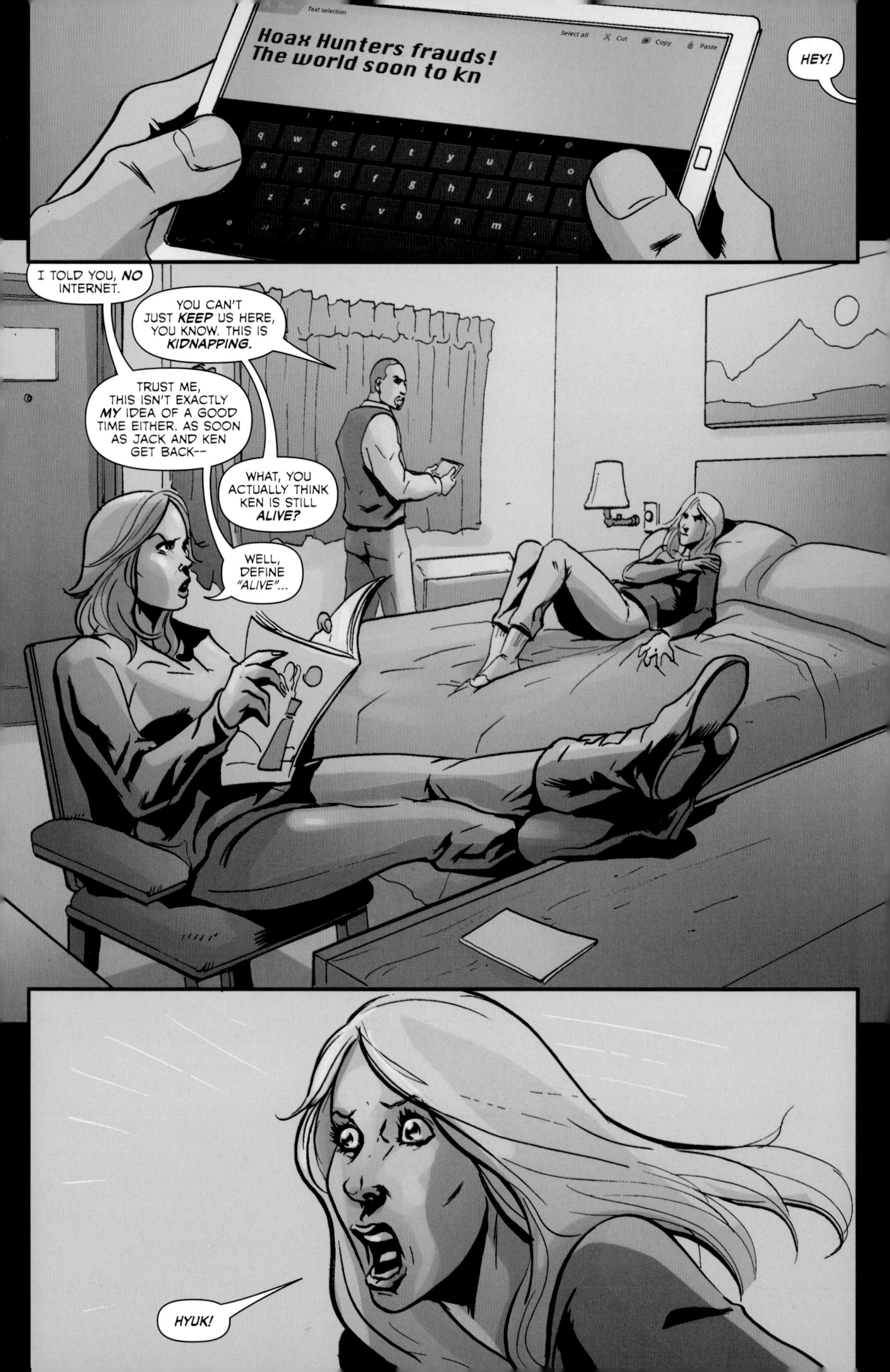
Text selection
Select all
Cut
Copy
Paste
Hoax Hunters frauds!
The world soon to kn
HEY!
I TOLD YOU, NO INTERNET.
YOU CAN'T JUST KEEP US HERE, YOU KNOW. THIS IS KIDNAPPING.
TRUST ME, THIS ISN'T EXACTLY MY IDEA OF A GOOD TIME EITHER. AS SOON AS JACK AND KEN GET BACK--
WHAT, YOU ACTUALLY THINK KEN IS STILL ALIVE?
WELL, DEFINE "ALIVE"...
HYUK!

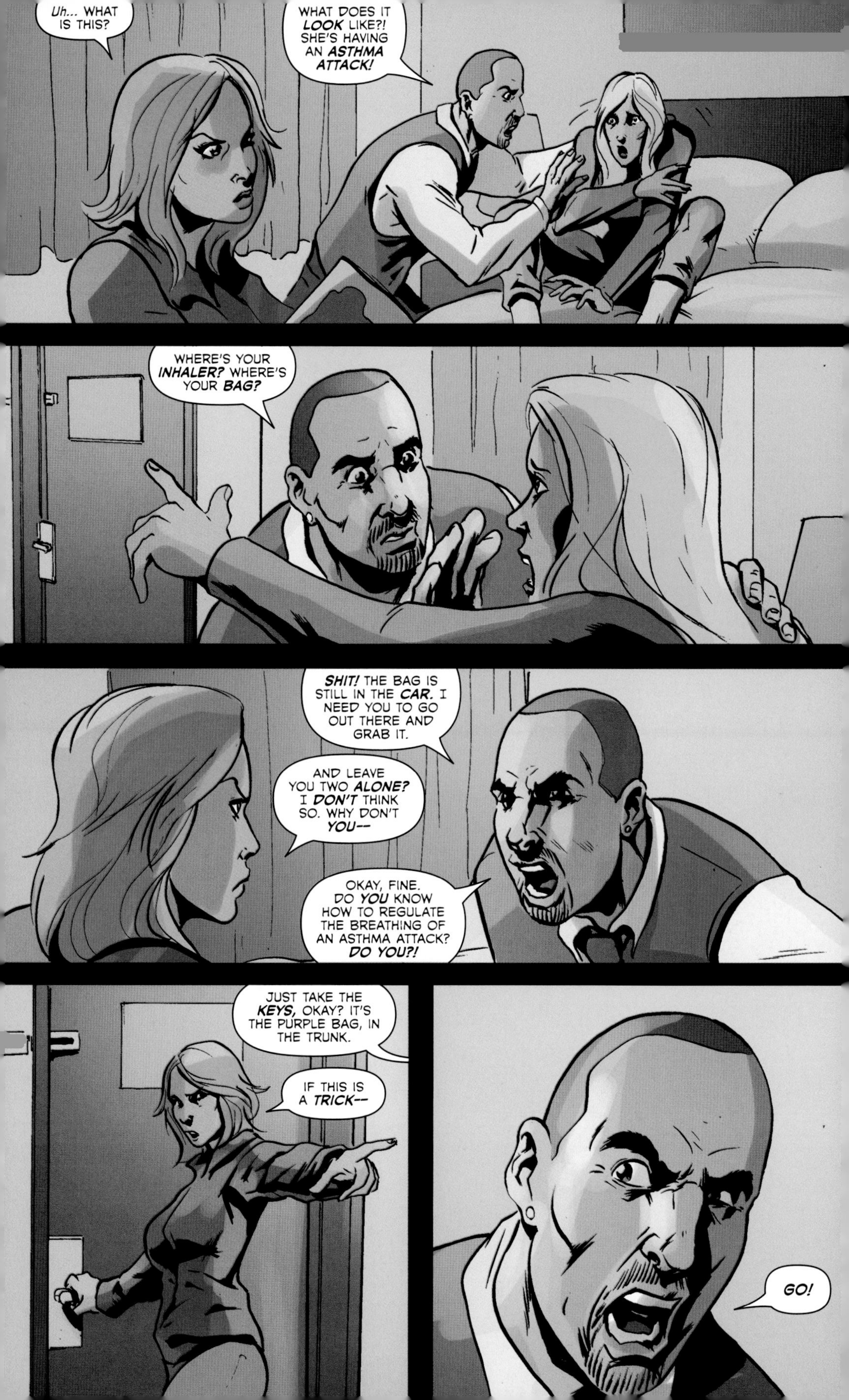
Uh... WHAT IS THIS?
WHAT DOES IT LOOK LIKE?! SHE'S HAVING AN ASTHMA ATTACK!
WHERE'S YOUR INHALER? WHERE'S YOUR BAG?
SHIT! THE BAG IS STILL IN THE CAR. I NEED YOU TO GO OUT THERE AND GRAB IT.
AND LEAVE YOU TWO ALONE? I DON'T THINK SO. WHY DON'T YOU--
OKAY, FINE. DO YOU KNOW HOW TO REGULATE THE BREATHING OF AN ASTHMA ATTACK? DO YOU?!
JUST TAKE THE KEYS, OKAY? IT'S THE PURPLE BAG, IN THE TRUNK.
IF THIS IS A TRICK--
GO!

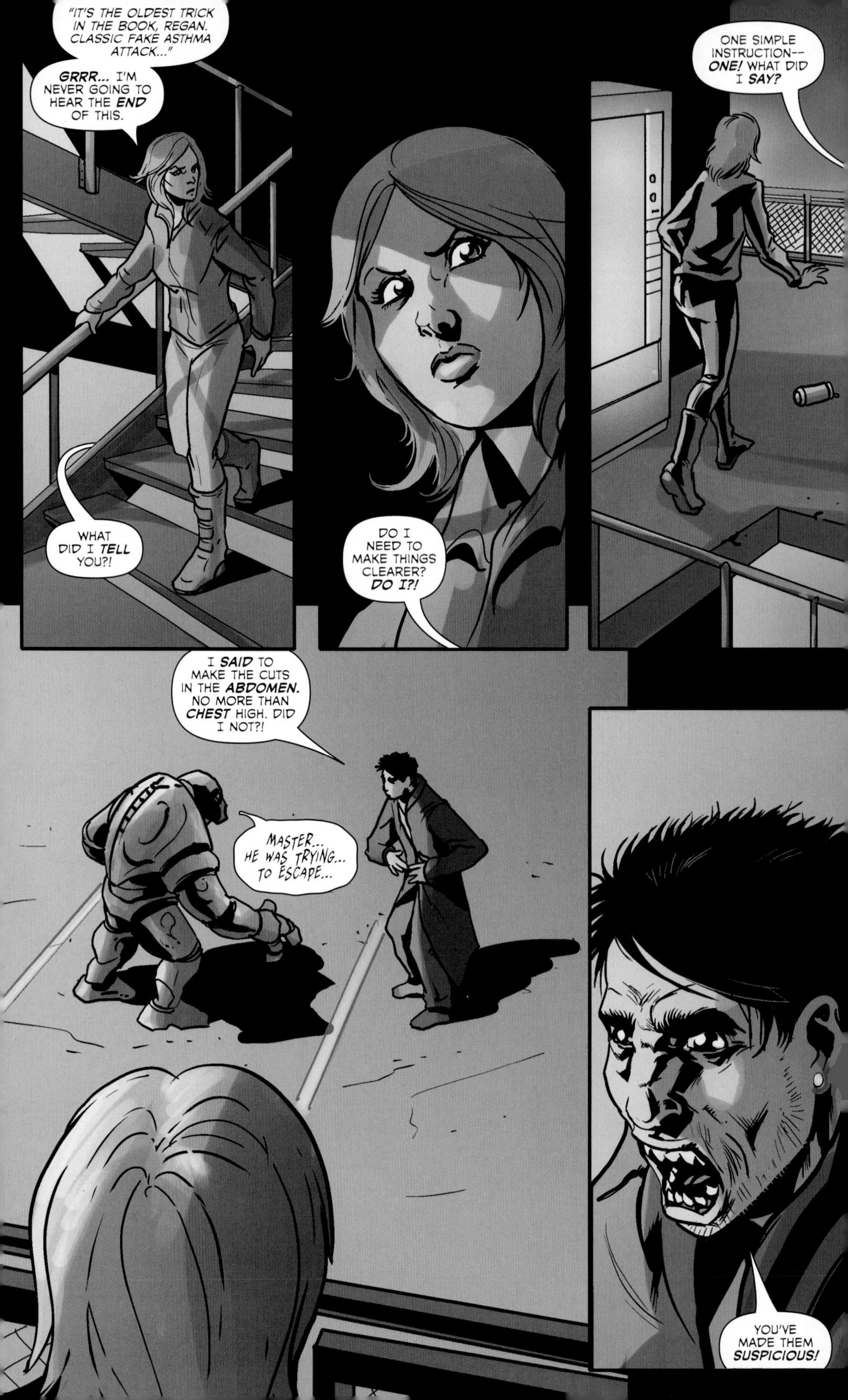
"IT'S THE OLDEST TRICK IN THE BOOK, REGAN. CLASSIC FAKE ASTHMA ATTACK..."
GRRR... I'M NEVER GOING TO HEAR THE END OF THIS.
WHAT DID I TELL YOU?!
DO I NEED TO MAKE THINGS CLEARER? DO I?!
ONE SIMPLE INSTRUCTION-- ONE! WHAT DID I SAY?
I SAID TO MAKE THE CUTS IN THE ABDOMEN. NO MORE THAN CHEST HIGH. DID I NOT?!
MASTER... HE WAS TRYING... TO ESCAPE...
YOU'VE MADE THEM SUSPICIOUS!

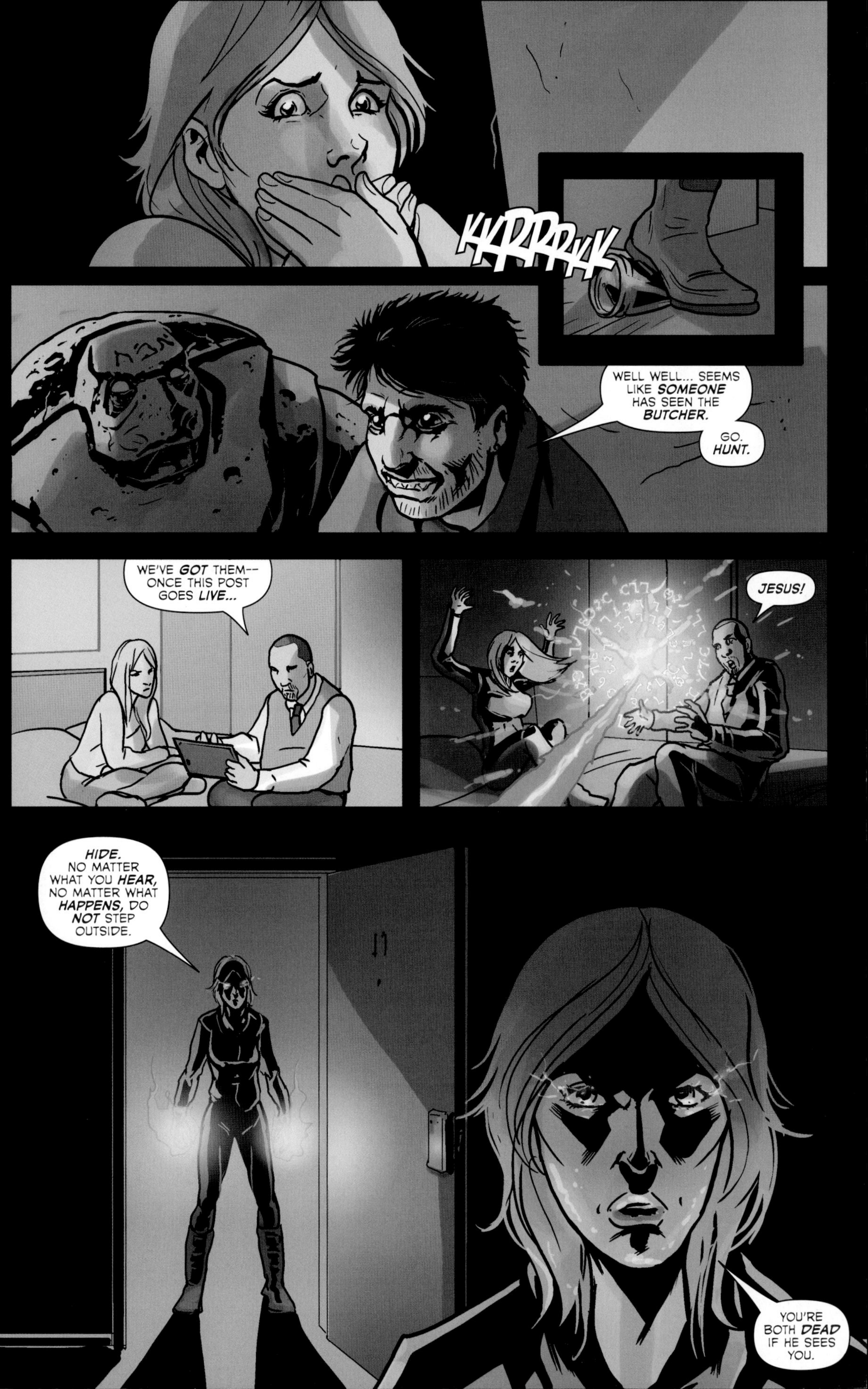

KKRRRRKK
WELL WELL... SEEMS LIKE SOMEONE HAS SEEN THE BUTCHER.
GO. HUNT.
WE'VE GOT THEM-- ONCE THIS POST GOES LIVE...
JESUS!
HIDE. NO MATTER WHAT YOU HEAR, NO MATTER WHAT HAPPENS, DO NOT STEP OUTSIDE.
YOU'RE BOTH DEAD IF HE SEES YOU.

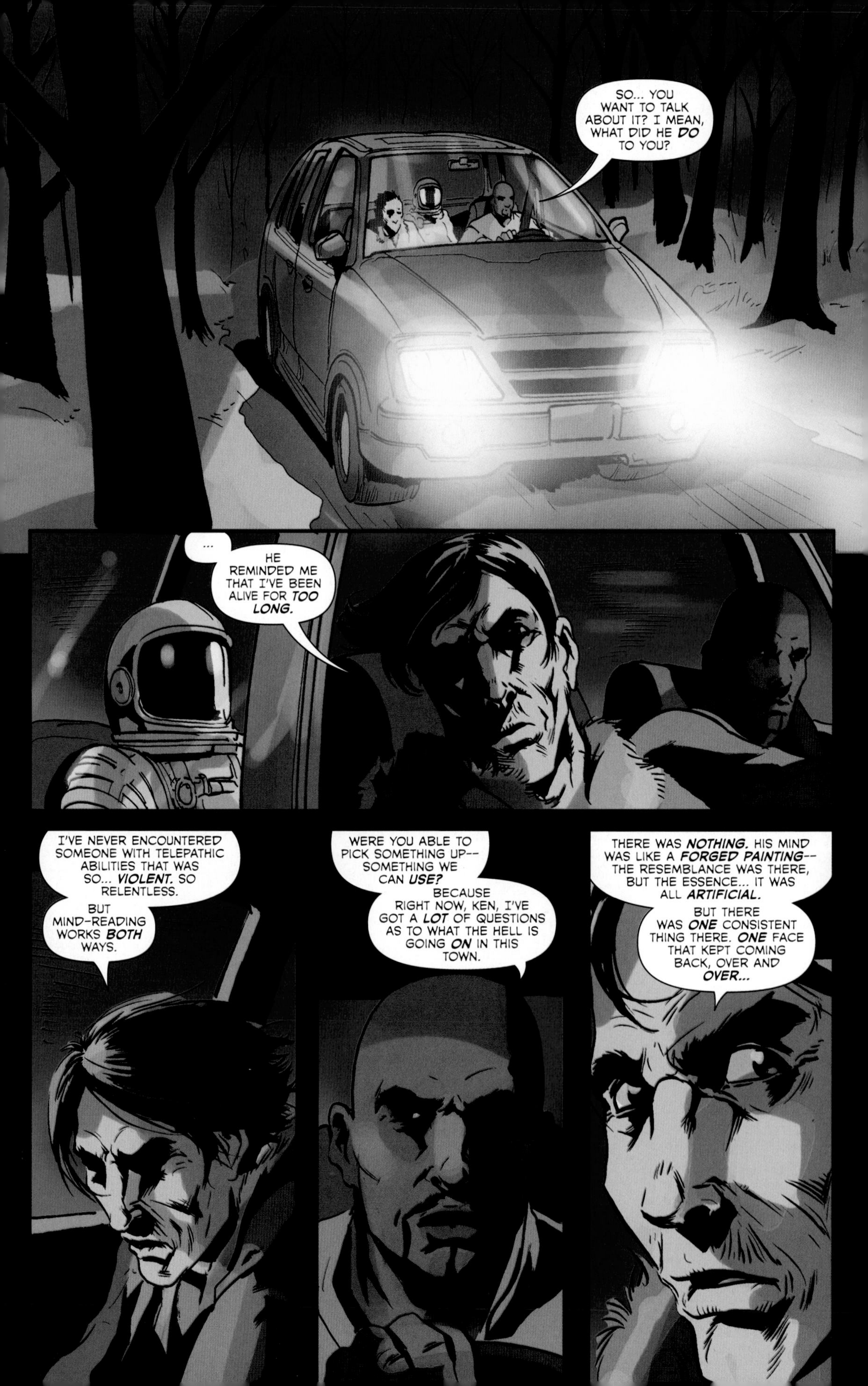
SO... YOU WANT TO TALK ABOUT IT? I MEAN, WHAT DID HE *DO* TO YOU?
...
HE REMINDED ME THAT I'VE BEEN ALIVE FOR *TOO LONG.*
I'VE NEVER ENCOUNTERED SOMEONE WITH TELEPATHIC ABILITIES THAT WAS SO... *VIOLENT.* SO RELENTLESS.
BUT MIND-READING WORKS *BOTH* WAYS.
WERE YOU ABLE TO PICK SOMETHING UP-- SOMETHING WE CAN *USE?*
BECAUSE RIGHT NOW, KEN, I'VE GOT A *LOT* OF QUESTIONS AS TO WHAT THE HELL IS GOING *ON* IN THIS TOWN.
THERE WAS *NOTHING.* HIS MIND WAS LIKE A *FORGED PAINTING*-- THE RESEMBLANCE WAS THERE, BUT THE ESSENCE... IT WAS ALL *ARTIFICIAL.*
BUT THERE WAS *ONE* CONSISTENT THING THERE. *ONE* FACE THAT KEPT COMING BACK, OVER AND *OVER...*

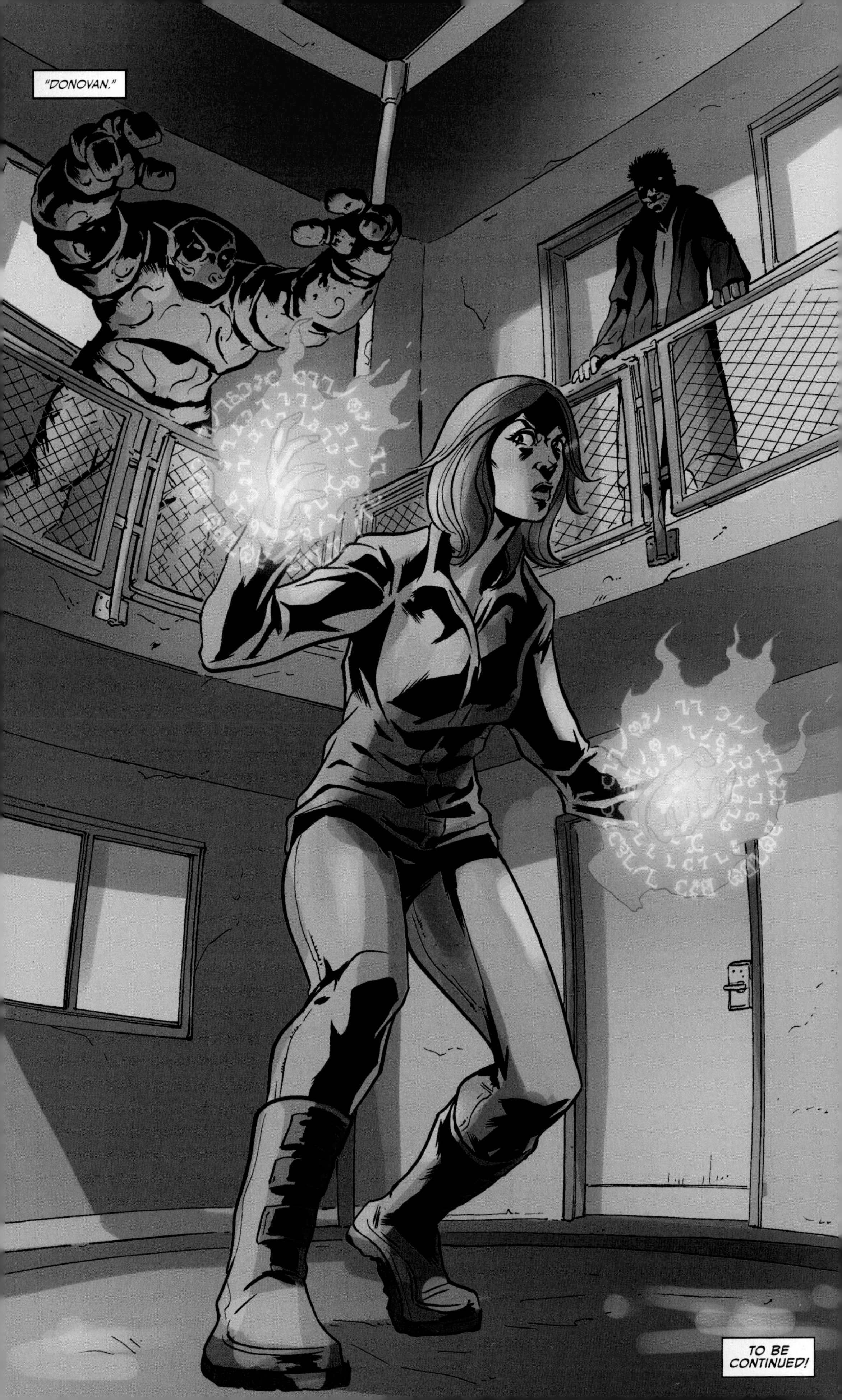
"DONOVAN."
TO BE CONTINUED!

HOAX HUNTERS

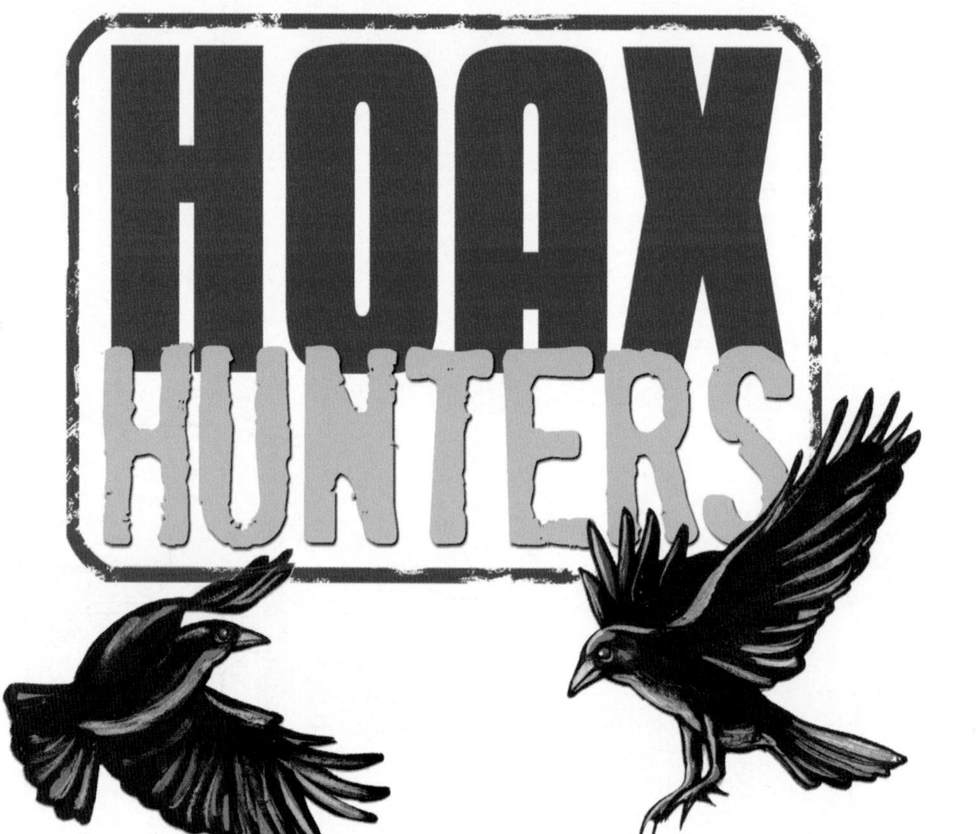

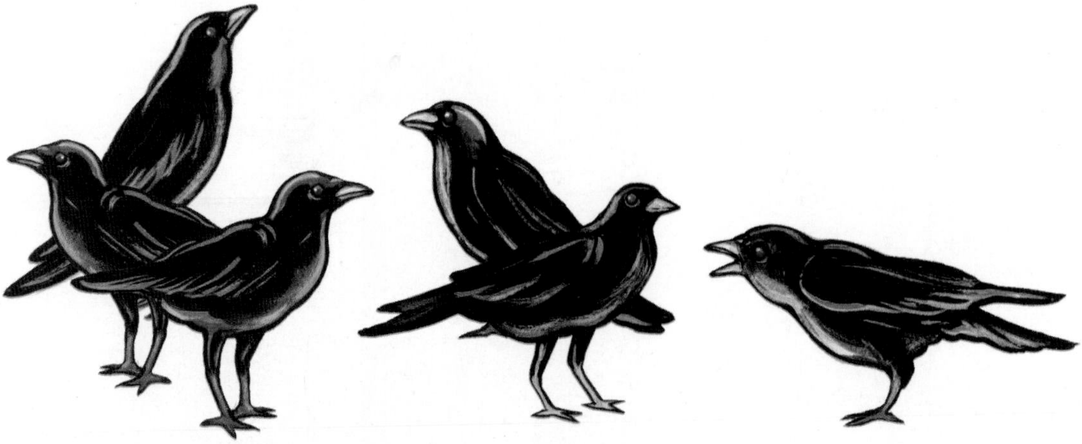

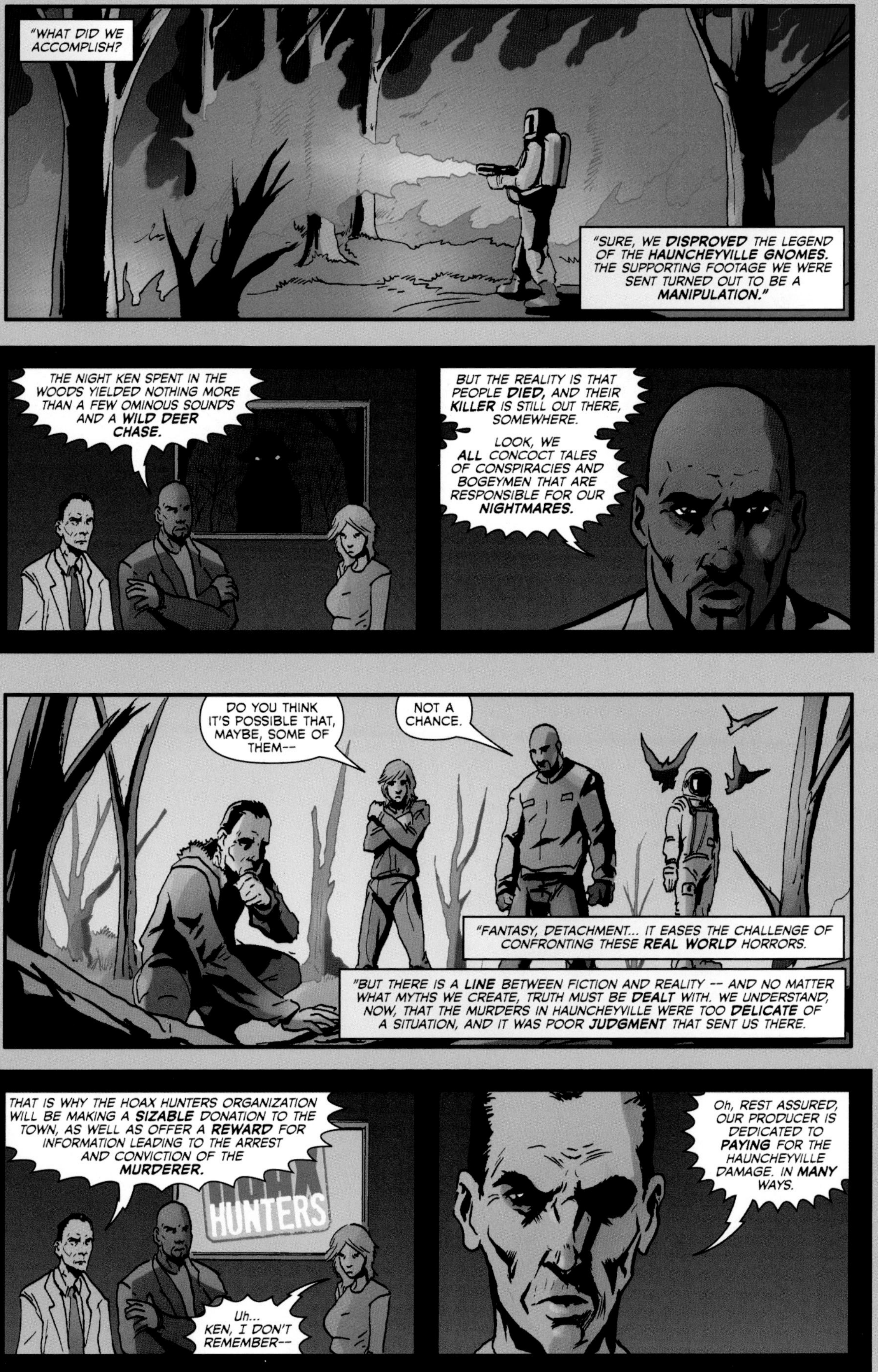
"WHAT DID WE ACCOMPLISH?
"SURE, WE **DISPROVED** THE LEGEND OF THE **HAUNCHEYVILLE GNOMES.** THE SUPPORTING FOOTAGE WE WERE SENT TURNED OUT TO BE A **MANIPULATION.**"
THE NIGHT KEN SPENT IN THE WOODS YIELDED NOTHING MORE THAN A FEW OMINOUS SOUNDS AND A **WILD DEER CHASE.**
BUT THE REALITY IS THAT PEOPLE **DIED,** AND THEIR **KILLER** IS STILL OUT THERE, SOMEWHERE.
LOOK, WE **ALL** CONCOCT TALES OF CONSPIRACIES AND BOGEYMEN THAT ARE RESPONSIBLE FOR OUR **NIGHTMARES.**
DO YOU THINK IT'S POSSIBLE THAT, MAYBE, SOME OF THEM--
NOT A CHANCE.
"FANTASY, DETACHMENT... IT EASES THE CHALLENGE OF CONFRONTING THESE **REAL WORLD** HORRORS.
"BUT THERE IS A **LINE** BETWEEN FICTION AND REALITY -- AND NO MATTER WHAT MYTHS WE CREATE, TRUTH MUST BE **DEALT** WITH. WE UNDERSTAND, NOW, THAT THE MURDERS IN HAUNCHEYVILLE WERE TOO **DELICATE** OF A SITUATION, AND IT WAS POOR **JUDGMENT** THAT SENT US THERE.
THAT IS WHY THE HOAX HUNTERS ORGANIZATION WILL BE MAKING A **SIZABLE** DONATION TO THE TOWN, AS WELL AS OFFER A **REWARD** FOR INFORMATION LEADING TO THE ARREST AND CONVICTION OF THE **MURDERER.**
HUNTERS
Uh... KEN, I DON'T REMEMBER--
Oh, REST ASSURED, OUR PRODUCER IS DEDICATED TO **PAYING** FOR THE HAUNCHEYVILLE DAMAGE. IN **MANY** WAYS.

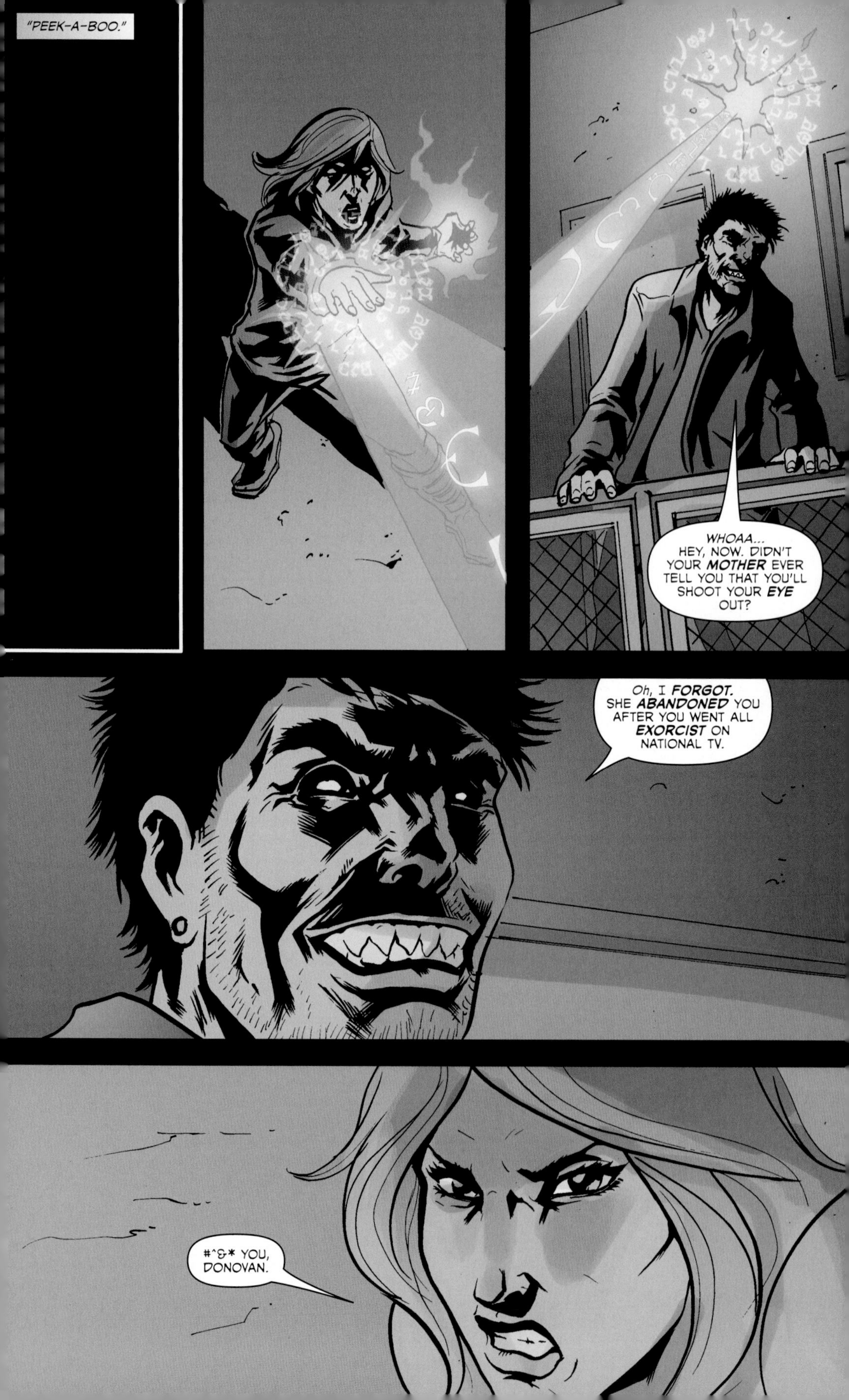
"PEEK-A-BOO."
WHOAA... HEY, NOW. DIDN'T YOUR MOTHER EVER TELL YOU THAT YOU'LL SHOOT YOUR EYE OUT?
Oh, I FORGOT. SHE ABANDONED YOU AFTER YOU WENT ALL EXORCIST ON NATIONAL TV.
#^&* YOU, DONOVAN.

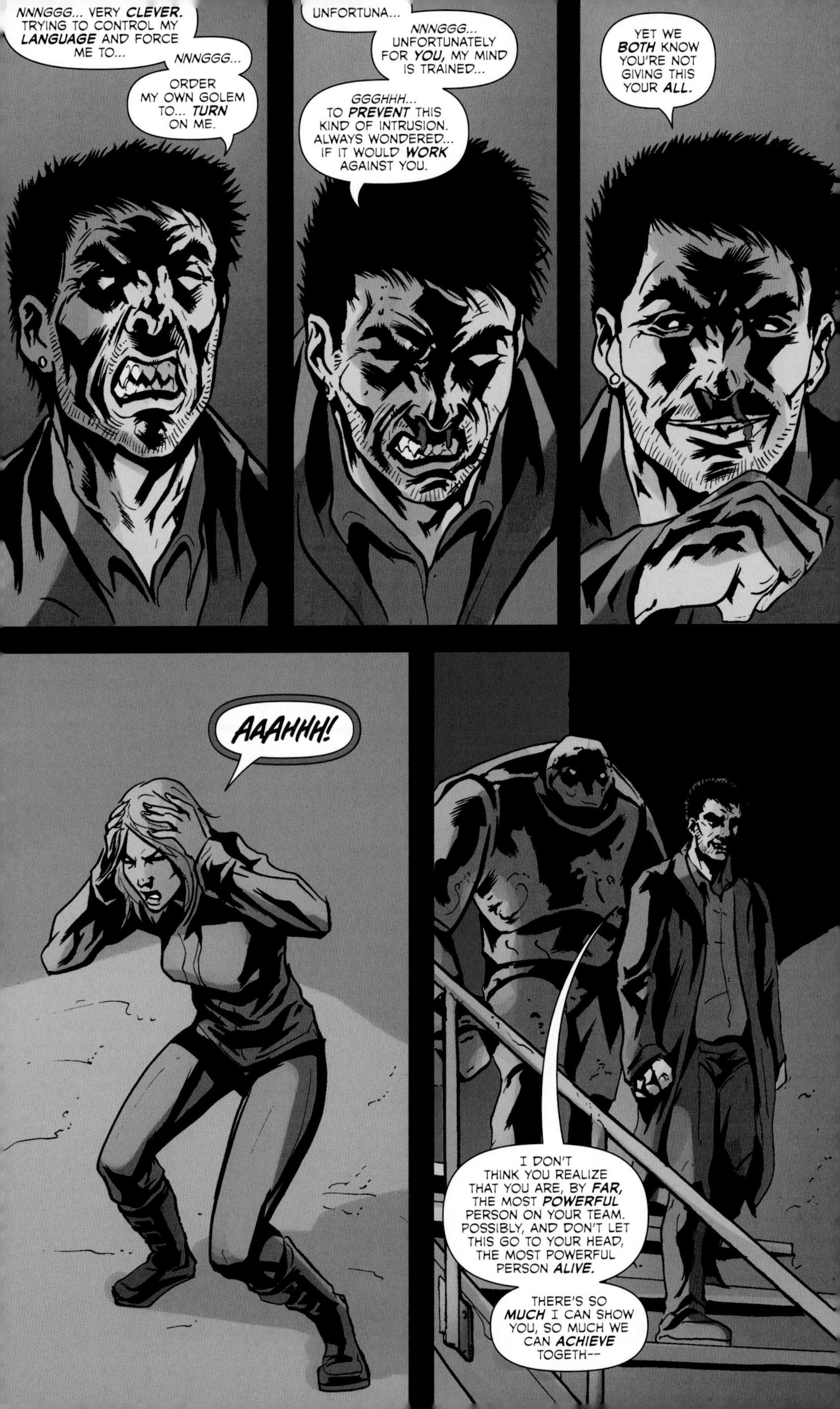
NNNGGG... VERY CLEVER. TRYING TO CONTROL MY LANGUAGE AND FORCE ME TO...
NNNGGG...
ORDER MY OWN GOLEM TO... TURN ON ME.
UNFORTUNA...
NNNGGG... UNFORTUNATELY FOR YOU, MY MIND IS TRAINED...
GGGHHH... TO PREVENT THIS KIND OF INTRUSION. ALWAYS WONDERED... IF IT WOULD WORK AGAINST YOU.
YET WE BOTH KNOW YOU'RE NOT GIVING THIS YOUR ALL.
AAAHHH!
I DON'T THINK YOU REALIZE THAT YOU ARE, BY FAR, THE MOST POWERFUL PERSON ON YOUR TEAM. POSSIBLY, AND DON'T LET THIS GO TO YOUR HEAD, THE MOST POWERFUL PERSON ALIVE.
THERE'S SO MUCH I CAN SHOW YOU, SO MUCH WE CAN ACHIEVE TOGETH--

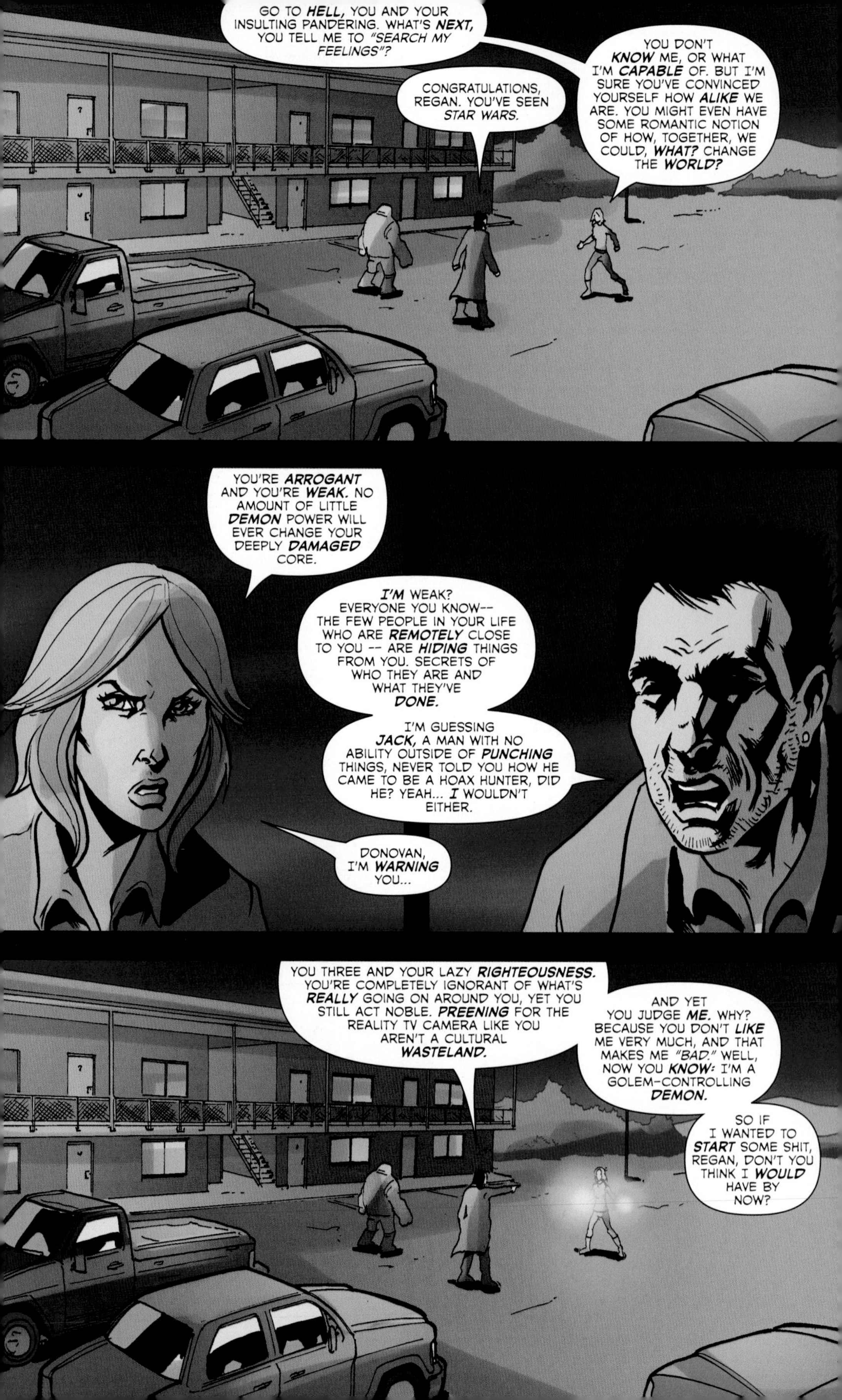

GO TO HELL, YOU AND YOUR INSULTING PANDERING. WHAT'S NEXT, YOU TELL ME TO "SEARCH MY FEELINGS"?
CONGRATULATIONS, REGAN. YOU'VE SEEN STAR WARS.
YOU DON'T KNOW ME, OR WHAT I'M CAPABLE OF. BUT I'M SURE YOU'VE CONVINCED YOURSELF HOW ALIKE WE ARE. YOU MIGHT EVEN HAVE SOME ROMANTIC NOTION OF HOW, TOGETHER, WE COULD, WHAT? CHANGE THE WORLD?
YOU'RE ARROGANT AND YOU'RE WEAK. NO AMOUNT OF LITTLE DEMON POWER WILL EVER CHANGE YOUR DEEPLY DAMAGED CORE.
I'M WEAK? EVERYONE YOU KNOW-- THE FEW PEOPLE IN YOUR LIFE WHO ARE REMOTELY CLOSE TO YOU -- ARE HIDING THINGS FROM YOU. SECRETS OF WHO THEY ARE AND WHAT THEY'VE DONE.
I'M GUESSING JACK, A MAN WITH NO ABILITY OUTSIDE OF PUNCHING THINGS, NEVER TOLD YOU HOW HE CAME TO BE A HOAX HUNTER, DID HE? YEAH... I WOULDN'T EITHER.
DONOVAN, I'M WARNING YOU...
YOU THREE AND YOUR LAZY RIGHTEOUSNESS. YOU'RE COMPLETELY IGNORANT OF WHAT'S REALLY GOING ON AROUND YOU, YET YOU STILL ACT NOBLE. PREENING FOR THE REALITY TV CAMERA LIKE YOU AREN'T A CULTURAL WASTELAND.
AND YET YOU JUDGE ME. WHY? BECAUSE YOU DON'T LIKE ME VERY MUCH, AND THAT MAKES ME "BAD." WELL, NOW YOU KNOW: I'M A GOLEM-CONTROLLING DEMON.
SO IF I WANTED TO START SOME SHIT, REGAN, DON'T YOU THINK I WOULD HAVE BY NOW?

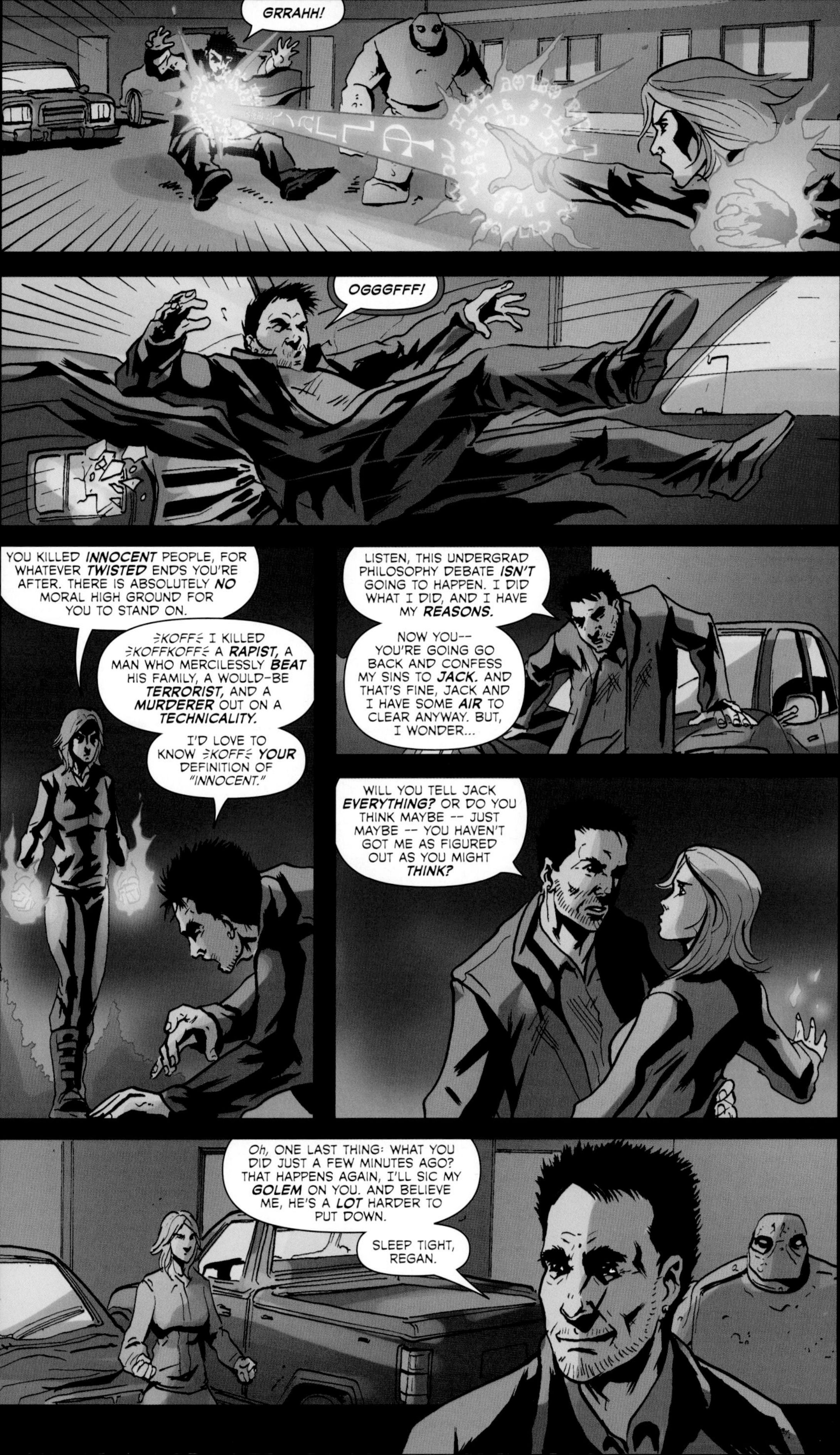
GRRAHH!
OGGGFFF!
YOU KILLED INNOCENT PEOPLE, FOR WHATEVER TWISTED ENDS YOU'RE AFTER. THERE IS ABSOLUTELY NO MORAL HIGH GROUND FOR YOU TO STAND ON.
≠KOFF≠ I KILLED ≠KOFFKOFF≠ A RAPIST, A MAN WHO MERCILESSLY BEAT HIS FAMILY, A WOULD-BE TERRORIST, AND A MURDERER OUT ON A TECHNICALITY.
I'D LOVE TO KNOW ≠KOFF≠ YOUR DEFINITION OF "INNOCENT."
LISTEN, THIS UNDERGRAD PHILOSOPHY DEBATE ISN'T GOING TO HAPPEN. I DID WHAT I DID, AND I HAVE MY REASONS.
NOW YOU-- YOU'RE GOING GO BACK AND CONFESS MY SINS TO JACK. AND THAT'S FINE, JACK AND I HAVE SOME AIR TO CLEAR ANYWAY. BUT, I WONDER...
WILL YOU TELL JACK EVERYTHING? OR DO YOU THINK MAYBE -- JUST MAYBE -- YOU HAVEN'T GOT ME AS FIGURED OUT AS YOU MIGHT THINK?
Oh, ONE LAST THING: WHAT YOU DID JUST A FEW MINUTES AGO? THAT HAPPENS AGAIN, I'LL SIC MY GOLEM ON YOU. AND BELIEVE ME, HE'S A LOT HARDER TO PUT DOWN.
SLEEP TIGHT, REGAN.

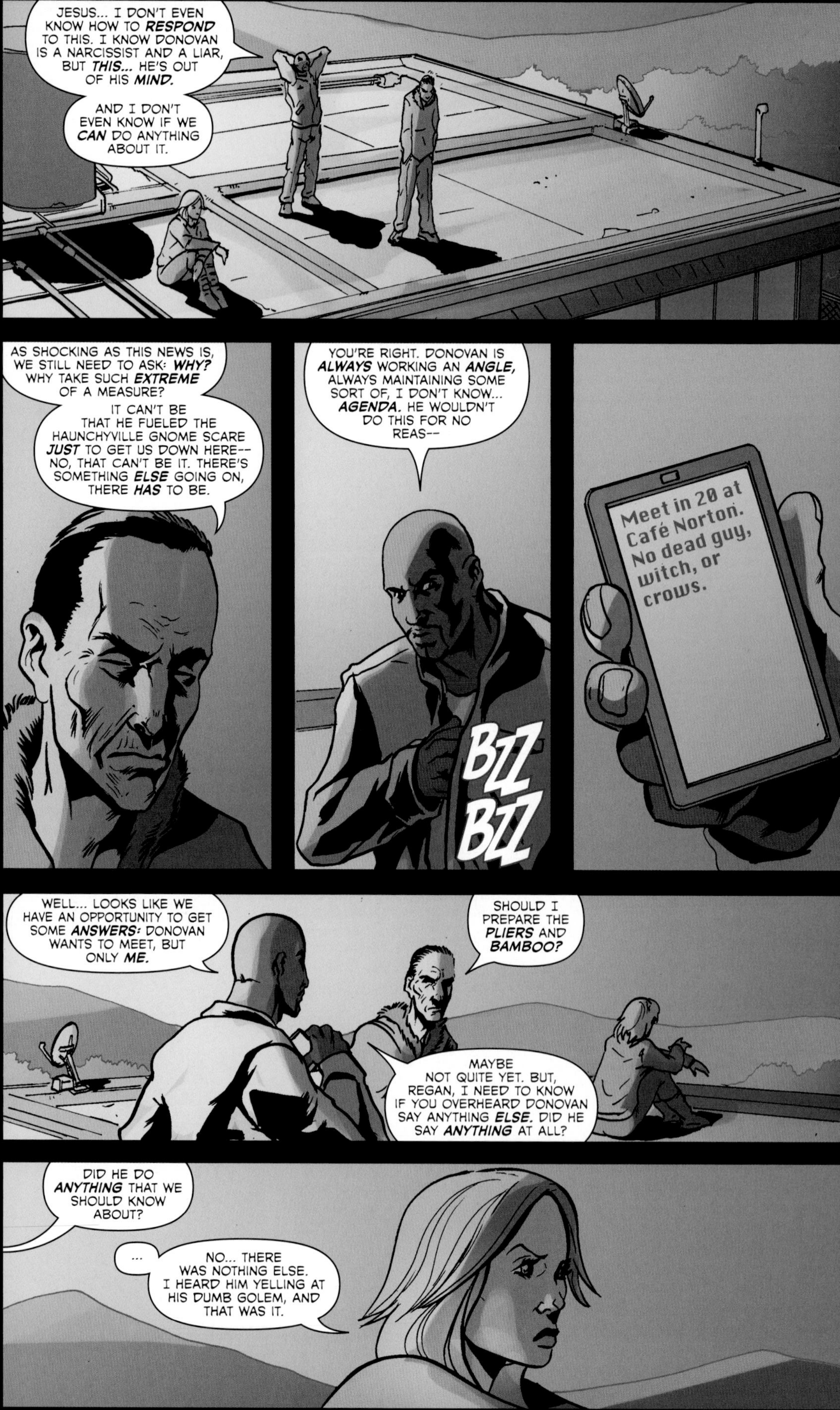
JESUS... I DON'T EVEN KNOW HOW TO RESPOND TO THIS. I KNOW DONOVAN IS A NARCISSIST AND A LIAR, BUT THIS... HE'S OUT OF HIS MIND.
AND I DON'T EVEN KNOW IF WE CAN DO ANYTHING ABOUT IT.
AS SHOCKING AS THIS NEWS IS, WE STILL NEED TO ASK: WHY? WHY TAKE SUCH EXTREME OF A MEASURE?
IT CAN'T BE THAT HE FUELED THE HAUNCHYVILLE GNOME SCARE JUST TO GET US DOWN HERE-- NO, THAT CAN'T BE IT. THERE'S SOMETHING ELSE GOING ON, THERE HAS TO BE.
YOU'RE RIGHT. DONOVAN IS ALWAYS WORKING AN ANGLE, ALWAYS MAINTAINING SOME SORT OF, I DON'T KNOW... AGENDA. HE WOULDN'T DO THIS FOR NO REAS--
BZZ BZZ
Meet in 20 at Café Norton. No dead guy, witch, or crows.
WELL... LOOKS LIKE WE HAVE AN OPPORTUNITY TO GET SOME ANSWERS: DONOVAN WANTS TO MEET, BUT ONLY ME.
SHOULD I PREPARE THE PLIERS AND BAMBOO?
MAYBE NOT QUITE YET. BUT, REGAN, I NEED TO KNOW IF YOU OVERHEARD DONOVAN SAY ANYTHING ELSE. DID HE SAY ANYTHING AT ALL?
DID HE DO ANYTHING THAT WE SHOULD KNOW ABOUT?
...
NO... THERE WAS NOTHING ELSE. I HEARD HIM YELLING AT HIS DUMB GOLEM, AND THAT WAS IT.

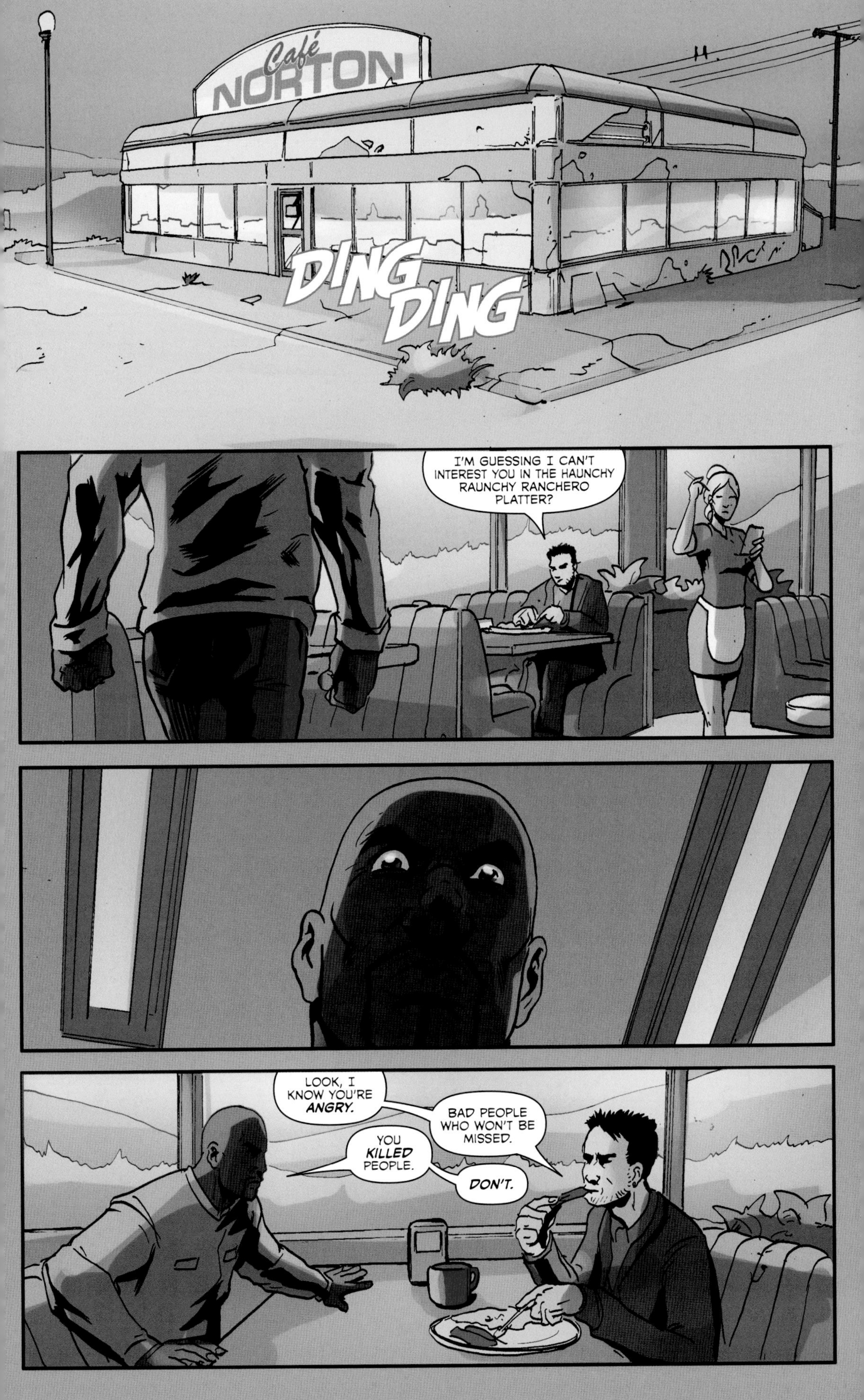

Café
NORTON
DING DING
I'M GUESSING I CAN'T INTEREST YOU IN THE HAUNCHY RAUNCHY RANCHERO PLATTER?
LOOK, I KNOW YOU'RE *ANGRY.*
BAD PEOPLE WHO WON'T BE MISSED.
YOU *KILLED* PEOPLE.
DON'T.

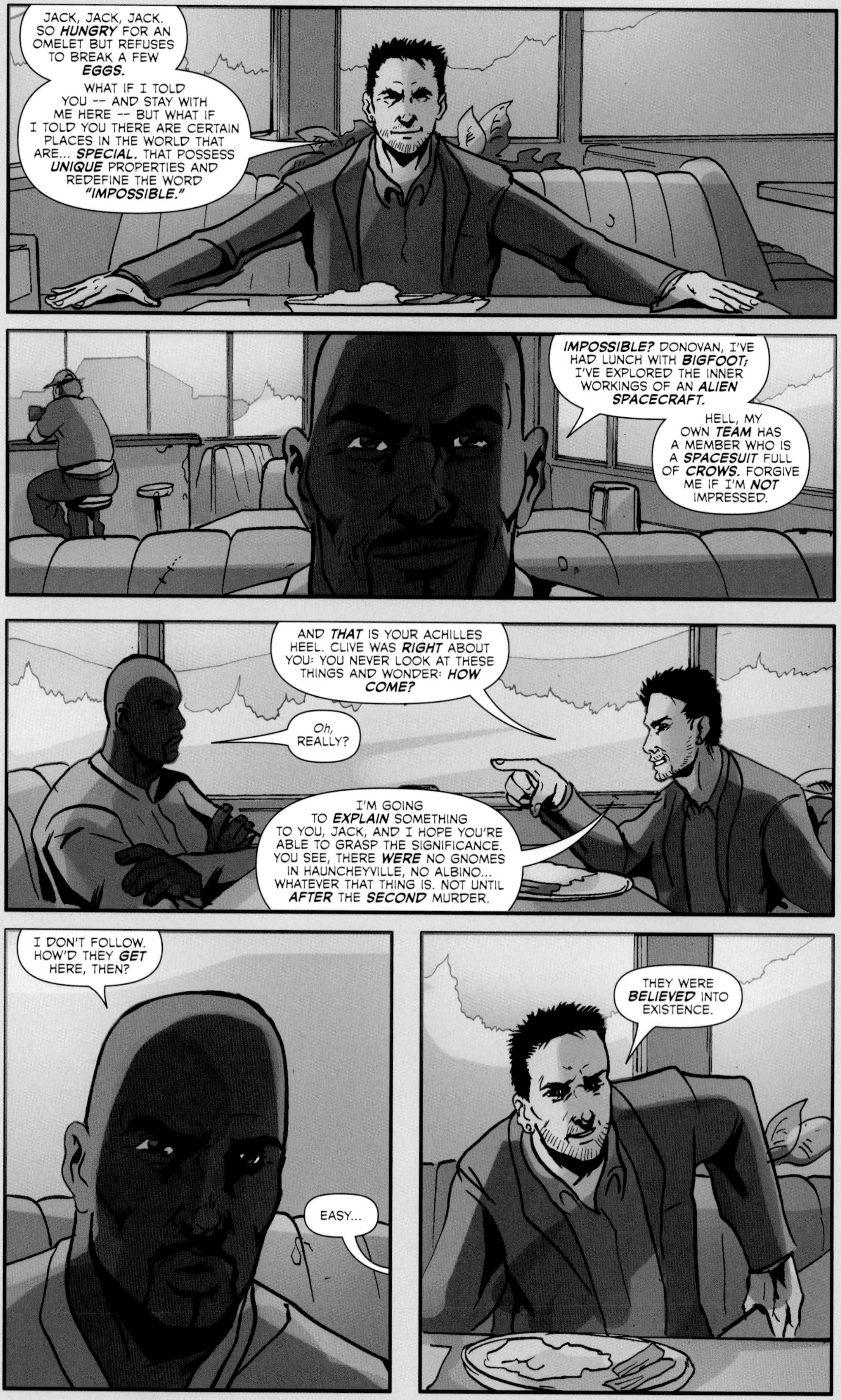
JACK, JACK, JACK. SO HUNGRY FOR AN OMELET BUT REFUSES TO BREAK A FEW EGGS.
WHAT IF I TOLD YOU -- AND STAY WITH ME HERE -- BUT WHAT IF I TOLD YOU THERE ARE CERTAIN PLACES IN THE WORLD THAT ARE... SPECIAL. THAT POSSESS UNIQUE PROPERTIES AND REDEFINE THE WORD "IMPOSSIBLE."
IMPOSSIBLE? DONOVAN, I'VE HAD LUNCH WITH BIGFOOT; I'VE EXPLORED THE INNER WORKINGS OF AN ALIEN SPACECRAFT.
HELL, MY OWN TEAM HAS A MEMBER WHO IS A SPACESUIT FULL OF CROWS. FORGIVE ME IF I'M NOT IMPRESSED.
AND THAT IS YOUR ACHILLES HEEL. CLIVE WAS RIGHT ABOUT YOU: YOU NEVER LOOK AT THESE THINGS AND WONDER: HOW COME?
Oh, REALLY?
I'M GOING TO EXPLAIN SOMETHING TO YOU, JACK, AND I HOPE YOU'RE ABLE TO GRASP THE SIGNIFICANCE. YOU SEE, THERE WERE NO GNOMES IN HAUNCHEYVILLE, NO ALBINO... WHATEVER THAT THING IS. NOT UNTIL AFTER THE SECOND MURDER.
I DON'T FOLLOW. HOW'D THEY GET HERE, THEN?
EASY...
THEY WERE BELIEVED INTO EXISTENCE.

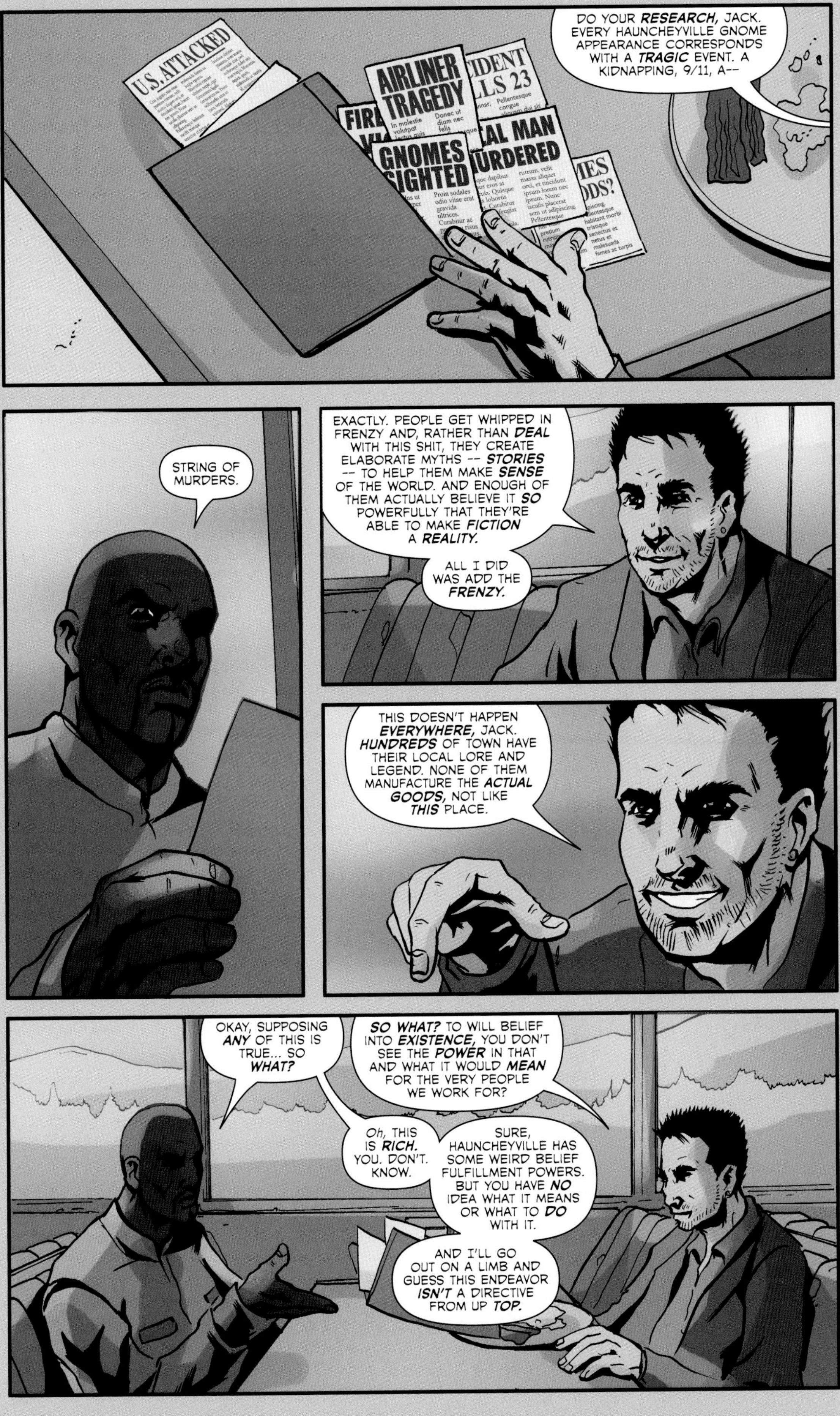
U.S. ATTACKED
AIRLINER TRAGEDY
GNOMES SIGHTED
DO YOUR RESEARCH, JACK. EVERY HAUNCHEYVILLE GNOME APPEARANCE CORRESPONDS WITH A TRAGIC EVENT. A KIDNAPPING, 9/11, A--
STRING OF MURDERS.
EXACTLY. PEOPLE GET WHIPPED IN FRENZY AND, RATHER THAN DEAL WITH THIS SHIT, THEY CREATE ELABORATE MYTHS -- STORIES -- TO HELP THEM MAKE SENSE OF THE WORLD. AND ENOUGH OF THEM ACTUALLY BELIEVE IT SO POWERFULLY THAT THEY'RE ABLE TO MAKE FICTION A REALITY.
ALL I DID WAS ADD THE FRENZY.
THIS DOESN'T HAPPEN EVERYWHERE, JACK. HUNDREDS OF TOWN HAVE THEIR LOCAL LORE AND LEGEND. NONE OF THEM MANUFACTURE THE ACTUAL GOODS, NOT LIKE THIS PLACE.
OKAY, SUPPOSING ANY OF THIS IS TRUE... SO WHAT?
SO WHAT? TO WILL BELIEF INTO EXISTENCE, YOU DON'T SEE THE POWER IN THAT AND WHAT IT WOULD MEAN FOR THE VERY PEOPLE WE WORK FOR?
Oh, THIS IS RICH. YOU. DON'T. KNOW.
SURE, HAUNCHEYVILLE HAS SOME WEIRD BELIEF FULFILLMENT POWERS. BUT YOU HAVE NO IDEA WHAT IT MEANS OR WHAT TO DO WITH IT.
AND I'LL GO OUT ON A LIMB AND GUESS THIS ENDEAVOR ISN'T A DIRECTIVE FROM UP TOP.

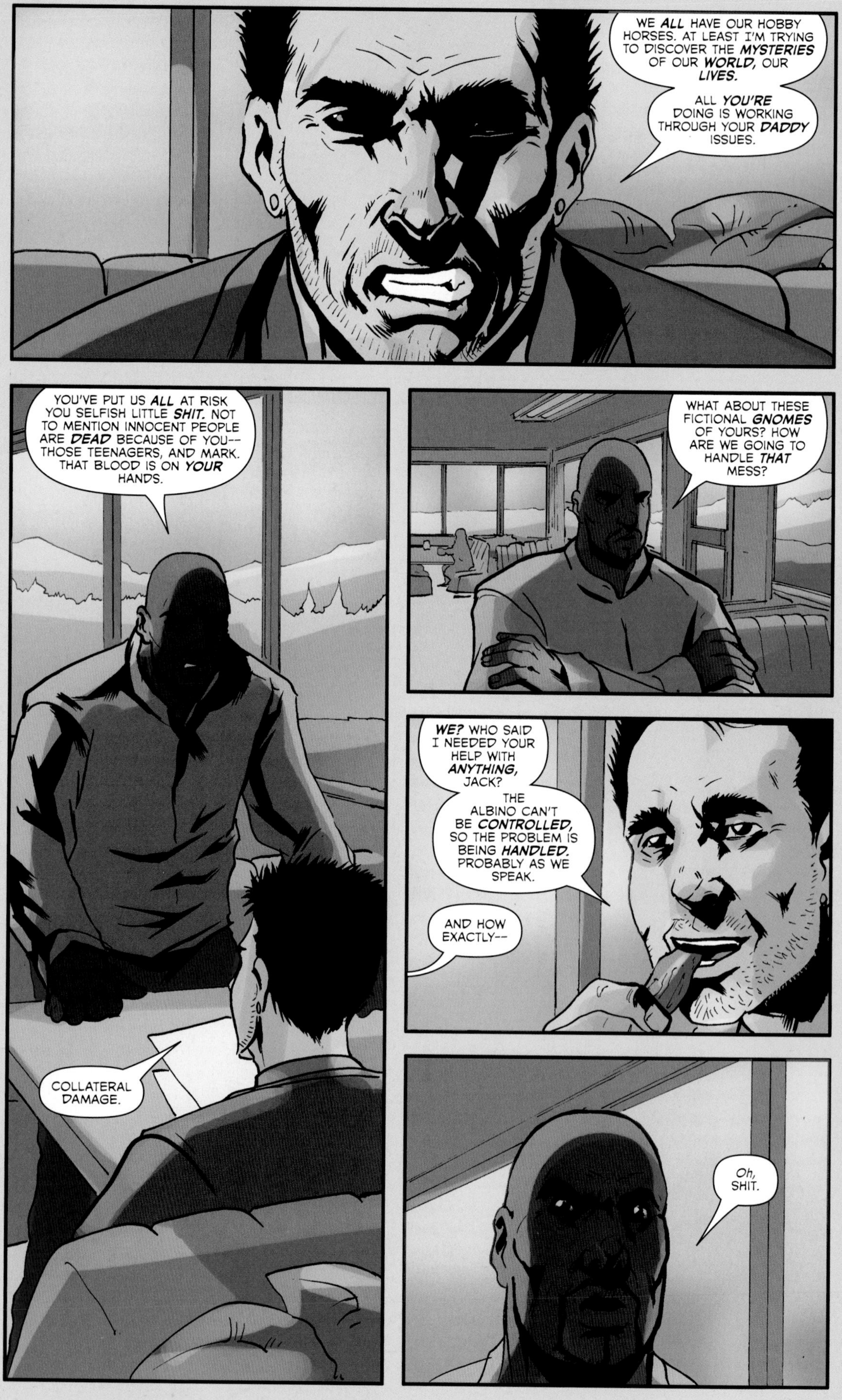
WE ALL HAVE OUR HOBBY HORSES. AT LEAST I'M TRYING TO DISCOVER THE MYSTERIES OF OUR WORLD, OUR LIVES.
ALL YOU'RE DOING IS WORKING THROUGH YOUR DADDY ISSUES.
YOU'VE PUT US ALL AT RISK YOU SELFISH LITTLE SHIT. NOT TO MENTION INNOCENT PEOPLE ARE DEAD BECAUSE OF YOU-- THOSE TEENAGERS, AND MARK. THAT BLOOD IS ON YOUR HANDS.
COLLATERAL DAMAGE.
WHAT ABOUT THESE FICTIONAL GNOMES OF YOURS? HOW ARE WE GOING TO HANDLE THAT MESS?
WE? WHO SAID I NEEDED YOUR HELP WITH ANYTHING, JACK?
THE ALBINO CAN'T BE CONTROLLED, SO THE PROBLEM IS BEING HANDLED. PROBABLY AS WE SPEAK.
AND HOW EXACTLY--
Oh, SHIT.

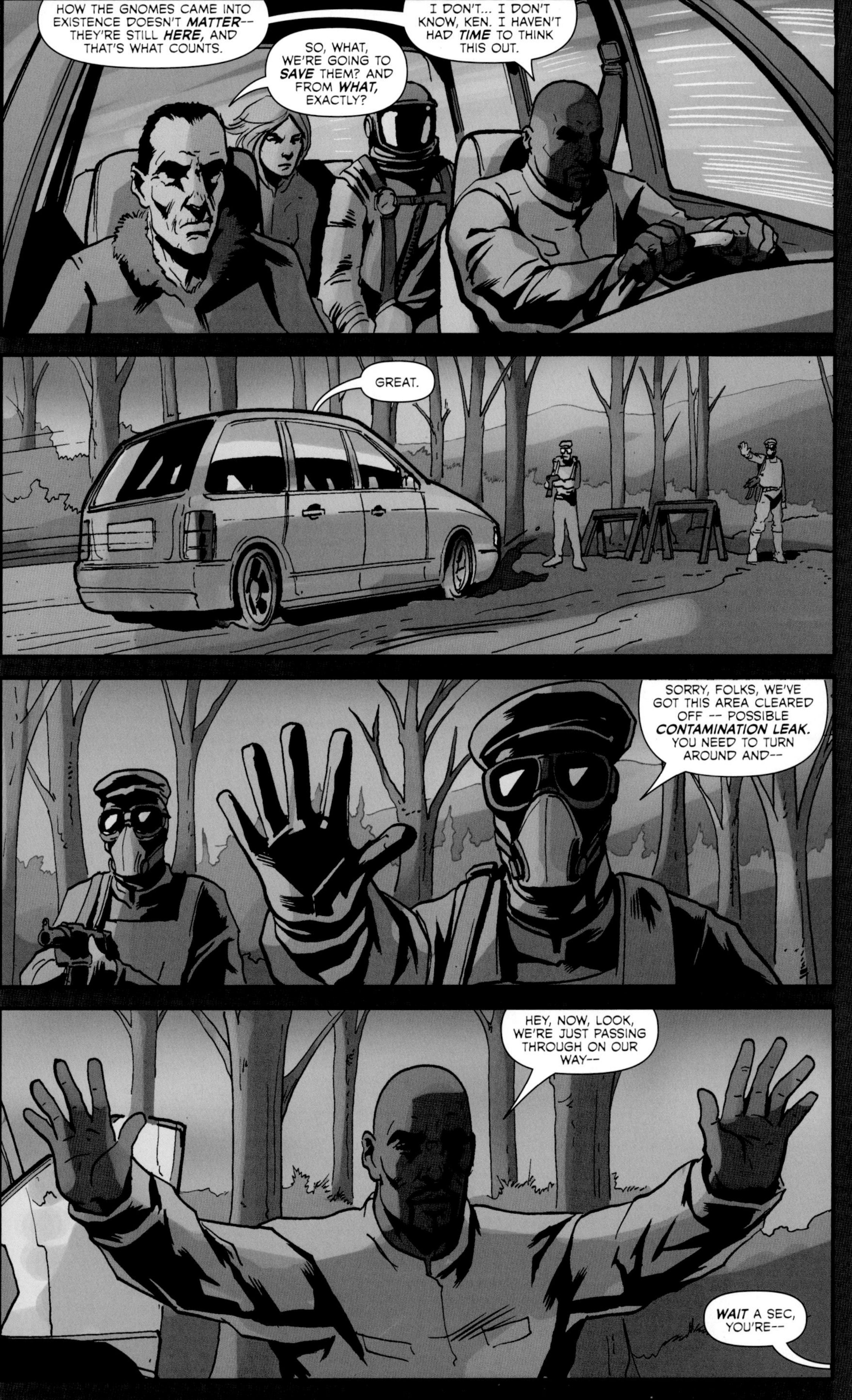
HOW THE GNOMES CAME INTO EXISTENCE DOESN'T MATTER-- THEY'RE STILL HERE, AND THAT'S WHAT COUNTS.
SO, WHAT, WE'RE GOING TO SAVE THEM? AND FROM WHAT, EXACTLY?
I DON'T... I DON'T KNOW, KEN. I HAVEN'T HAD TIME TO THINK THIS OUT.
GREAT.
SORRY, FOLKS, WE'VE GOT THIS AREA CLEARED OFF -- POSSIBLE CONTAMINATION LEAK. YOU NEED TO TURN AROUND AND--
HEY, NOW, LOOK, WE'RE JUST PASSING THROUGH ON OUR WAY--
WAIT A SEC, YOU'RE--

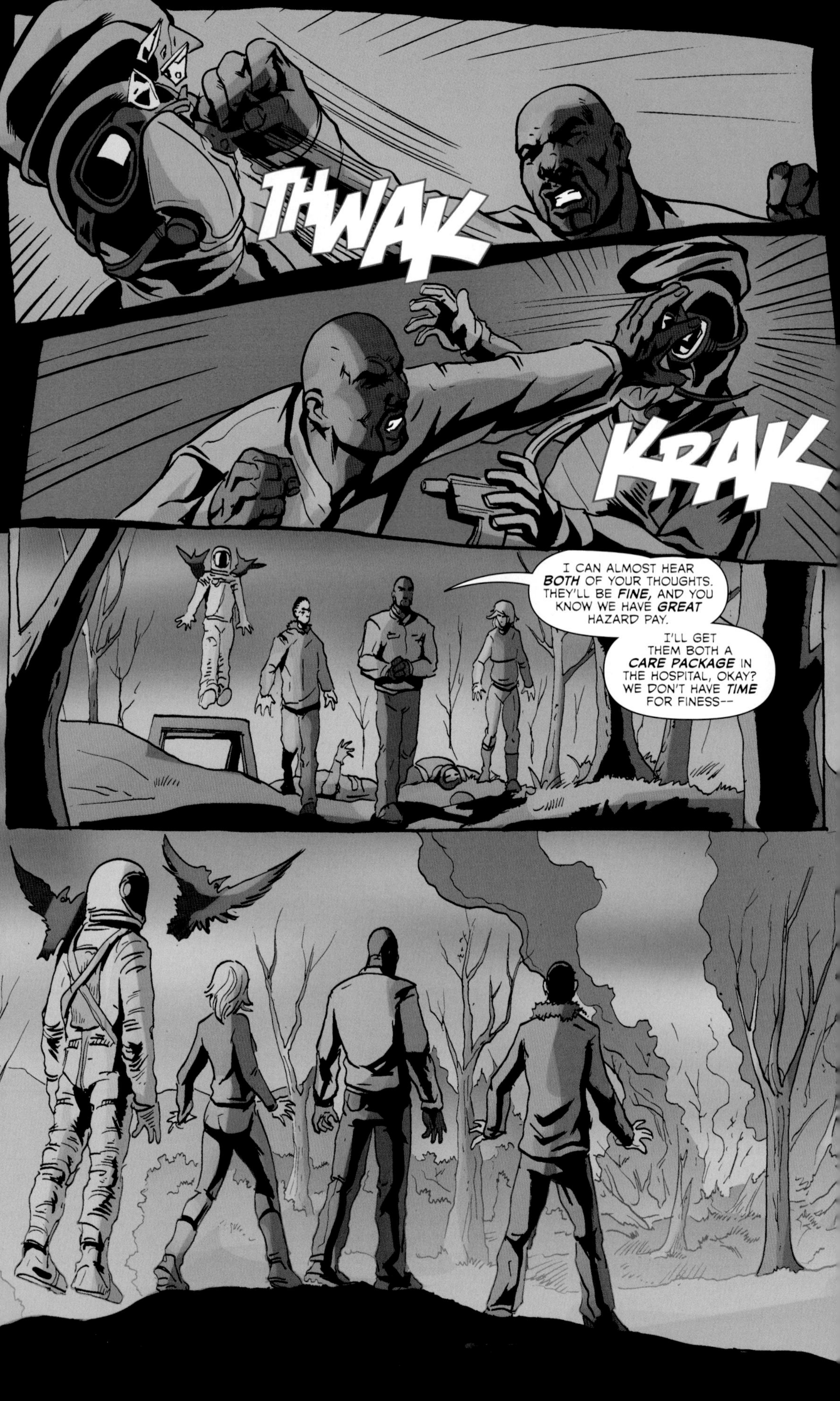
THWAK
KRAK
I CAN ALMOST HEAR BOTH OF YOUR THOUGHTS. THEY'LL BE FINE, AND YOU KNOW WE HAVE GREAT HAZARD PAY.
I'LL GET THEM BOTH A CARE PACKAGE IN THE HOSPITAL, OKAY? WE DON'T HAVE TIME FOR FINESS--

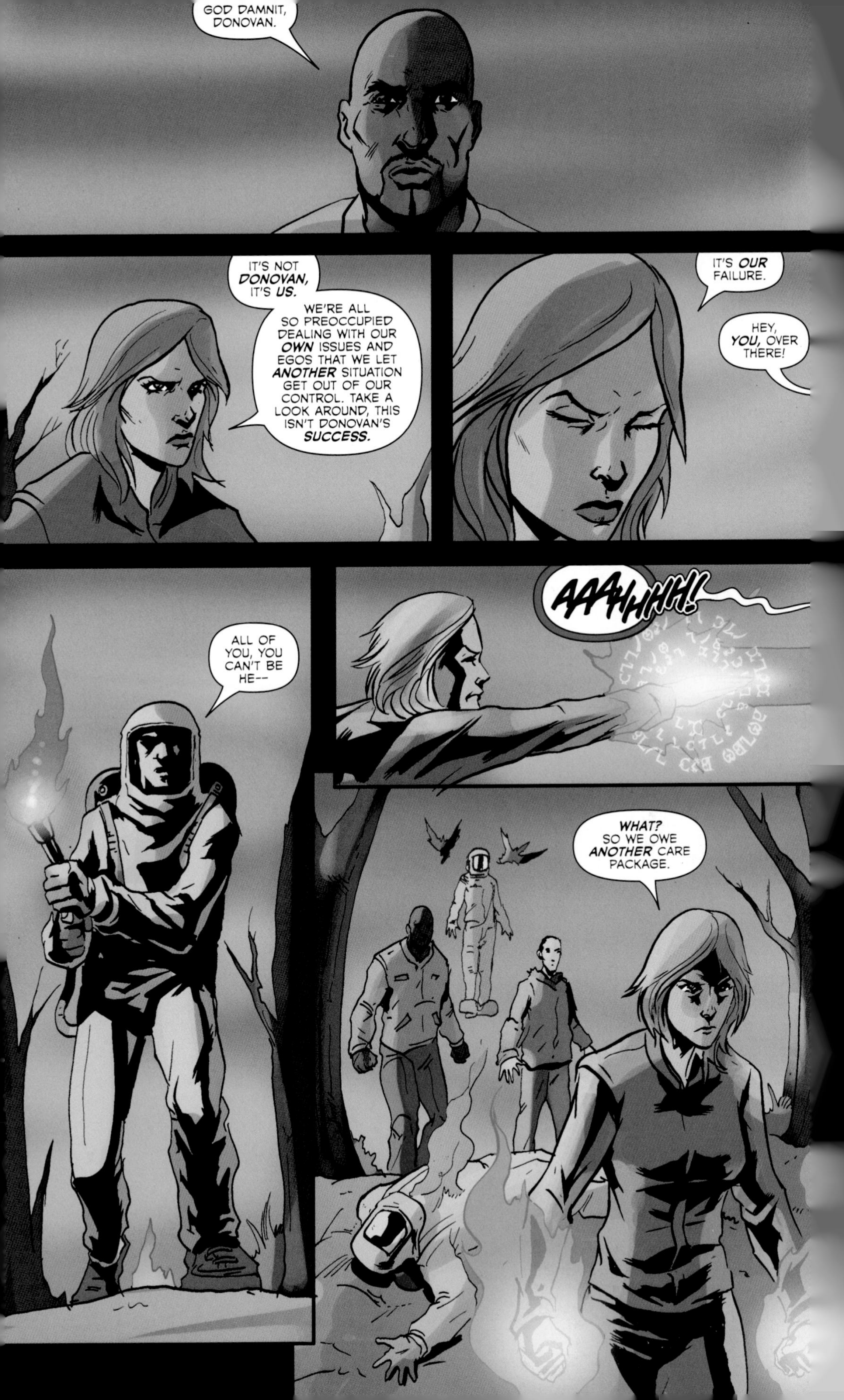
GOD DAMNIT, DONOVAN.
IT'S NOT DONOVAN, IT'S US.
WE'RE ALL SO PREOCCUPIED DEALING WITH OUR OWN ISSUES AND EGOS THAT WE LET ANOTHER SITUATION GET OUT OF OUR CONTROL. TAKE A LOOK AROUND, THIS ISN'T DONOVAN'S SUCCESS.
IT'S OUR FAILURE.
HEY, YOU, OVER THERE!
ALL OF YOU, YOU CAN'T BE HE--
AAAHHHH!
WHAT? SO WE OWE ANOTHER CARE PACKAGE.

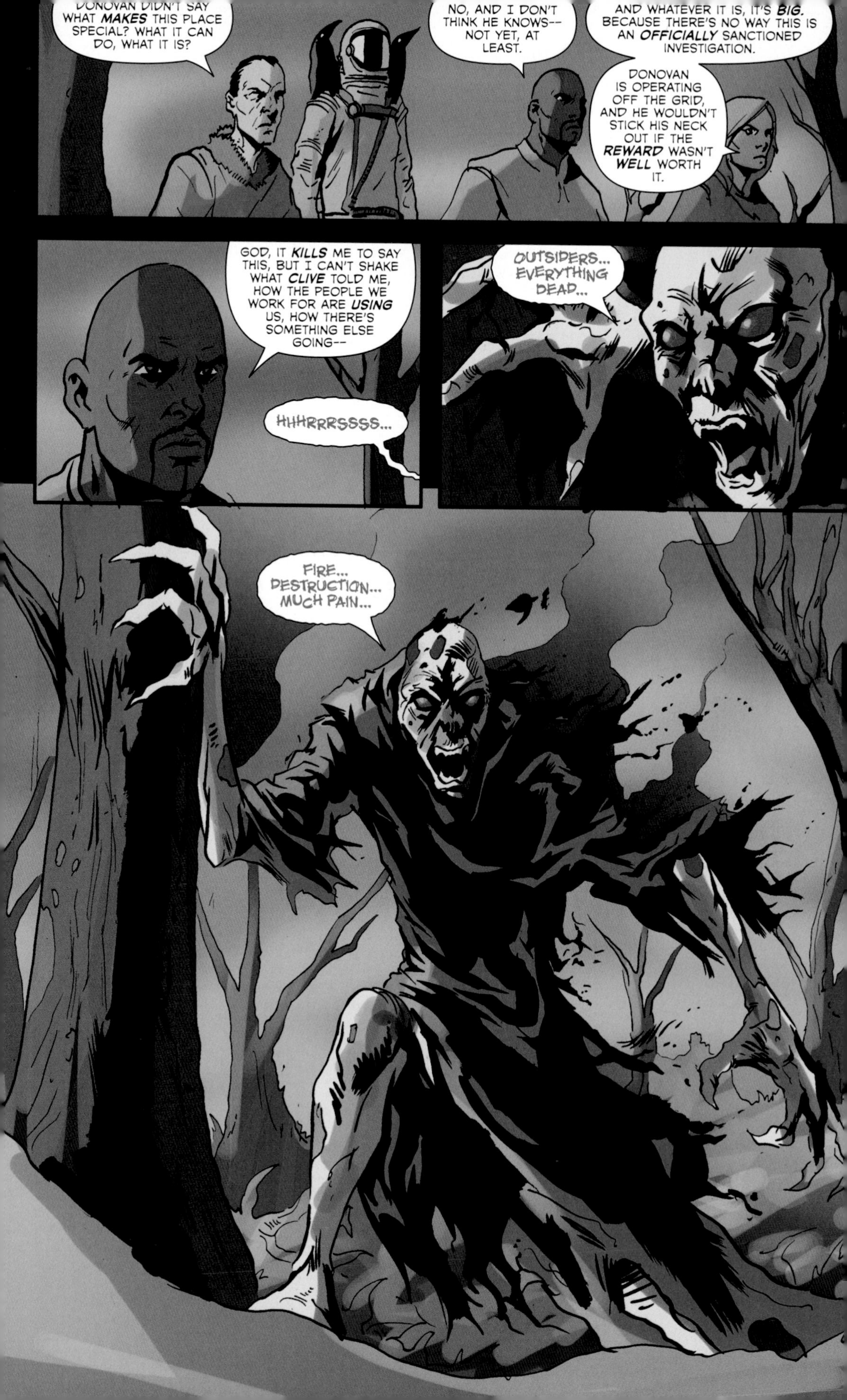
DONOVAN DIDN'T SAY WHAT MAKES THIS PLACE SPECIAL? WHAT IT CAN DO, WHAT IT IS?
NO, AND I DON'T THINK HE KNOWS-- NOT YET, AT LEAST.
AND WHATEVER IT IS, IT'S BIG. BECAUSE THERE'S NO WAY THIS IS AN OFFICIALLY SANCTIONED INVESTIGATION.
DONOVAN IS OPERATING OFF THE GRID, AND HE WOULDN'T STICK HIS NECK OUT IF THE REWARD WASN'T WELL WORTH IT.
GOD, IT KILLS ME TO SAY THIS, BUT I CAN'T SHAKE WHAT CLIVE TOLD ME, HOW THE PEOPLE WE WORK FOR ARE USING US, HOW THERE'S SOMETHING ELSE GOING--
HHHRRRSSSS...
OUTSIDERS... EVERYTHING DEAD...
FIRE... DESTRUCTION... MUCH PAIN...

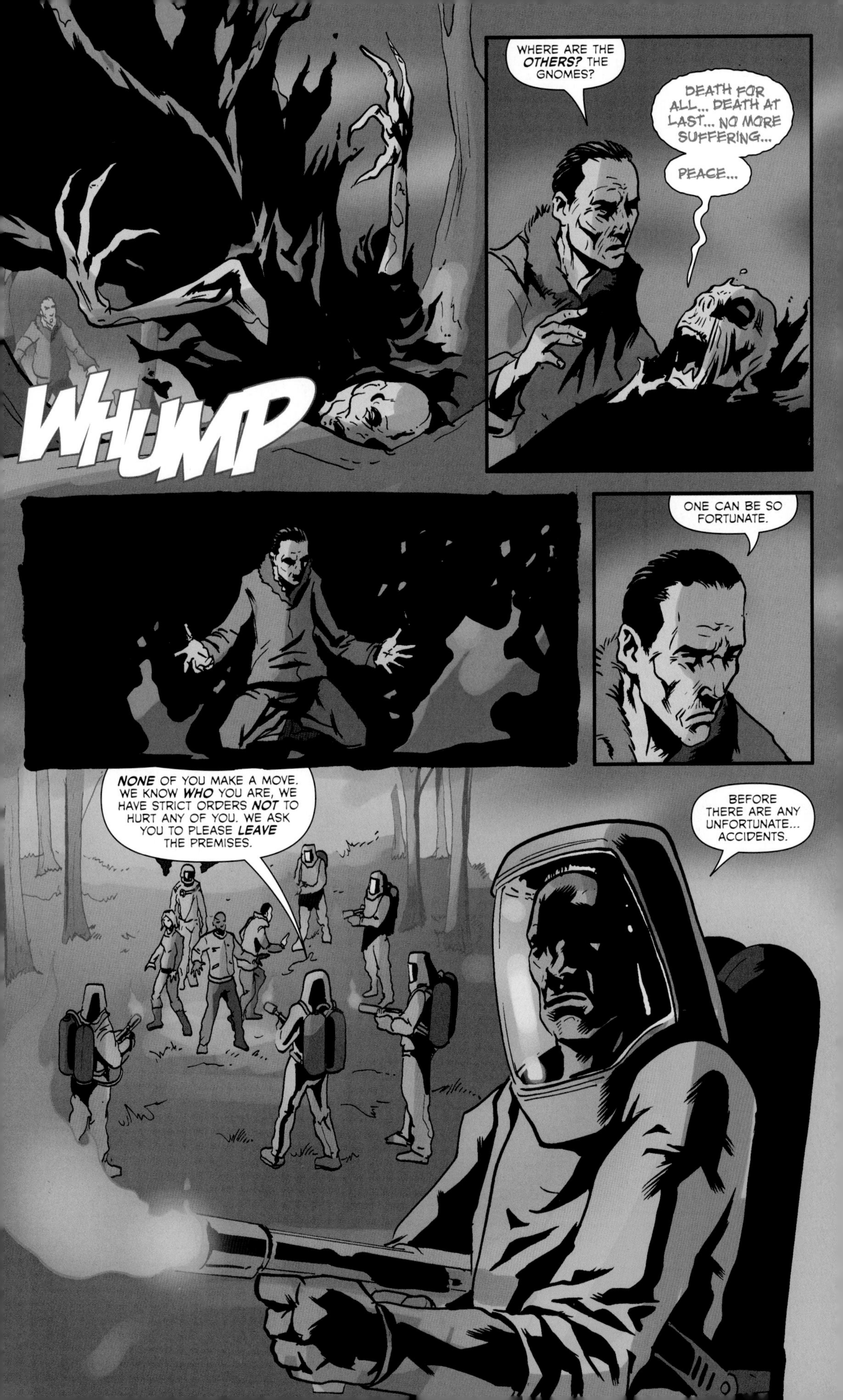
WHUMP
WHERE ARE THE OTHERS? THE GNOMES?
DEATH FOR ALL... DEATH AT LAST... NO MORE SUFFERING...
PEACE...
ONE CAN BE SO FORTUNATE.
NONE OF YOU MAKE A MOVE. WE KNOW WHO YOU ARE, WE HAVE STRICT ORDERS NOT TO HURT ANY OF YOU. WE ASK YOU TO PLEASE LEAVE THE PREMISES.
BEFORE THERE ARE ANY UNFORTUNATE... ACCIDENTS.

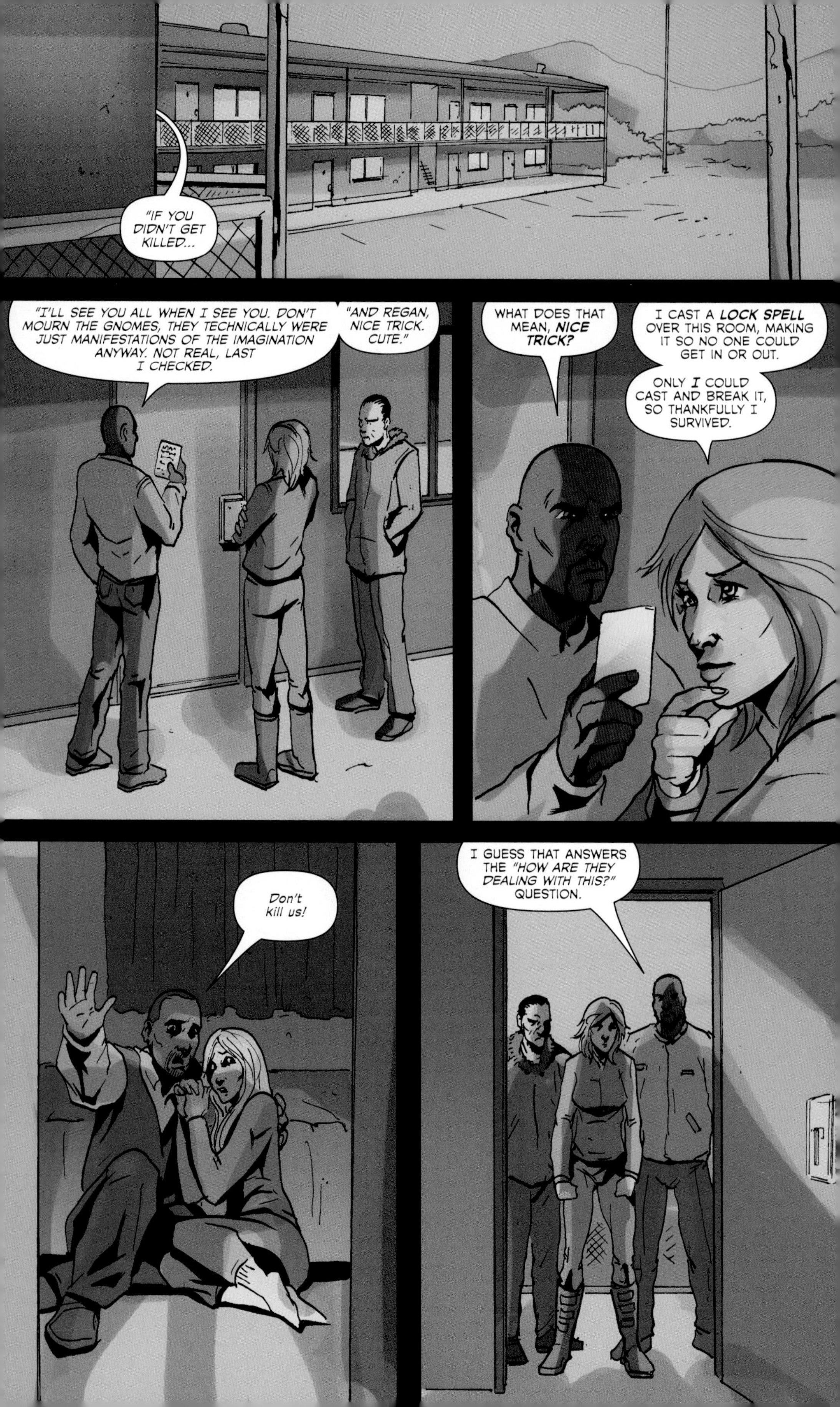
"IF YOU DIDN'T GET KILLED...
"I'LL SEE YOU ALL WHEN I SEE YOU. DON'T MOURN THE GNOMES, THEY TECHNICALLY WERE JUST MANIFESTATIONS OF THE IMAGINATION ANYWAY. NOT REAL, LAST I CHECKED.
"AND REGAN, NICE TRICK. CUTE."
WHAT DOES THAT MEAN, NICE TRICK?
I CAST A LOCK SPELL OVER THIS ROOM, MAKING IT SO NO ONE COULD GET IN OR OUT.
ONLY I COULD CAST AND BREAK IT, SO THANKFULLY I SURVIVED.
Don't kill us!
I GUESS THAT ANSWERS THE "HOW ARE THEY DEALING WITH THIS?" QUESTION.

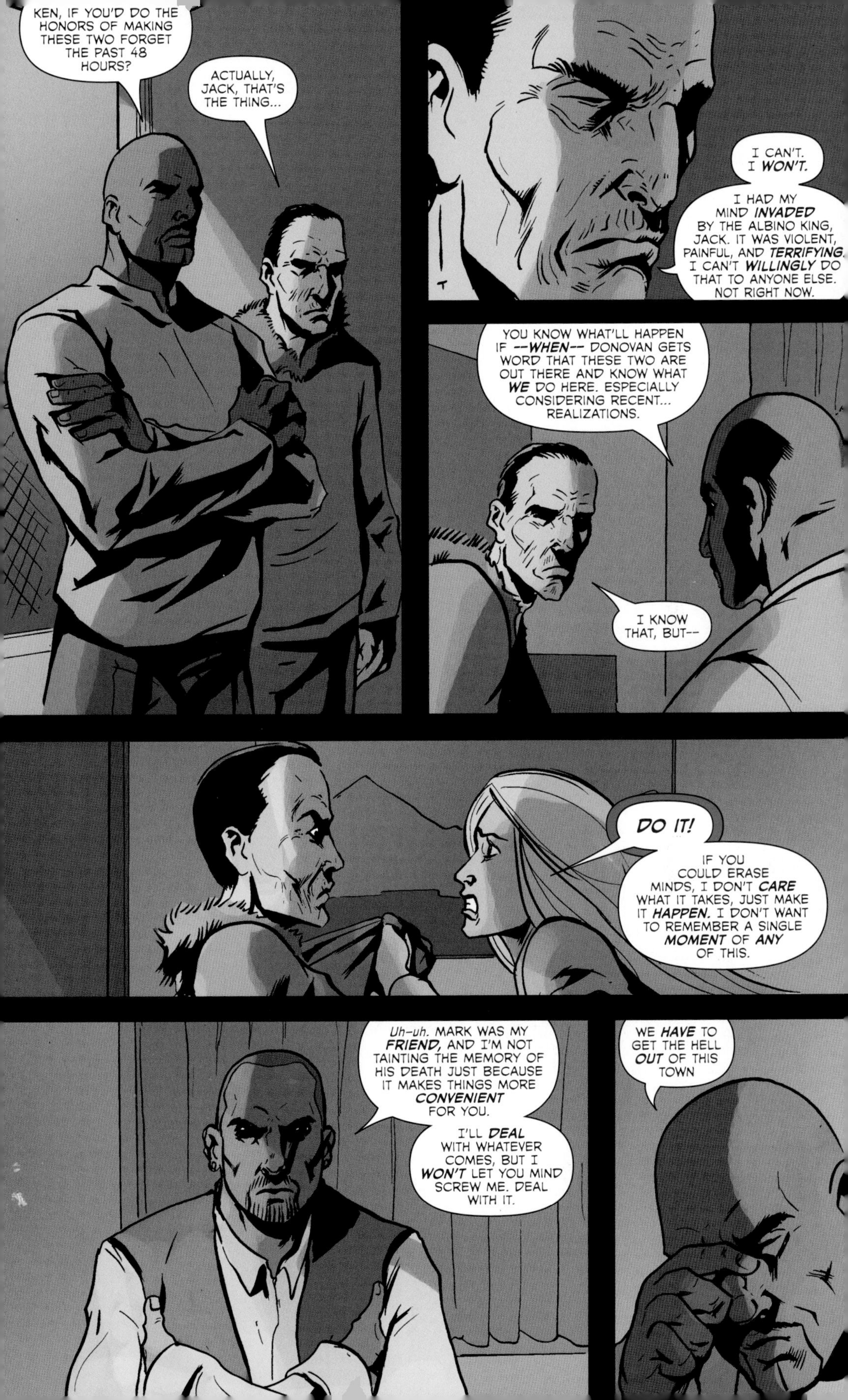
KEN, IF YOU'D DO THE HONORS OF MAKING THESE TWO FORGET THE PAST 48 HOURS?
ACTUALLY, JACK, THAT'S THE THING...
I CAN'T. I WON'T.
I HAD MY MIND INVADED BY THE ALBINO KING, JACK. IT WAS VIOLENT, PAINFUL, AND TERRIFYING. I CAN'T WILLINGLY DO THAT TO ANYONE ELSE. NOT RIGHT NOW.
YOU KNOW WHAT'LL HAPPEN IF --WHEN-- DONOVAN GETS WORD THAT THESE TWO ARE OUT THERE AND KNOW WHAT WE DO HERE. ESPECIALLY CONSIDERING RECENT... REALIZATIONS.
I KNOW THAT, BUT--
DO IT!
IF YOU COULD ERASE MINDS, I DON'T CARE WHAT IT TAKES, JUST MAKE IT HAPPEN. I DON'T WANT TO REMEMBER A SINGLE MOMENT OF ANY OF THIS.
Uh-uh. MARK WAS MY FRIEND, AND I'M NOT TAINTING THE MEMORY OF HIS DEATH JUST BECAUSE IT MAKES THINGS MORE CONVENIENT FOR YOU.
I'LL DEAL WITH WHATEVER COMES, BUT I WON'T LET YOU MIND SCREW ME. DEAL WITH IT.
WE HAVE TO GET THE HELL OUT OF THIS TOWN

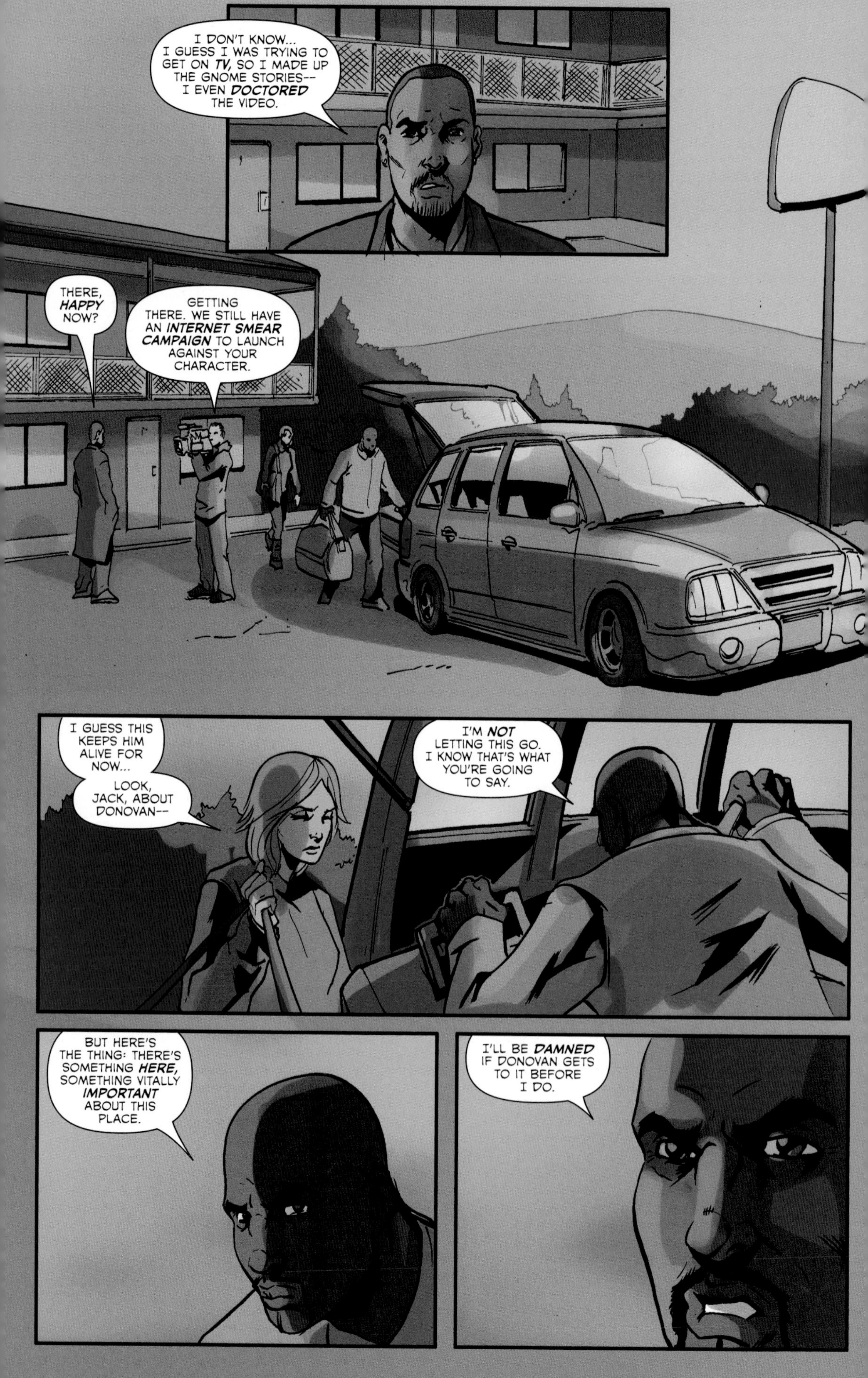
I DON'T KNOW... I GUESS I WAS TRYING TO GET ON *TV,* SO I MADE UP THE GNOME STORIES-- I EVEN *DOCTORED* THE VIDEO.
THERE, *HAPPY* NOW?
GETTING THERE. WE STILL HAVE AN *INTERNET SMEAR CAMPAIGN* TO LAUNCH AGAINST YOUR CHARACTER.
I GUESS THIS KEEPS HIM ALIVE FOR NOW...
LOOK, JACK, ABOUT DONOVAN--
I'M *NOT* LETTING THIS GO. I KNOW THAT'S WHAT YOU'RE GOING TO SAY.
BUT HERE'S THE THING: THERE'S SOMETHING *HERE,* SOMETHING VITALLY *IMPORTANT* ABOUT THIS PLACE.
I'LL BE *DAMNED* IF DONOVAN GETS TO IT BEFORE I DO.

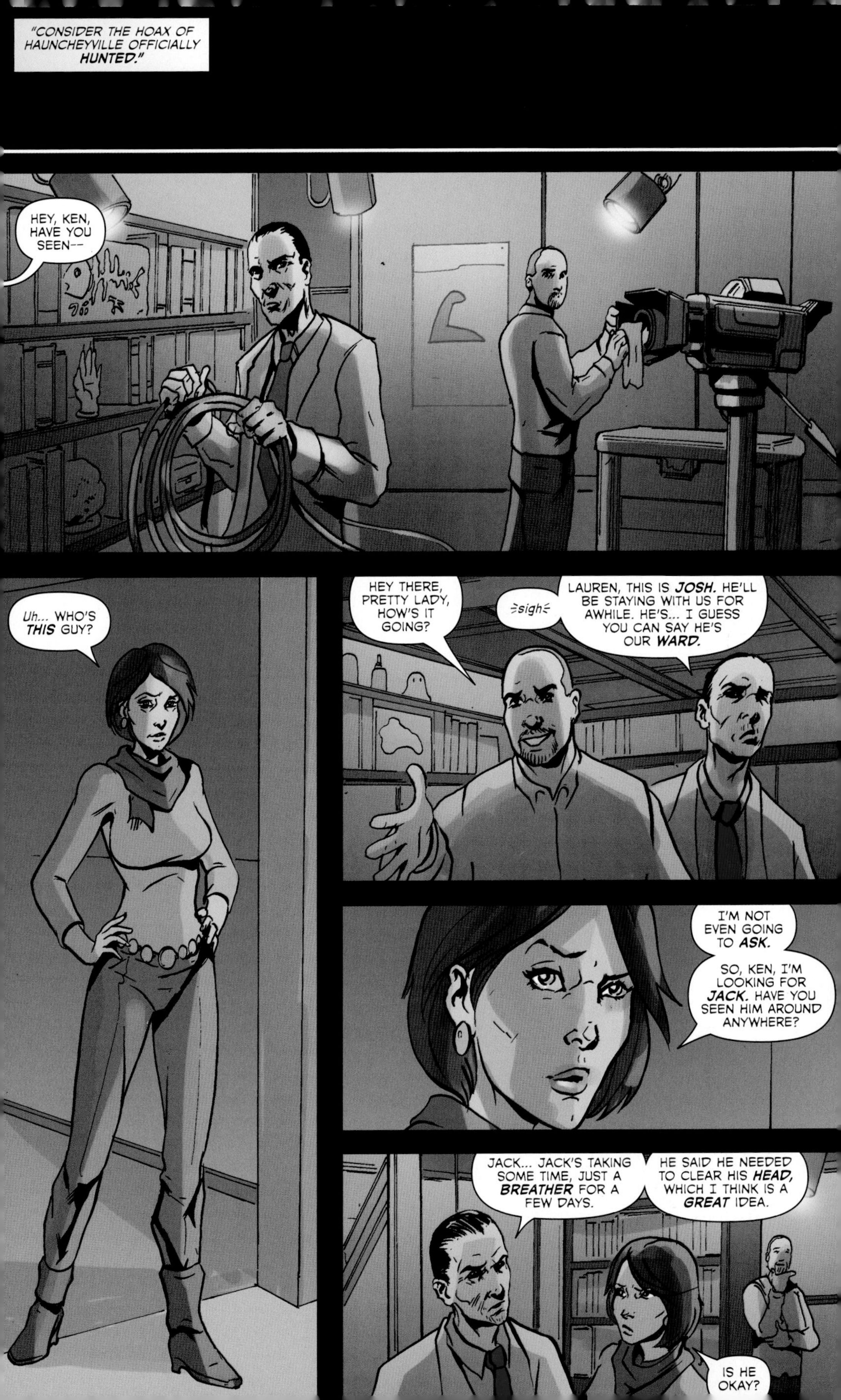
"CONSIDER THE HOAX OF HAUNCHEYVILLE OFFICIALLY HUNTED."
HEY, KEN, HAVE YOU SEEN--
Uh... WHO'S THIS GUY?
HEY THERE, PRETTY LADY, HOW'S IT GOING?
≥sigh≤
LAUREN, THIS IS JOSH. HE'LL BE STAYING WITH US FOR AWHILE. HE'S... I GUESS YOU CAN SAY HE'S OUR WARD.
I'M NOT EVEN GOING TO ASK.
SO, KEN, I'M LOOKING FOR JACK. HAVE YOU SEEN HIM AROUND ANYWHERE?
JACK... JACK'S TAKING SOME TIME, JUST A BREATHER FOR A FEW DAYS.
HE SAID HE NEEDED TO CLEAR HIS HEAD, WHICH I THINK IS A GREAT IDEA.
IS HE OKAY?

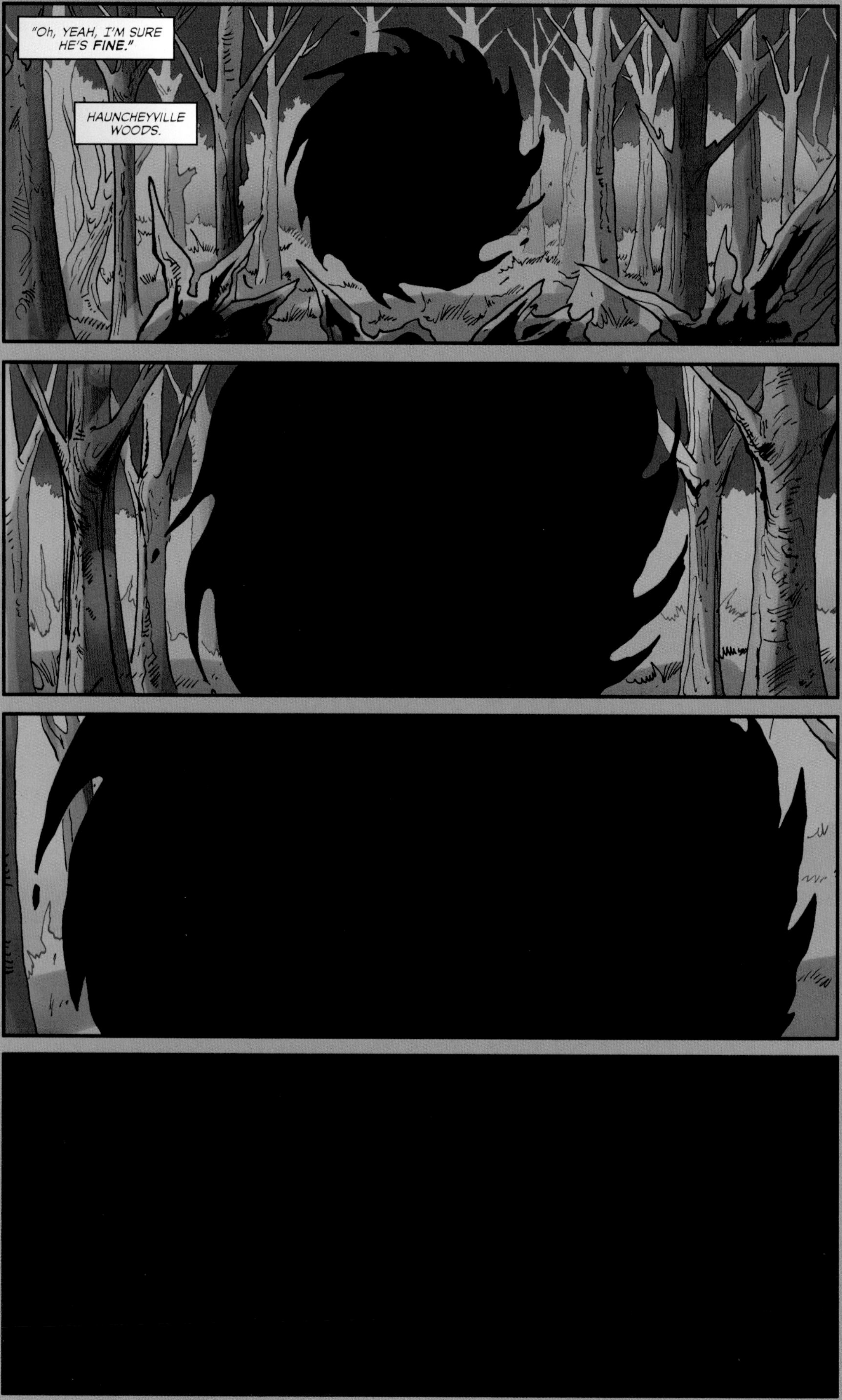
"Oh, YEAH, I'M SURE HE'S FINE."
HAUNCHEYVILLE WOODS.

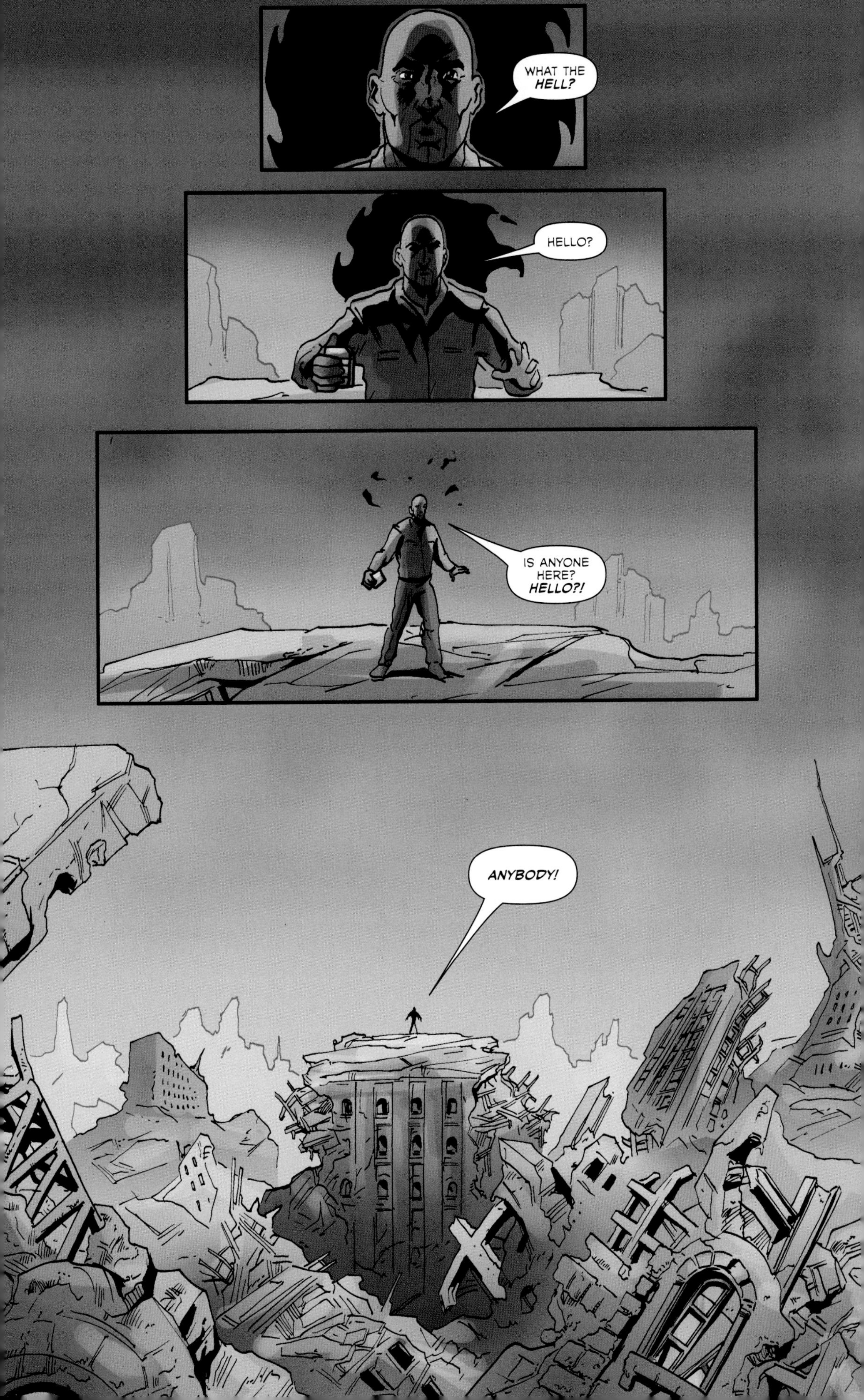
WHAT THE *HELL?*
HELLO?
IS ANYONE HERE? *HELLO?!*
ANYBODY!

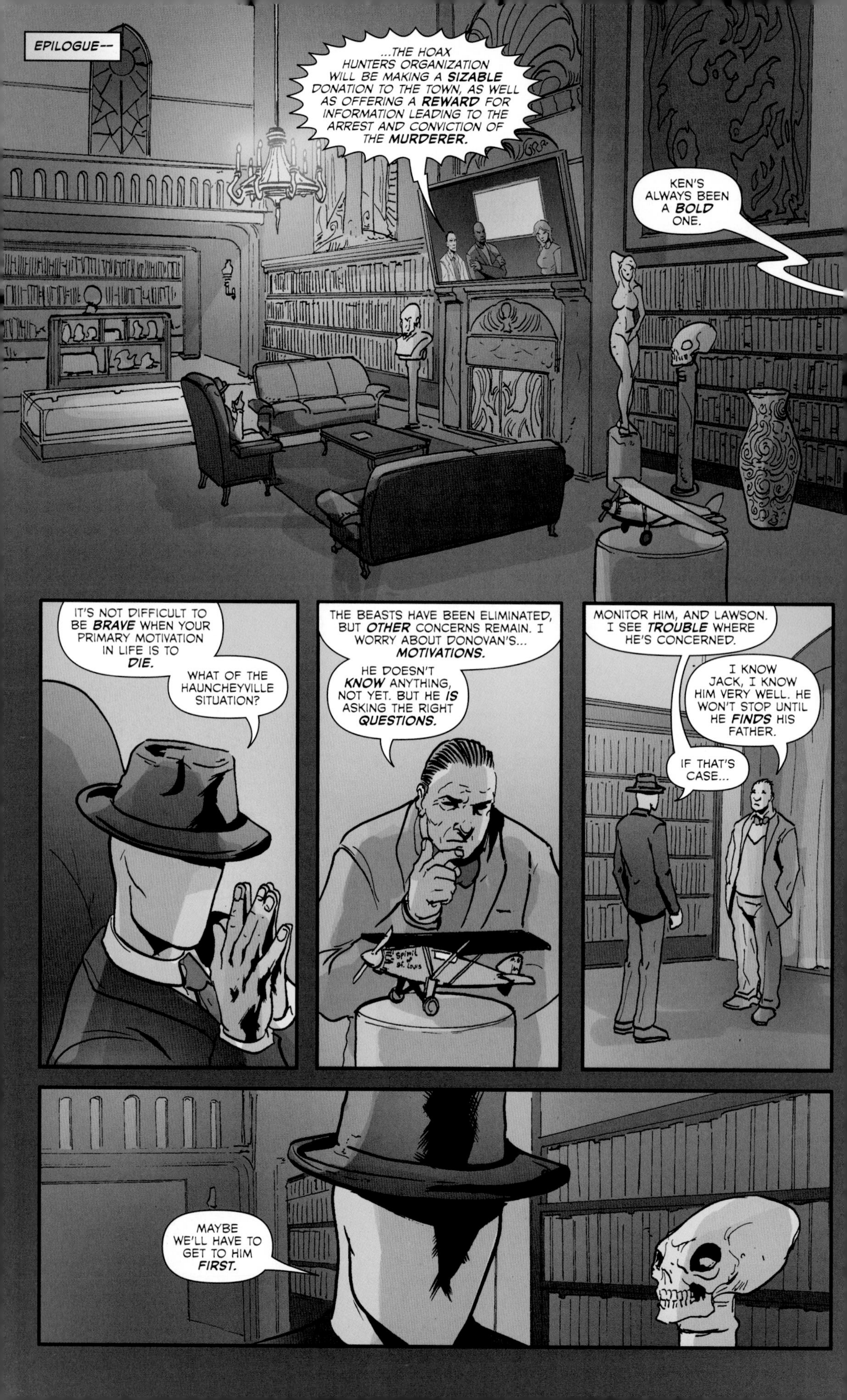
EPILOGUE--
...THE HOAX HUNTERS ORGANIZATION WILL BE MAKING A SIZABLE DONATION TO THE TOWN, AS WELL AS OFFERING A REWARD FOR INFORMATION LEADING TO THE ARREST AND CONVICTION OF THE MURDERER.
KEN'S ALWAYS BEEN A BOLD ONE.
IT'S NOT DIFFICULT TO BE BRAVE WHEN YOUR PRIMARY MOTIVATION IN LIFE IS TO DIE.
WHAT OF THE HAUNCHEYVILLE SITUATION?
THE BEASTS HAVE BEEN ELIMINATED, BUT OTHER CONCERNS REMAIN. I WORRY ABOUT DONOVAN'S... MOTIVATIONS.
HE DOESN'T KNOW ANYTHING, NOT YET. BUT HE IS ASKING THE RIGHT QUESTIONS.
Spirit of St. Louis
MONITOR HIM, AND LAWSON. I SEE TROUBLE WHERE HE'S CONCERNED.
I KNOW JACK, I KNOW HIM VERY WELL. HE WON'T STOP UNTIL HE FINDS HIS FATHER.
IF THAT'S CASE...
MAYBE WE'LL HAVE TO GET TO HIM FIRST.

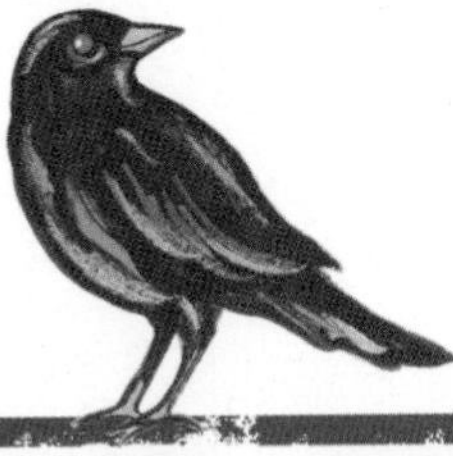

HOAX HUNTERS

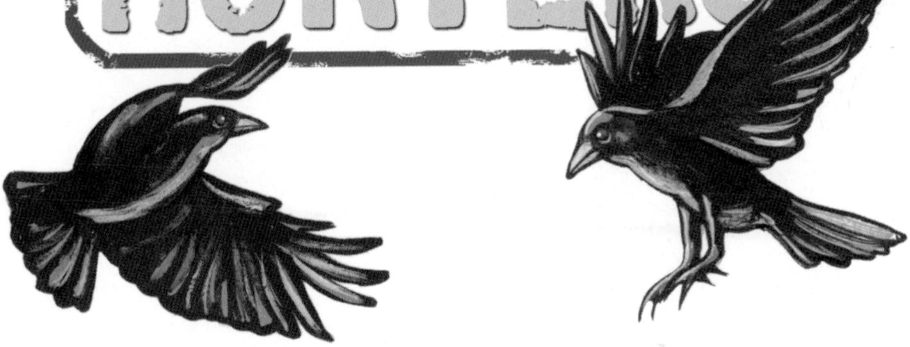

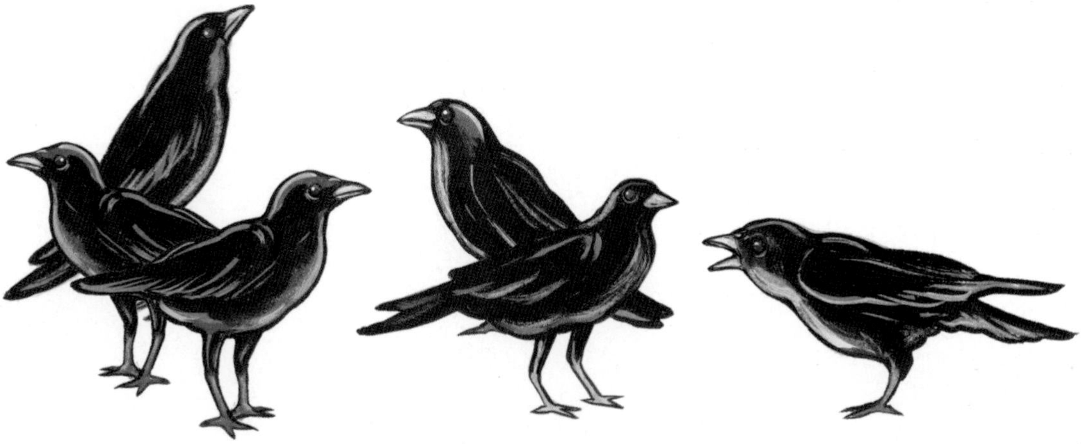

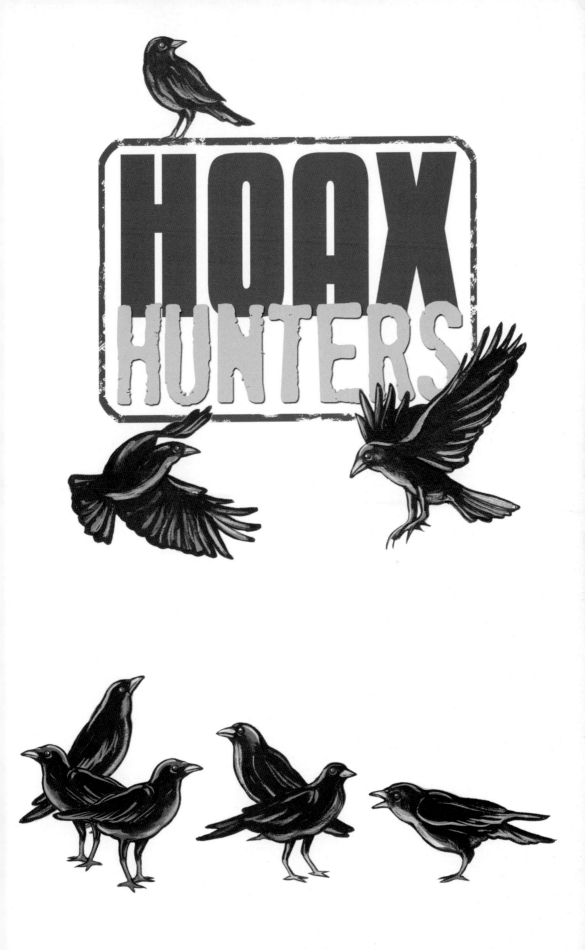

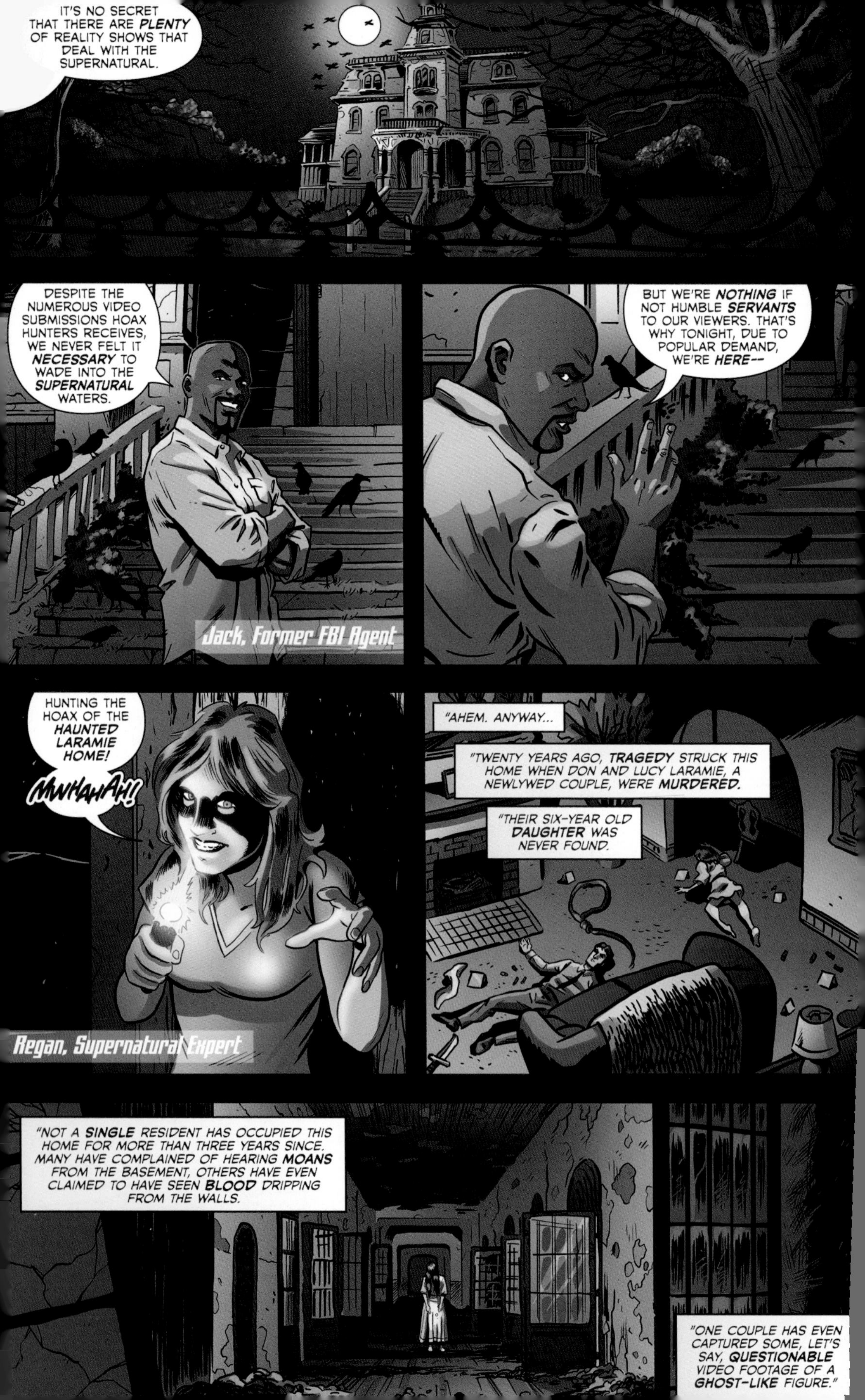

IT'S NO SECRET THAT THERE ARE PLENTY OF REALITY SHOWS THAT DEAL WITH THE SUPERNATURAL.
DESPITE THE NUMEROUS VIDEO SUBMISSIONS HOAX HUNTERS RECEIVES, WE NEVER FELT IT NECESSARY TO WADE INTO THE SUPERNATURAL WATERS.
Jack, Former FBI Agent
BUT WE'RE NOTHING IF NOT HUMBLE SERVANTS TO OUR VIEWERS. THAT'S WHY TONIGHT, DUE TO POPULAR DEMAND, WE'RE HERE--
HUNTING THE HOAX OF THE HAUNTED LARAMIE HOME!
MWHAHAH!
Regan, Supernatural Expert
"AHEM. ANYWAY...
"TWENTY YEARS AGO, TRAGEDY STRUCK THIS HOME WHEN DON AND LUCY LARAMIE, A NEWLYWED COUPLE, WERE MURDERED.
"THEIR SIX-YEAR OLD DAUGHTER WAS NEVER FOUND.
"NOT A SINGLE RESIDENT HAS OCCUPIED THIS HOME FOR MORE THAN THREE YEARS SINCE. MANY HAVE COMPLAINED OF HEARING MOANS FROM THE BASEMENT, OTHERS HAVE EVEN CLAIMED TO HAVE SEEN BLOOD DRIPPING FROM THE WALLS.
"ONE COUPLE HAS EVEN CAPTURED SOME, LET'S SAY, QUESTIONABLE VIDEO FOOTAGE OF A GHOST-LIKE FIGURE."

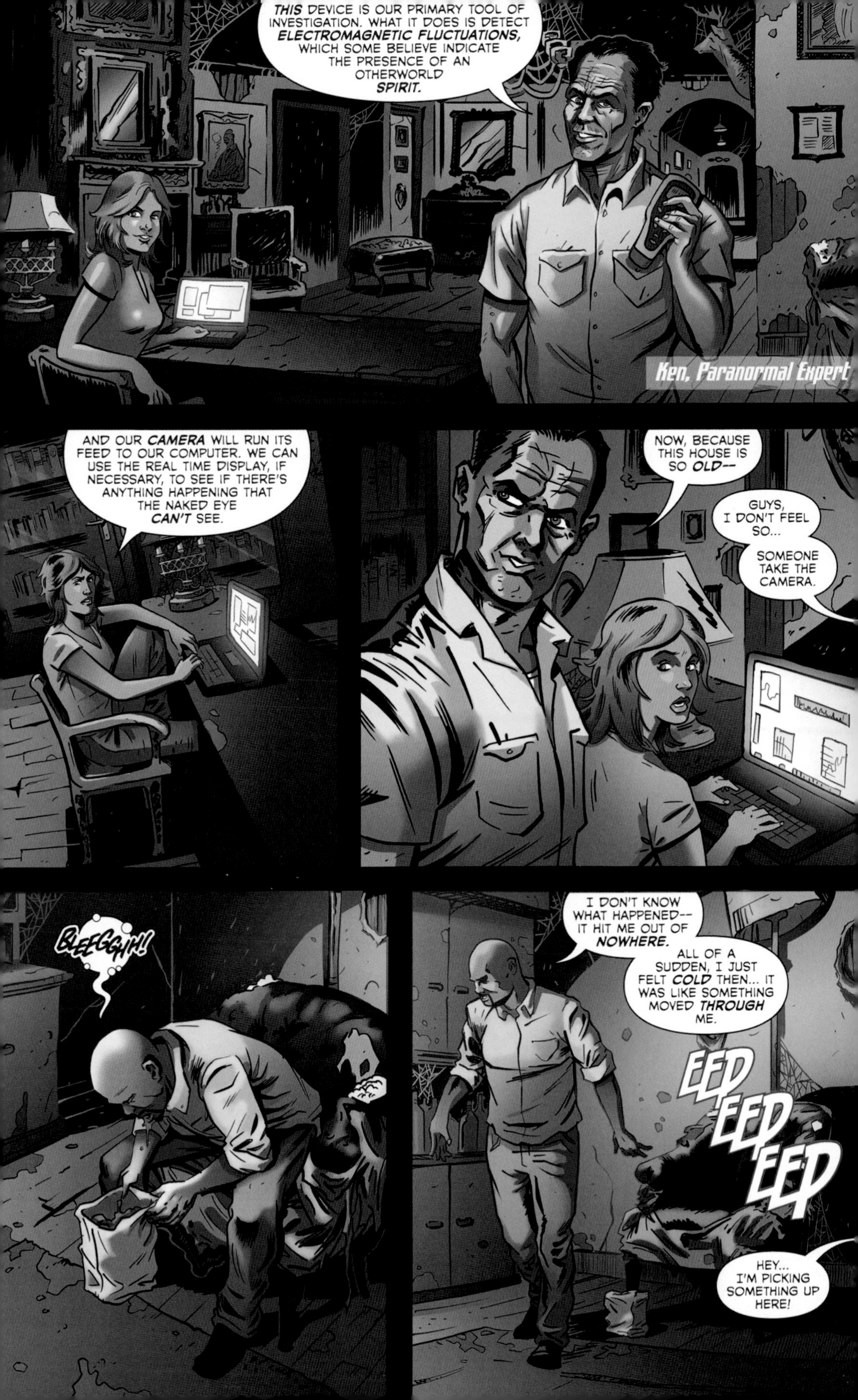
THIS DEVICE IS OUR PRIMARY TOOL OF INVESTIGATION. WHAT IT DOES IS DETECT ELECTROMAGNETIC FLUCTUATIONS, WHICH SOME BELIEVE INDICATE THE PRESENCE OF AN OTHERWORLD SPIRIT.
Ken, Paranormal Expert
AND OUR CAMERA WILL RUN ITS FEED TO OUR COMPUTER. WE CAN USE THE REAL TIME DISPLAY, IF NECESSARY, TO SEE IF THERE'S ANYTHING HAPPENING THAT THE NAKED EYE CAN'T SEE.
NOW, BECAUSE THIS HOUSE IS SO OLD--
GUYS, I DON'T FEEL SO...
SOMEONE TAKE THE CAMERA.
BLEEGGHH!
I DON'T KNOW WHAT HAPPENED-- IT HIT ME OUT OF NOWHERE.
ALL OF A SUDDEN, I JUST FELT COLD THEN... IT WAS LIKE SOMETHING MOVED THROUGH ME.
EEP EEP EEP
HEY... I'M PICKING SOMETHING UP HERE!

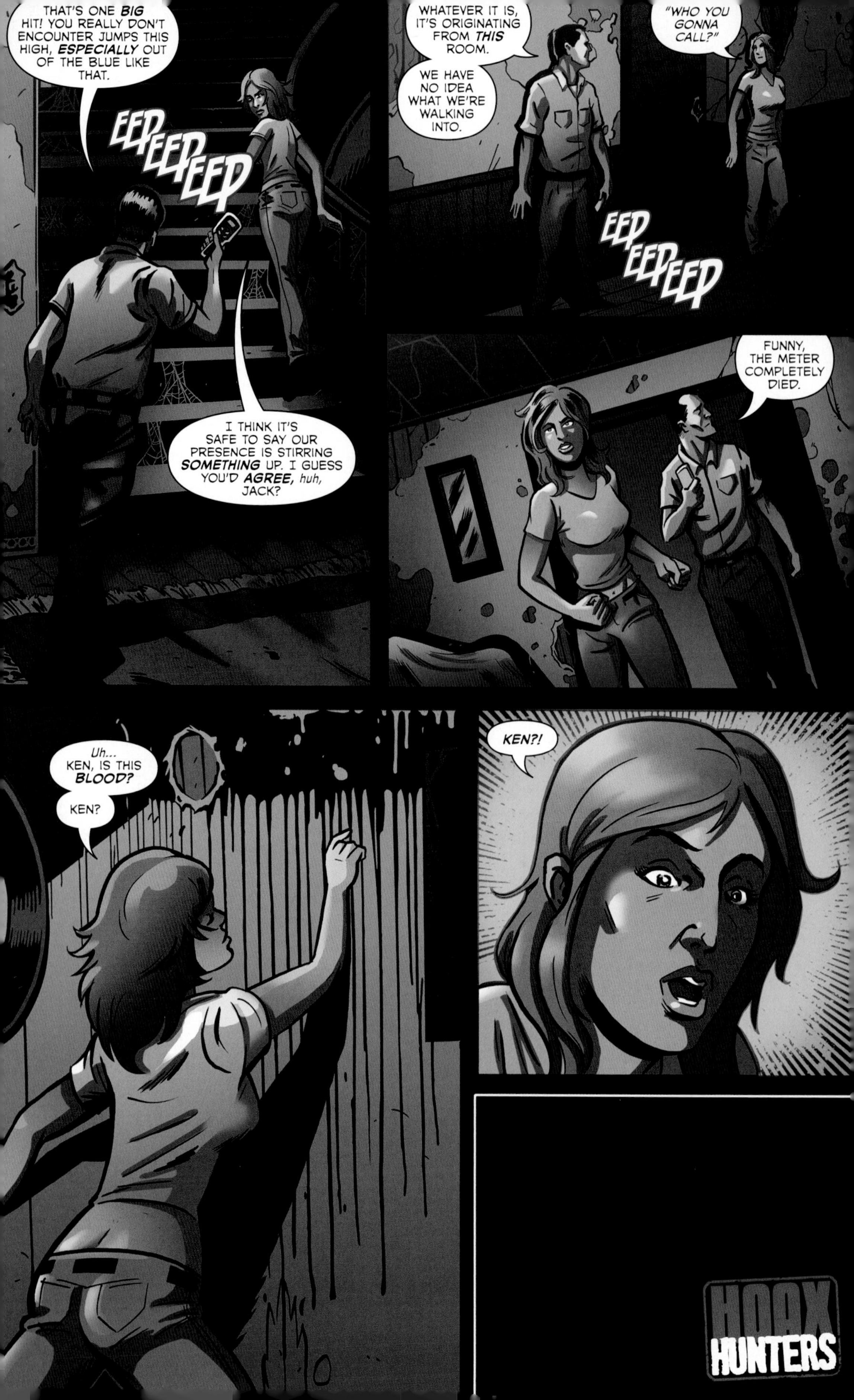
THAT'S ONE BIG HIT! YOU REALLY DON'T ENCOUNTER JUMPS THIS HIGH, ESPECIALLY OUT OF THE BLUE LIKE THAT.
EEP EEP EEP EEP
I THINK IT'S SAFE TO SAY OUR PRESENCE IS STIRRING SOMETHING UP. I GUESS YOU'D AGREE, huh, JACK?
WHATEVER IT IS, IT'S ORIGINATING FROM THIS ROOM.
WE HAVE NO IDEA WHAT WE'RE WALKING INTO.
"WHO YOU GONNA CALL?"
EEP EEP EEP EEP
FUNNY, THE METER COMPLETELY DIED.
Uh... KEN, IS THIS BLOOD?
KEN?
KEN?!
HOAX HUNTERS

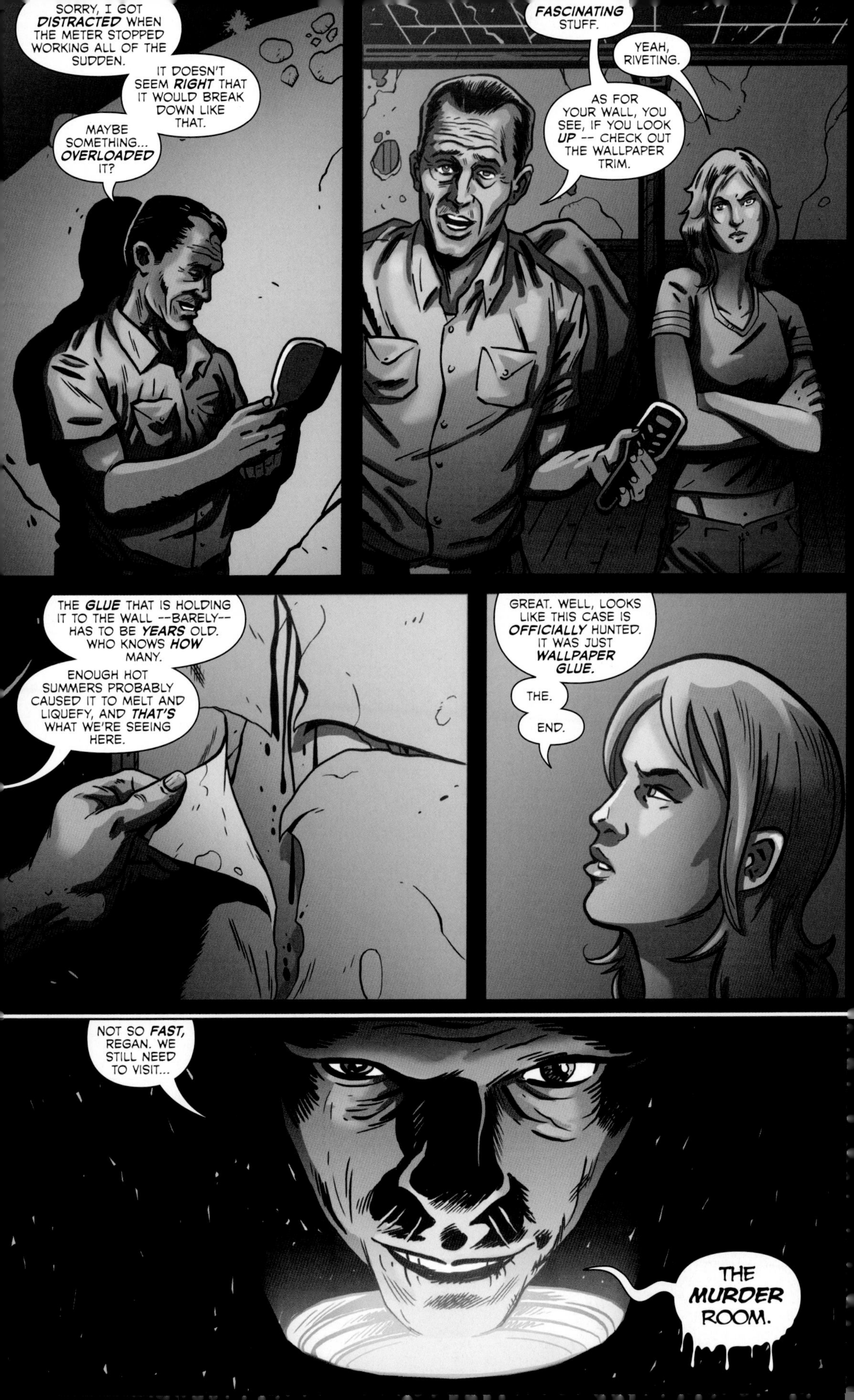
SORRY, I GOT DISTRACTED WHEN THE METER STOPPED WORKING ALL OF THE SUDDEN.
IT DOESN'T SEEM RIGHT THAT IT WOULD BREAK DOWN LIKE THAT.
MAYBE SOMETHING... OVERLOADED IT?
FASCINATING STUFF.
YEAH, RIVETING.
AS FOR YOUR WALL, YOU SEE, IF YOU LOOK UP -- CHECK OUT THE WALLPAPER TRIM.
THE GLUE THAT IS HOLDING IT TO THE WALL --BARELY-- HAS TO BE YEARS OLD. WHO KNOWS HOW MANY.
ENOUGH HOT SUMMERS PROBABLY CAUSED IT TO MELT AND LIQUEFY, AND THAT'S WHAT WE'RE SEEING HERE.
GREAT. WELL, LOOKS LIKE THIS CASE IS OFFICIALLY HUNTED. IT WAS JUST WALLPAPER GLUE.
THE.
END.
NOT SO FAST, REGAN. WE STILL NEED TO VISIT...
THE MURDER ROOM.

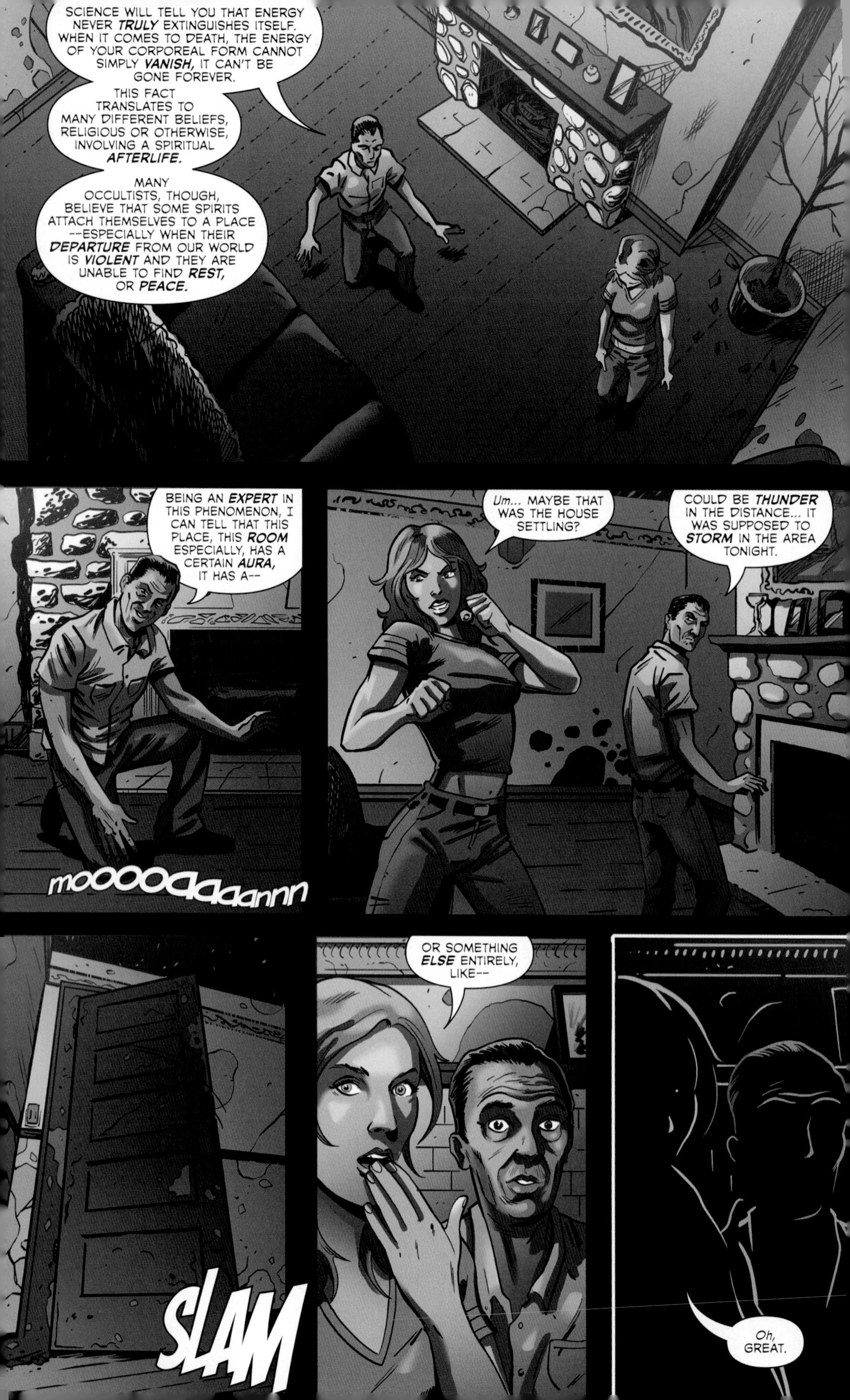
SCIENCE WILL TELL YOU THAT ENERGY NEVER TRULY EXTINGUISHES ITSELF. WHEN IT COMES TO DEATH, THE ENERGY OF YOUR CORPOREAL FORM CANNOT SIMPLY VANISH, IT CAN'T BE GONE FOREVER.
THIS FACT TRANSLATES TO MANY DIFFERENT BELIEFS, RELIGIOUS OR OTHERWISE, INVOLVING A SPIRITUAL AFTERLIFE.
MANY OCCULTISTS, THOUGH, BELIEVE THAT SOME SPIRITS ATTACH THEMSELVES TO A PLACE --ESPECIALLY WHEN THEIR DEPARTURE FROM OUR WORLD IS VIOLENT AND THEY ARE UNABLE TO FIND REST, OR PEACE.
BEING AN EXPERT IN THIS PHENOMENON, I CAN TELL THAT THIS PLACE, THIS ROOM ESPECIALLY, HAS A CERTAIN AURA, IT HAS A--
mooooaaaannn
Um... MAYBE THAT WAS THE HOUSE SETTLING?
COULD BE THUNDER IN THE DISTANCE... IT WAS SUPPOSED TO STORM IN THE AREA TONIGHT.
SLAM
OR SOMETHING ELSE ENTIRELY, LIKE--
Oh, GREAT.

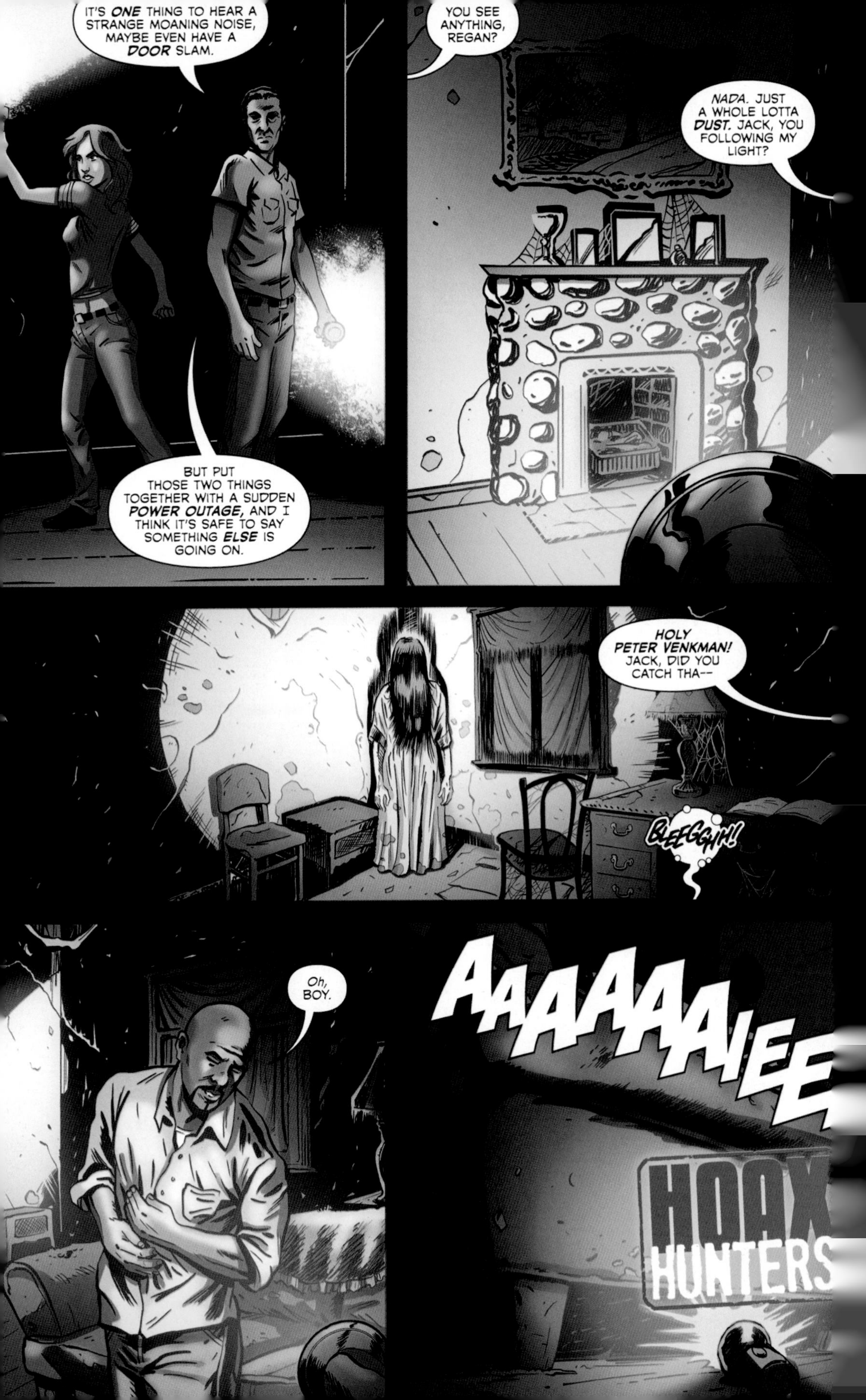
IT'S ONE THING TO HEAR A STRANGE MOANING NOISE, MAYBE EVEN HAVE A DOOR SLAM.
BUT PUT THOSE TWO THINGS TOGETHER WITH A SUDDEN POWER OUTAGE, AND I THINK IT'S SAFE TO SAY SOMETHING ELSE IS GOING ON.
YOU SEE ANYTHING, REGAN?
NADA. JUST A WHOLE LOTTA DUST. JACK, YOU FOLLOWING MY LIGHT?
HOLY PETER VENKMAN! JACK, DID YOU CATCH THA--
BLEEGGHH!
Oh, BOY.
AAAAAAIEEE
HOAX HUNTERS

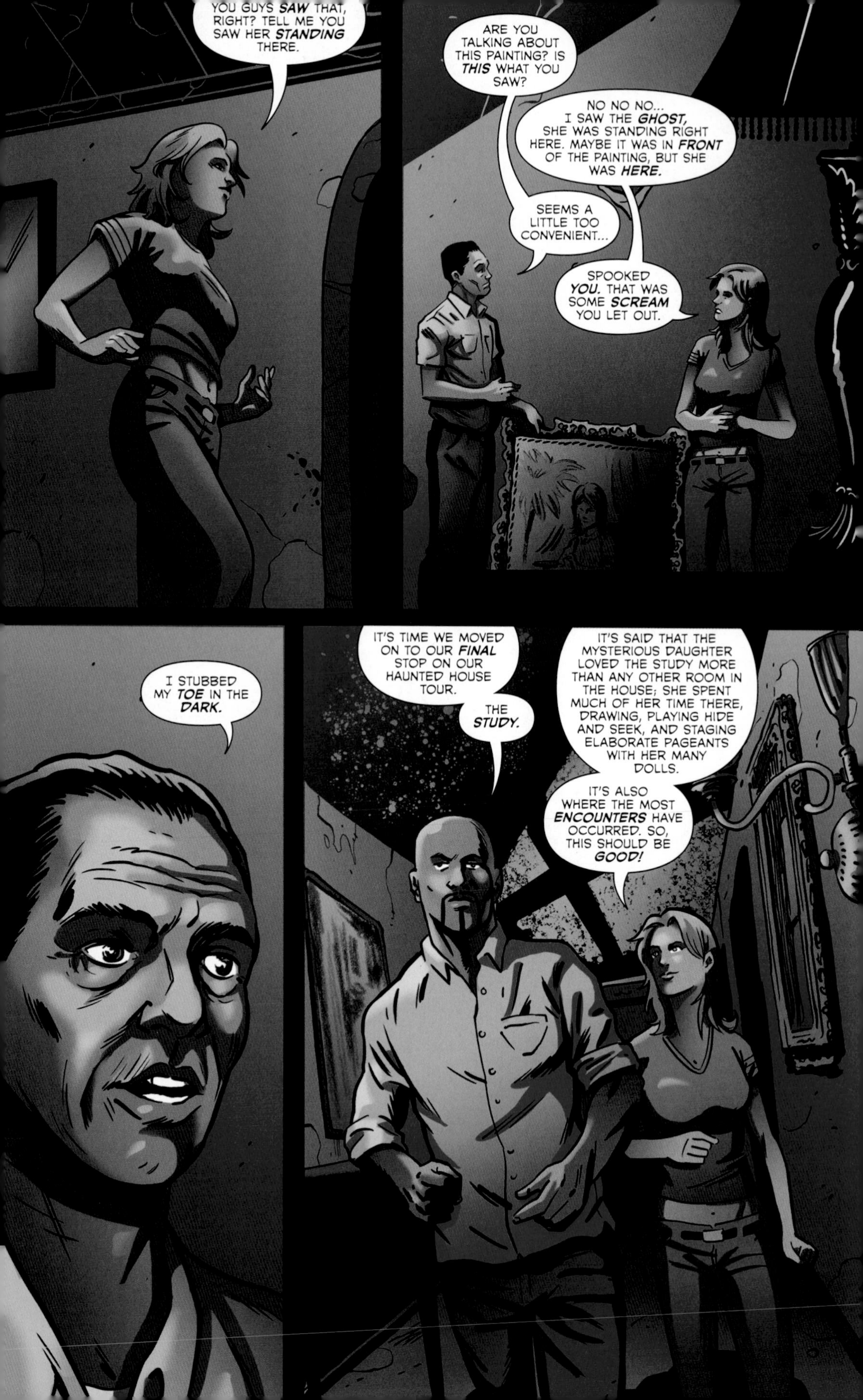
YOU GUYS SAW THAT, RIGHT? TELL ME YOU SAW HER STANDING THERE.
ARE YOU TALKING ABOUT THIS PAINTING? IS THIS WHAT YOU SAW?
NO NO NO... I SAW THE GHOST, SHE WAS STANDING RIGHT HERE. MAYBE IT WAS IN FRONT OF THE PAINTING, BUT SHE WAS HERE.
SEEMS A LITTLE TOO CONVENIENT...
SPOOKED YOU. THAT WAS SOME SCREAM YOU LET OUT.
I STUBBED MY TOE IN THE DARK.
IT'S TIME WE MOVED ON TO OUR FINAL STOP ON OUR HAUNTED HOUSE TOUR.
THE STUDY.
IT'S SAID THAT THE MYSTERIOUS DAUGHTER LOVED THE STUDY MORE THAN ANY OTHER ROOM IN THE HOUSE; SHE SPENT MUCH OF HER TIME THERE, DRAWING, PLAYING HIDE AND SEEK, AND STAGING ELABORATE PAGEANTS WITH HER MANY DOLLS.
IT'S ALSO WHERE THE MOST ENCOUNTERS HAVE OCCURRED. SO, THIS SHOULD BE GOOD!

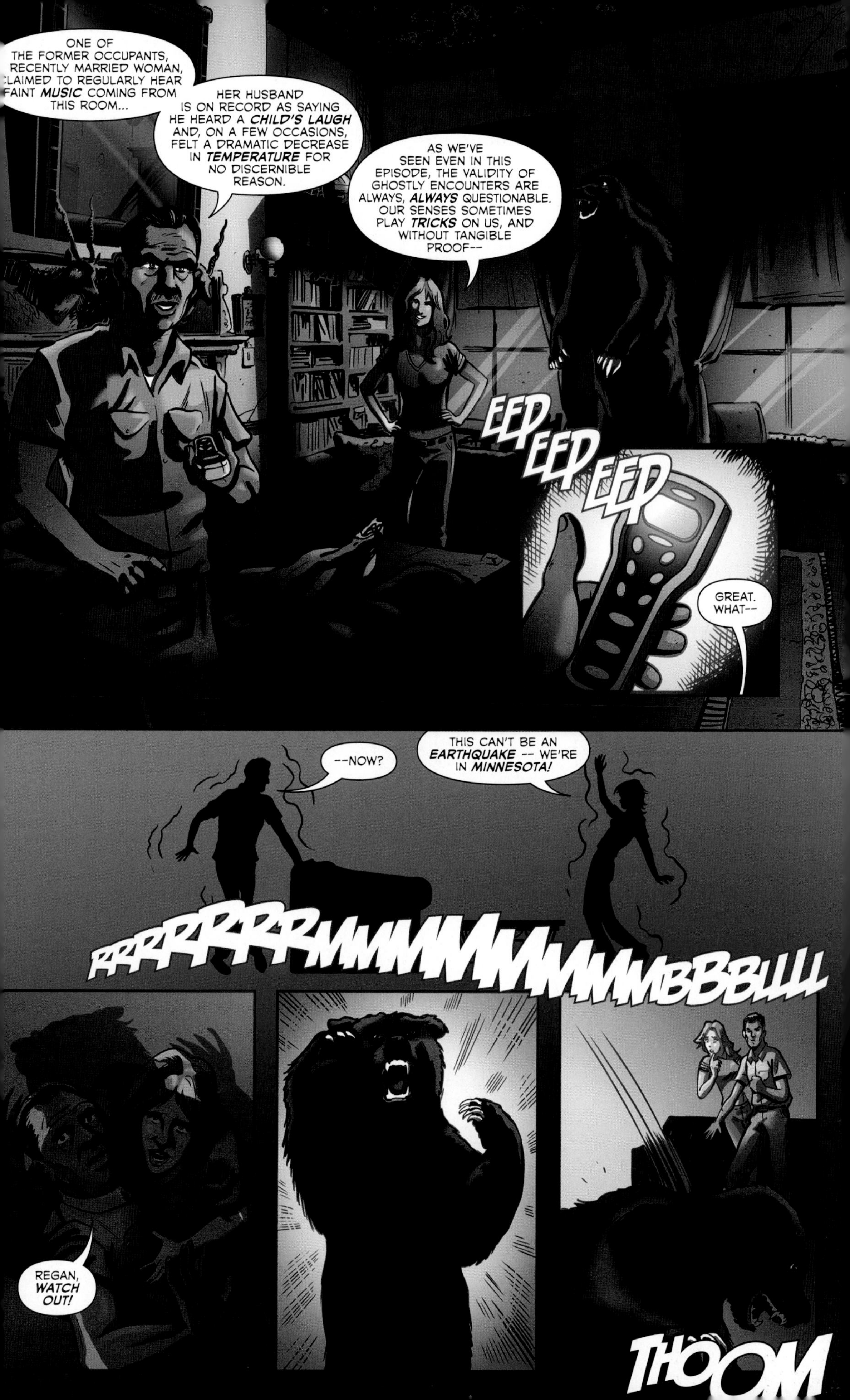
ONE OF THE FORMER OCCUPANTS, RECENTLY MARRIED WOMAN, CLAIMED TO REGULARLY HEAR FAINT MUSIC COMING FROM THIS ROOM...
HER HUSBAND IS ON RECORD AS SAYING HE HEARD A CHILD'S LAUGH AND, ON A FEW OCCASIONS, FELT A DRAMATIC DECREASE IN TEMPERATURE FOR NO DISCERNIBLE REASON.
AS WE'VE SEEN EVEN IN THIS EPISODE, THE VALIDITY OF GHOSTLY ENCOUNTERS ARE ALWAYS, ALWAYS QUESTIONABLE. OUR SENSES SOMETIMES PLAY TRICKS ON US, AND WITHOUT TANGIBLE PROOF--
EEP EEP EEP
GREAT. WHAT--
--NOW?
THIS CAN'T BE AN EARTHQUAKE -- WE'RE IN MINNESOTA!
RRRRRRRRMMMMMMMMMMMBBBLLLL
REGAN, WATCH OUT!
THOOM

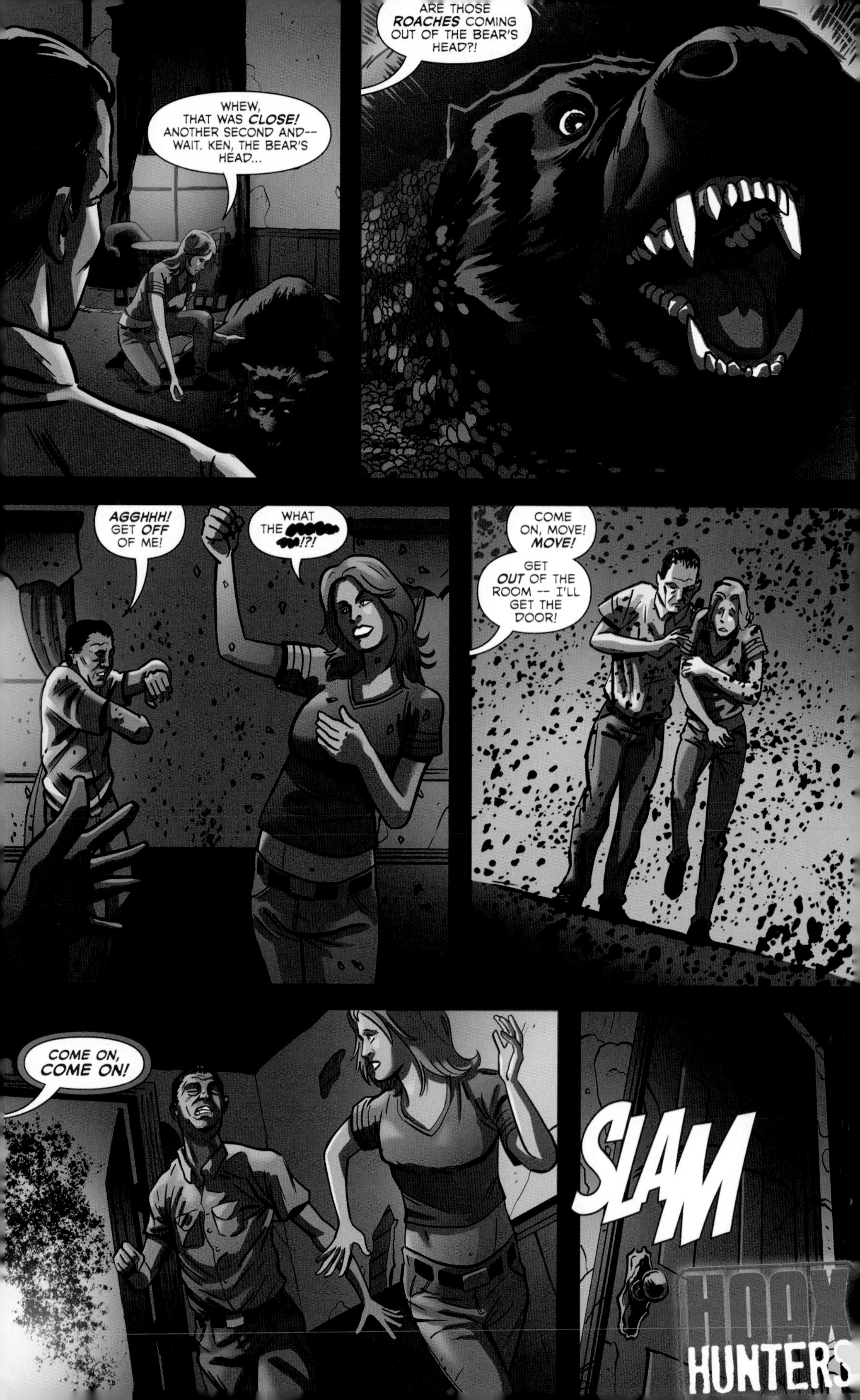

WHEW, THAT WAS CLOSE! ANOTHER SECOND AND-- WAIT. KEN, THE BEAR'S HEAD...
ARE THOSE ROACHES COMING OUT OF THE BEAR'S HEAD?!
AGGHHH! GET OFF OF ME!
WHAT THE [redacted]!?!
COME ON, MOVE! MOVE!
GET OUT OF THE ROOM -- I'LL GET THE DOOR!
COME ON, COME ON!
SLAM
HOAX HUNTERS

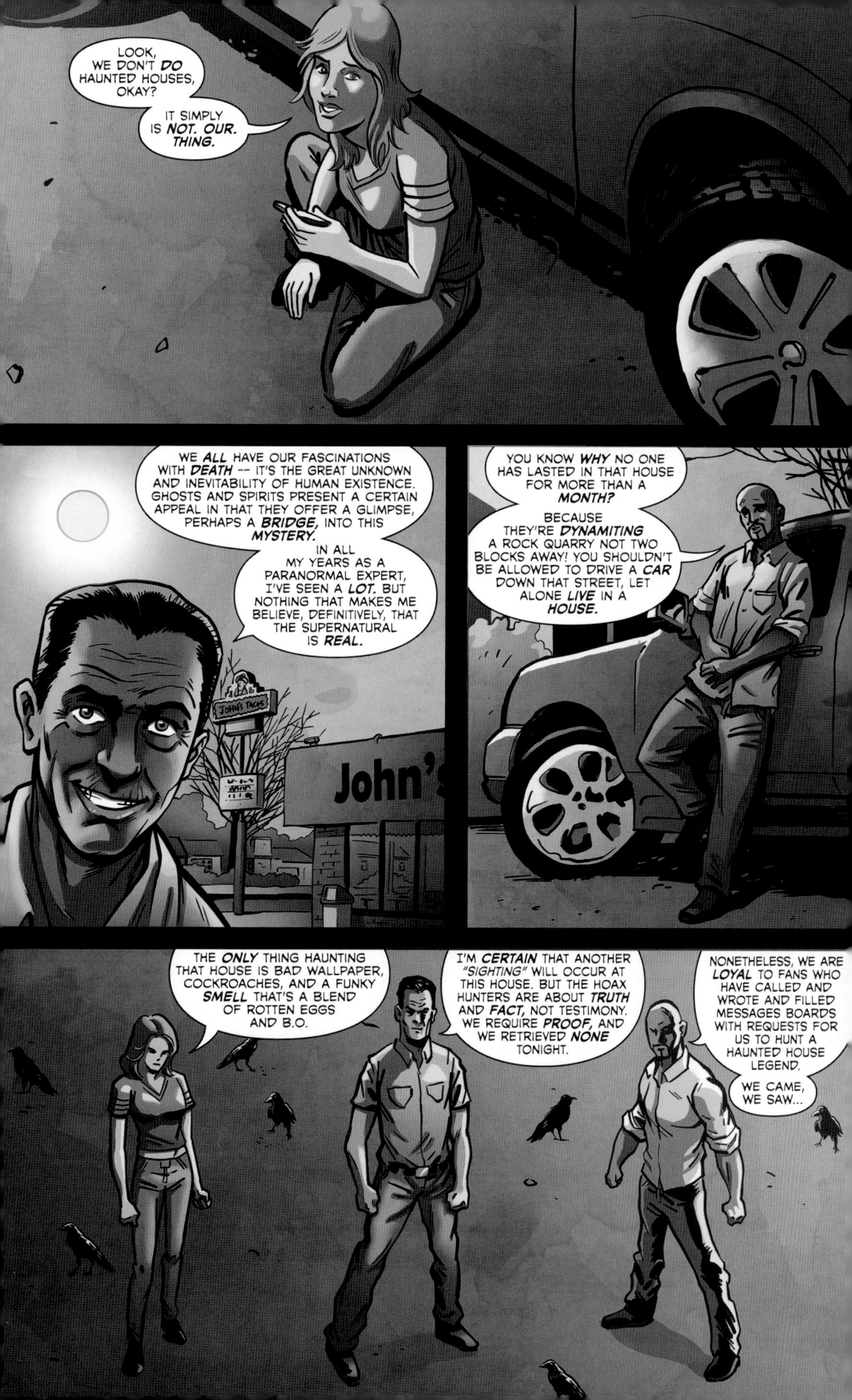

LOOK, WE DON'T DO HAUNTED HOUSES, OKAY?
IT SIMPLY IS NOT. OUR. THING.
WE ALL HAVE OUR FASCINATIONS WITH DEATH -- IT'S THE GREAT UNKNOWN AND INEVITABILITY OF HUMAN EXISTENCE. GHOSTS AND SPIRITS PRESENT A CERTAIN APPEAL IN THAT THEY OFFER A GLIMPSE, PERHAPS A BRIDGE, INTO THIS MYSTERY.
IN ALL MY YEARS AS A PARANORMAL EXPERT, I'VE SEEN A LOT. BUT NOTHING THAT MAKES ME BELIEVE, DEFINITIVELY, THAT THE SUPERNATURAL IS REAL.
John's
YOU KNOW WHY NO ONE HAS LASTED IN THAT HOUSE FOR MORE THAN A MONTH?
BECAUSE THEY'RE DYNAMITING A ROCK QUARRY NOT TWO BLOCKS AWAY! YOU SHOULDN'T BE ALLOWED TO DRIVE A CAR DOWN THAT STREET, LET ALONE LIVE IN A HOUSE.
THE ONLY THING HAUNTING THAT HOUSE IS BAD WALLPAPER, COCKROACHES, AND A FUNKY SMELL THAT'S A BLEND OF ROTTEN EGGS AND B.O.
I'M CERTAIN THAT ANOTHER "SIGHTING" WILL OCCUR AT THIS HOUSE. BUT THE HOAX HUNTERS ARE ABOUT TRUTH AND FACT, NOT TESTIMONY. WE REQUIRE PROOF, AND WE RETRIEVED NONE TONIGHT.
NONETHELESS, WE ARE LOYAL TO FANS WHO HAVE CALLED AND WROTE AND FILLED MESSAGES BOARDS WITH REQUESTS FOR US TO HUNT A HAUNTED HOUSE LEGEND.
WE CAME, WE SAW...

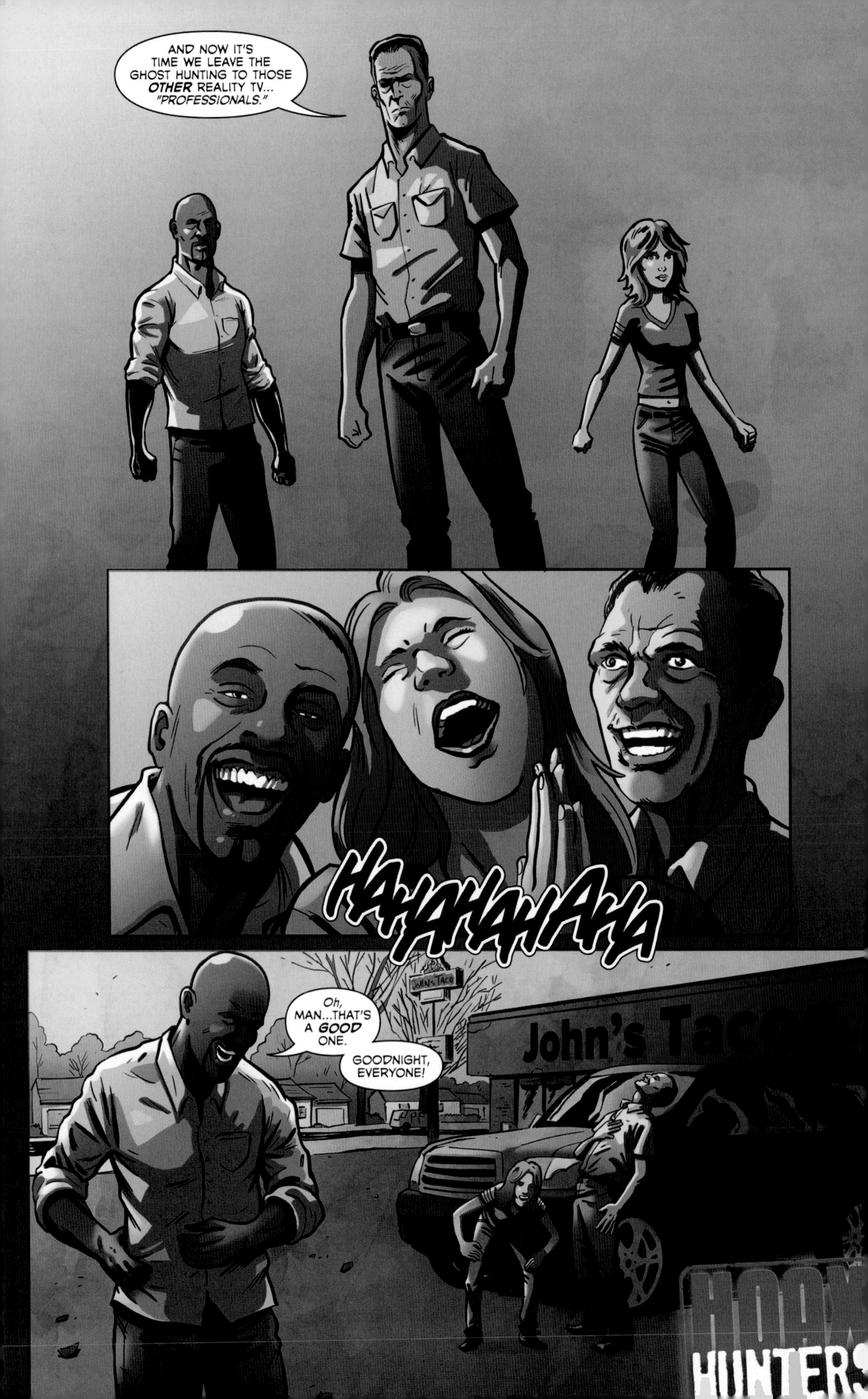
AND NOW IT'S TIME WE LEAVE THE GHOST HUNTING TO THOSE OTHER REALITY TV... "PROFESSIONALS."
HAHAHAHAHAHA
JOHN'S TACO
John's Ta
Oh, MAN...THAT'S A GOOD ONE.
GOODNIGHT, EVERYONE!
HUNTERS

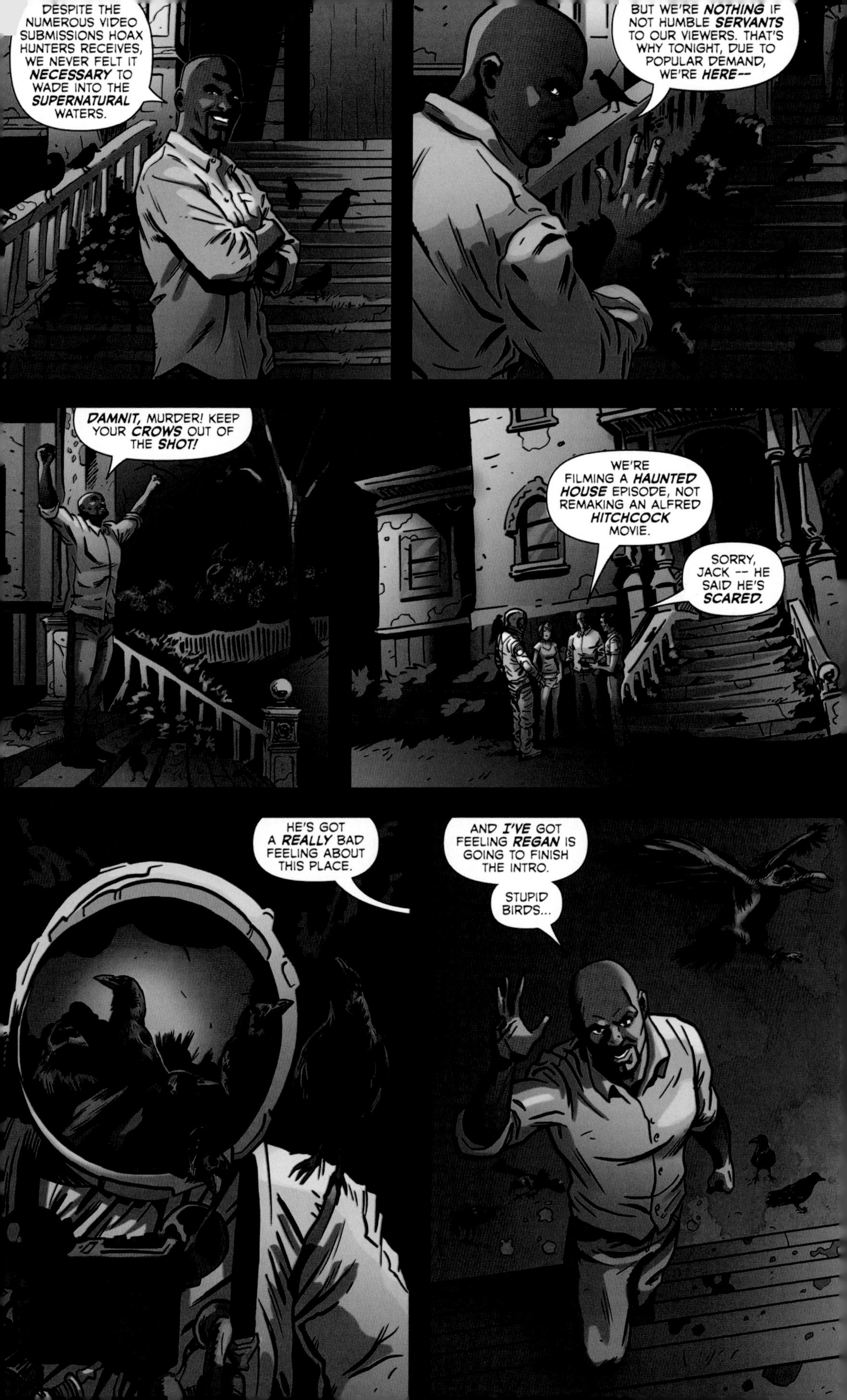
DESPITE THE NUMEROUS VIDEO SUBMISSIONS HOAX HUNTERS RECEIVES, WE NEVER FELT IT NECESSARY TO WADE INTO THE SUPERNATURAL WATERS.
BUT WE'RE NOTHING IF NOT HUMBLE SERVANTS TO OUR VIEWERS. THAT'S WHY TONIGHT, DUE TO POPULAR DEMAND, WE'RE HERE--
DAMNIT, MURDER! KEEP YOUR CROWS OUT OF THE SHOT!
WE'RE FILMING A HAUNTED HOUSE EPISODE, NOT REMAKING AN ALFRED HITCHCOCK MOVIE.
SORRY, JACK -- HE SAID HE'S SCARED.
HE'S GOT A REALLY BAD FEELING ABOUT THIS PLACE.
AND I'VE GOT FEELING REGAN IS GOING TO FINISH THE INTRO.
STUPID BIRDS...

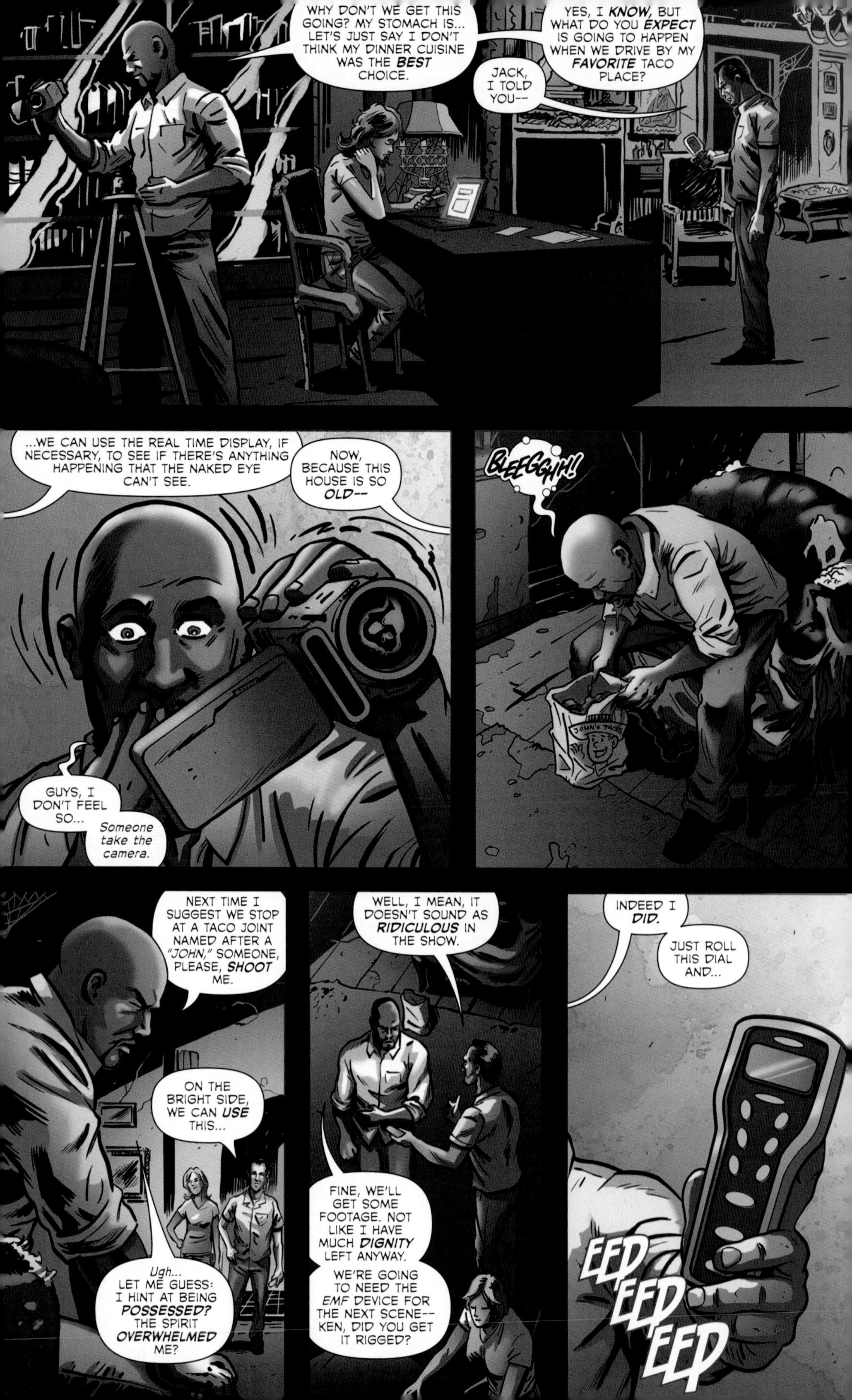
WHY DON'T WE GET THIS GOING? MY STOMACH IS... LET'S JUST SAY I DON'T THINK MY DINNER CUISINE WAS THE BEST CHOICE.
JACK, I TOLD YOU--
YES, I KNOW, BUT WHAT DO YOU EXPECT IS GOING TO HAPPEN WHEN WE DRIVE BY MY FAVORITE TACO PLACE?
...WE CAN USE THE REAL TIME DISPLAY, IF NECESSARY, TO SEE IF THERE'S ANYTHING HAPPENING THAT THE NAKED EYE CAN'T SEE.
NOW, BECAUSE THIS HOUSE IS SO OLD--
GUYS, I DON'T FEEL SO... Someone take the camera.
BLEEGGHH!
JOHN'S TACOS
NEXT TIME I SUGGEST WE STOP AT A TACO JOINT NAMED AFTER A "JOHN," SOMEONE, PLEASE, SHOOT ME.
ON THE BRIGHT SIDE, WE CAN USE THIS...
Ugh... LET ME GUESS: I HINT AT BEING POSSESSED? THE SPIRIT OVERWHELMED ME?
WELL, I MEAN, IT DOESN'T SOUND AS RIDICULOUS IN THE SHOW.
FINE, WE'LL GET SOME FOOTAGE. NOT LIKE I HAVE MUCH DIGNITY LEFT ANYWAY.
WE'RE GOING TO NEED THE EMF DEVICE FOR THE NEXT SCENE-- KEN, DID YOU GET IT RIGGED?
INDEED I DID.
JUST ROLL THIS DIAL AND...
EEP EEP EEP

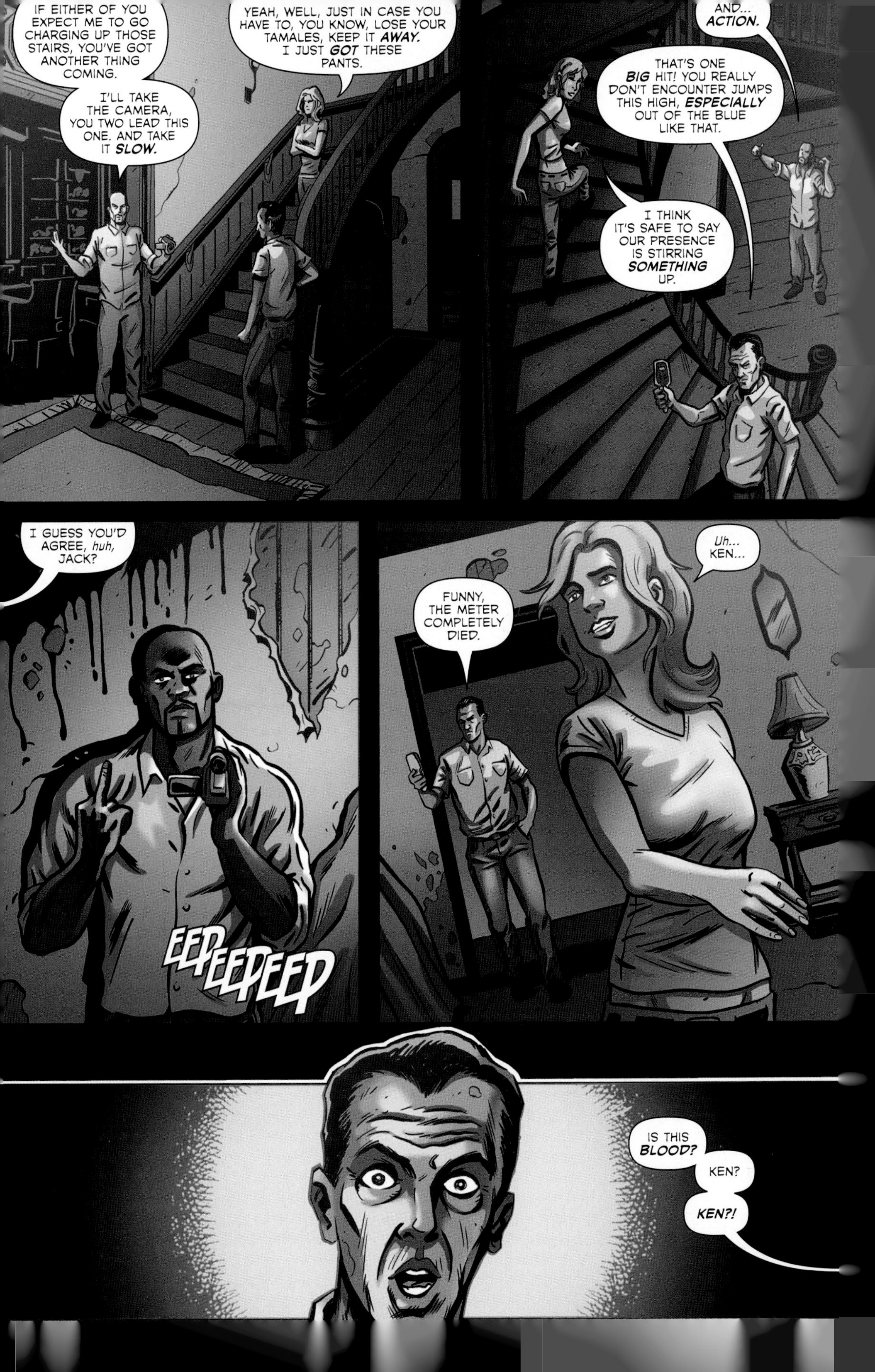
IF EITHER OF YOU EXPECT ME TO GO CHARGING UP THOSE STAIRS, YOU'VE GOT ANOTHER THING COMING.
YEAH, WELL, JUST IN CASE YOU HAVE TO, YOU KNOW, LOSE YOUR TAMALES, KEEP IT **AWAY.** I JUST **GOT** THESE PANTS.
I'LL TAKE THE CAMERA, YOU TWO LEAD THIS ONE. AND TAKE IT **SLOW.**
AND... **ACTION.**
THAT'S ONE **BIG** HIT! YOU REALLY DON'T ENCOUNTER JUMPS THIS HIGH, **ESPECIALLY** OUT OF THE BLUE LIKE THAT.
I THINK IT'S SAFE TO SAY OUR PRESENCE IS STIRRING **SOMETHING** UP.
I GUESS YOU'D AGREE, *huh,* JACK?
EEDEEDEED
Uh... KEN...
FUNNY, THE METER COMPLETELY DIED.
IS THIS **BLOOD?**
KEN?
KEN?!

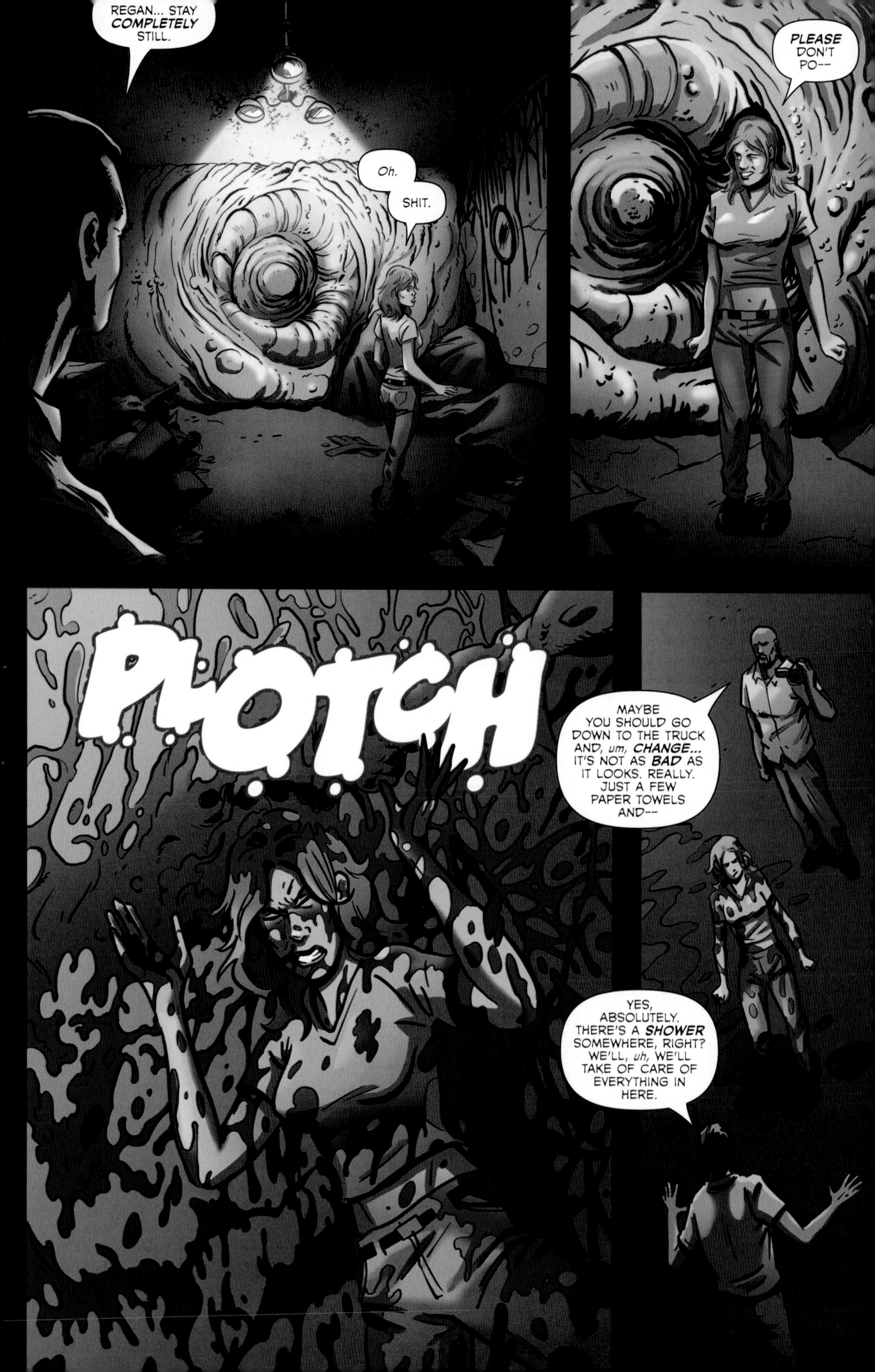
REGAN... STAY COMPLETELY STILL.
Oh.
SHIT.
PLEASE DON'T PO--
PLOTCH
MAYBE YOU SHOULD GO DOWN TO THE TRUCK AND, um, CHANGE... IT'S NOT AS BAD AS IT LOOKS. REALLY. JUST A FEW PAPER TOWELS AND--
YES, ABSOLUTELY. THERE'S A SHOWER SOMEWHERE, RIGHT? WE'LL, uh, WE'LL TAKE OF CARE OF EVERYTHING IN HERE.

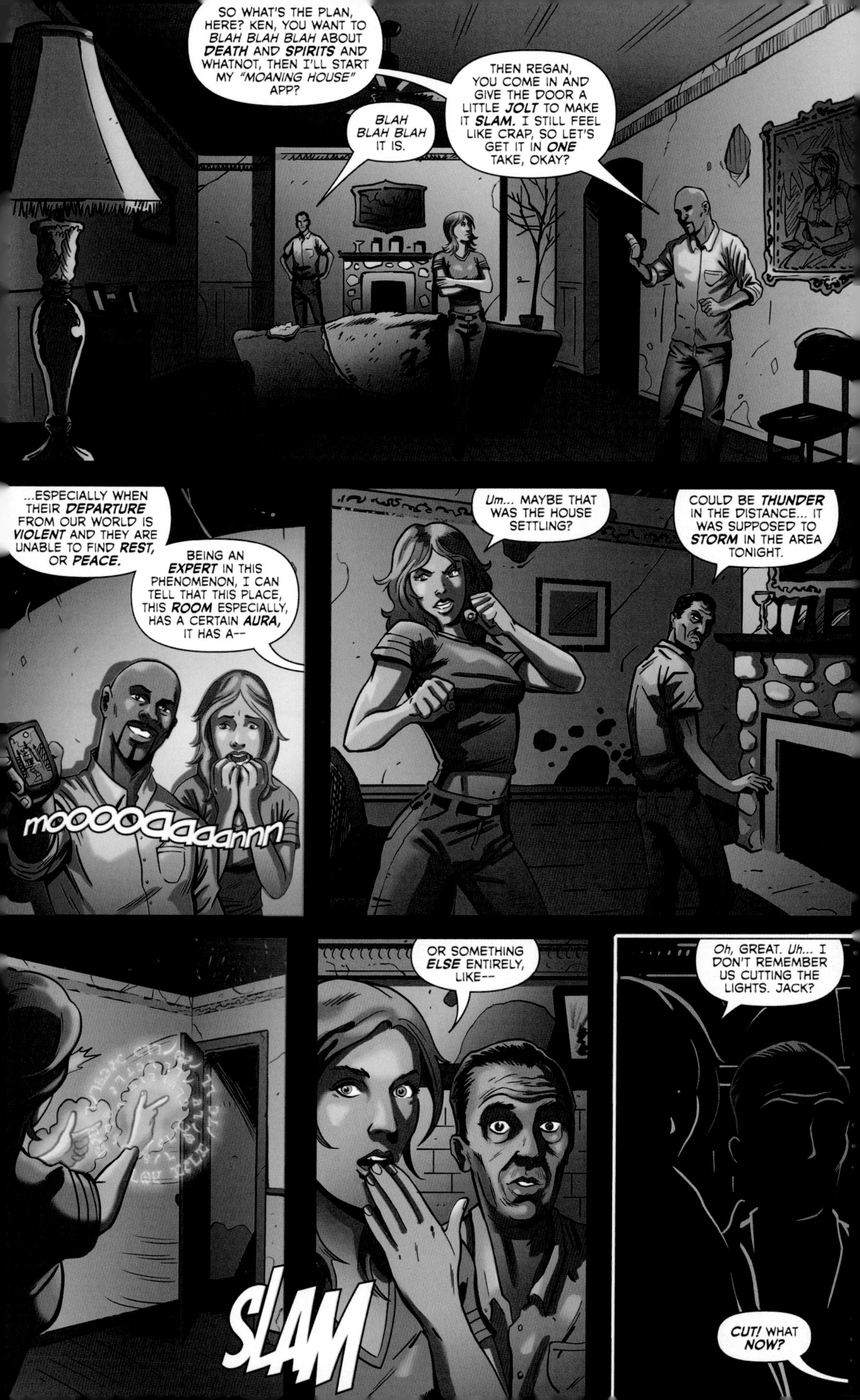
SO WHAT'S THE PLAN, HERE? KEN, YOU WANT TO *BLAH BLAH BLAH* ABOUT ***DEATH*** AND ***SPIRITS*** AND WHATNOT, THEN I'LL START MY *"MOANING HOUSE"* APP?
BLAH BLAH BLAH IT IS.
THEN REGAN, YOU COME IN AND GIVE THE DOOR A LITTLE ***JOLT*** TO MAKE IT ***SLAM.*** I STILL FEEL LIKE CRAP, SO LET'S GET IT IN ***ONE*** TAKE, OKAY?
...ESPECIALLY WHEN THEIR ***DEPARTURE*** FROM OUR WORLD IS ***VIOLENT*** AND THEY ARE UNABLE TO FIND ***REST,*** OR ***PEACE.***
BEING AN ***EXPERT*** IN THIS PHENOMENON, I CAN TELL THAT THIS PLACE, THIS ***ROOM*** ESPECIALLY, HAS A CERTAIN ***AURA,*** IT HAS A--
moooooaaaannn
Um... MAYBE THAT WAS THE HOUSE SETTLING?
COULD BE ***THUNDER*** IN THE DISTANCE... IT WAS SUPPOSED TO ***STORM*** IN THE AREA TONIGHT.
OR SOMETHING ***ELSE*** ENTIRELY, LIKE--
SLAM
Oh, GREAT. *Uh...* I DON'T REMEMBER US CUTTING THE LIGHTS. JACK?
CUT! WHAT ***NOW?***

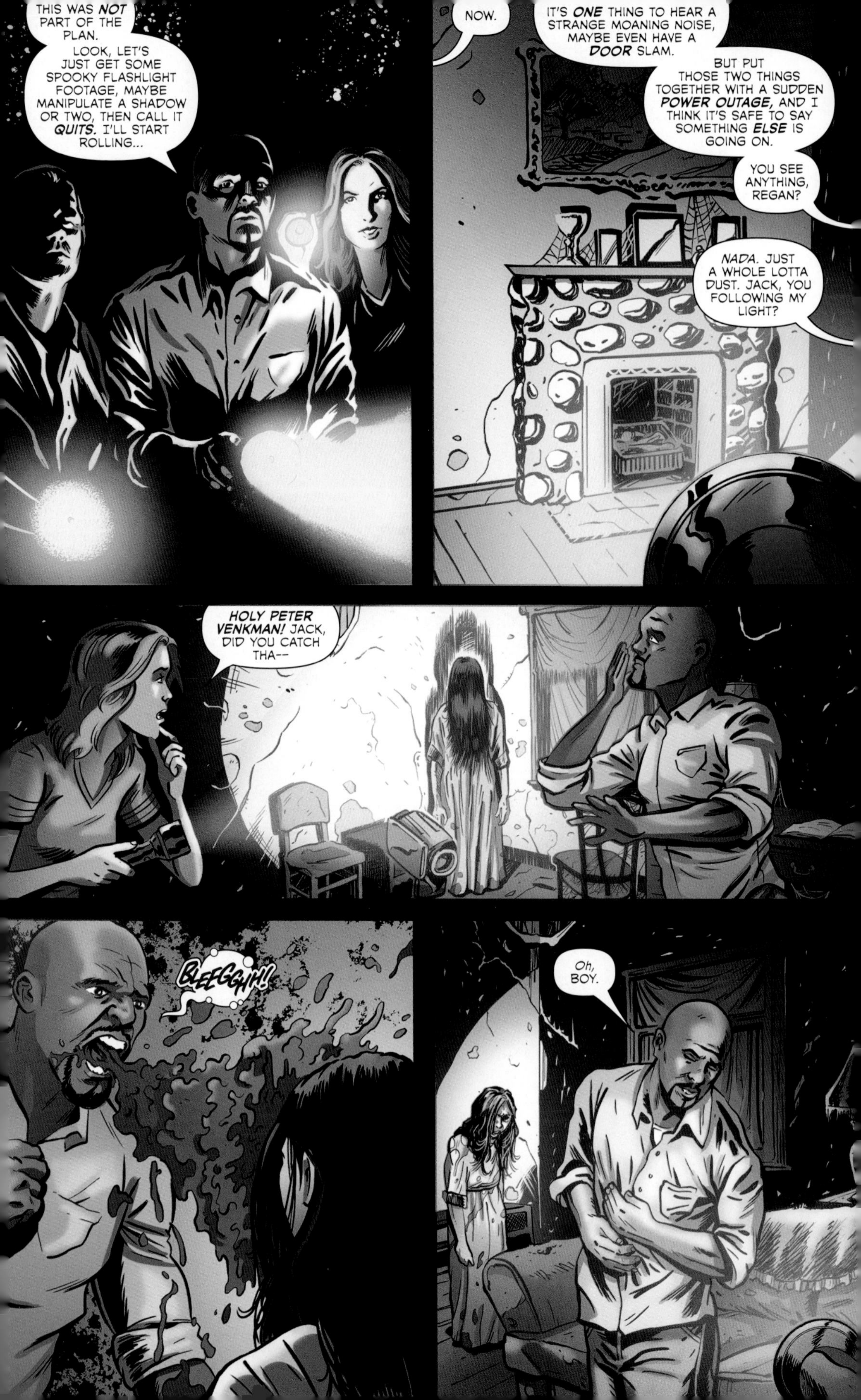
THIS WAS NOT PART OF THE PLAN.
LOOK, LET'S JUST GET SOME SPOOKY FLASHLIGHT FOOTAGE, MAYBE MANIPULATE A SHADOW OR TWO, THEN CALL IT QUITS. I'LL START ROLLING...
NOW.
IT'S ONE THING TO HEAR A STRANGE MOANING NOISE, MAYBE EVEN HAVE A DOOR SLAM.
BUT PUT THOSE TWO THINGS TOGETHER WITH A SUDDEN POWER OUTAGE, AND I THINK IT'S SAFE TO SAY SOMETHING ELSE IS GOING ON.
YOU SEE ANYTHING, REGAN?
NADA. JUST A WHOLE LOTTA DUST. JACK, YOU FOLLOWING MY LIGHT?
HOLY PETER VENKMAN! JACK, DID YOU CATCH THA--
BLEEGGHH!
Oh, BOY.

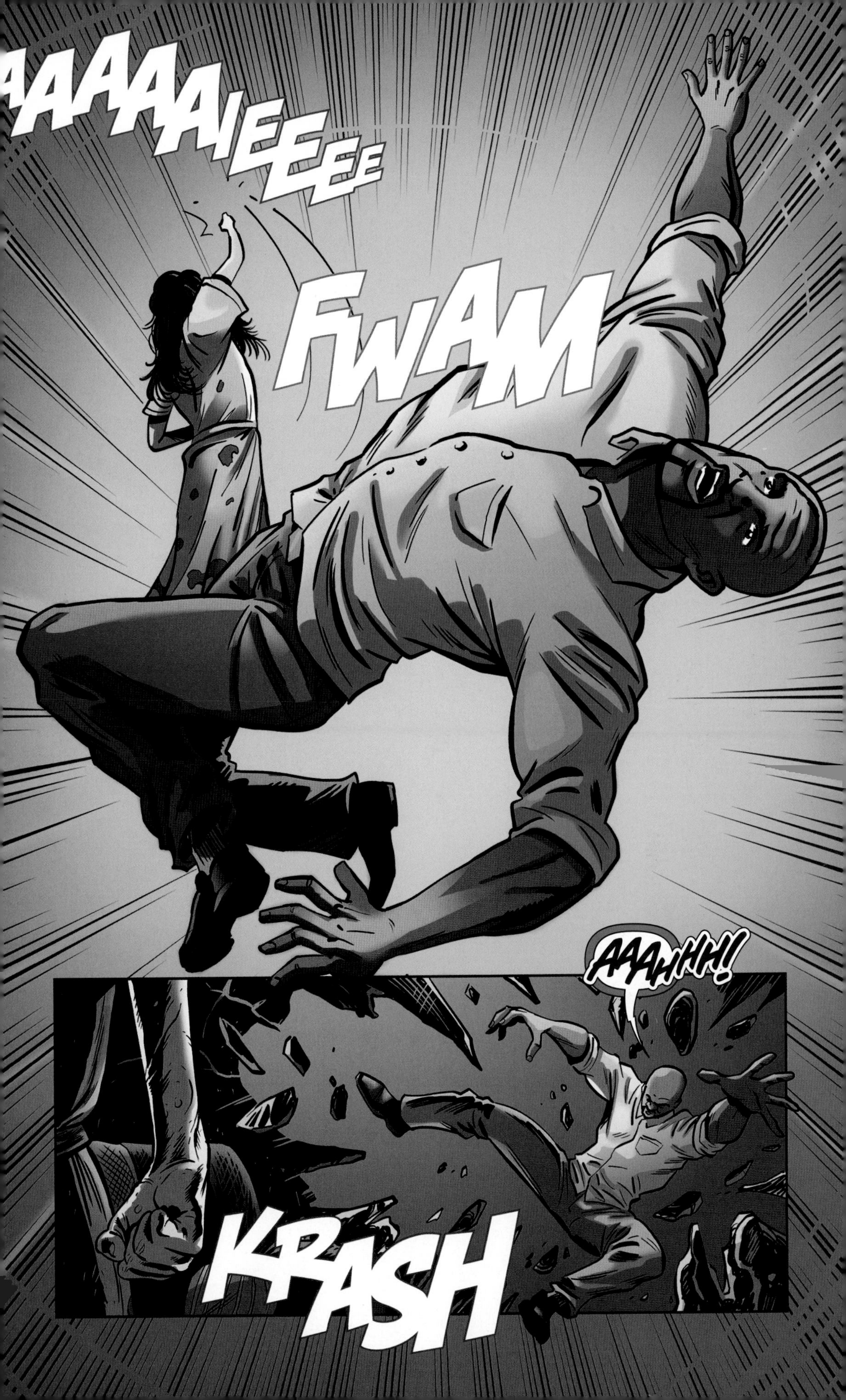
AAAAAIEEEE
FWAM
AAAHHH!
KRASH

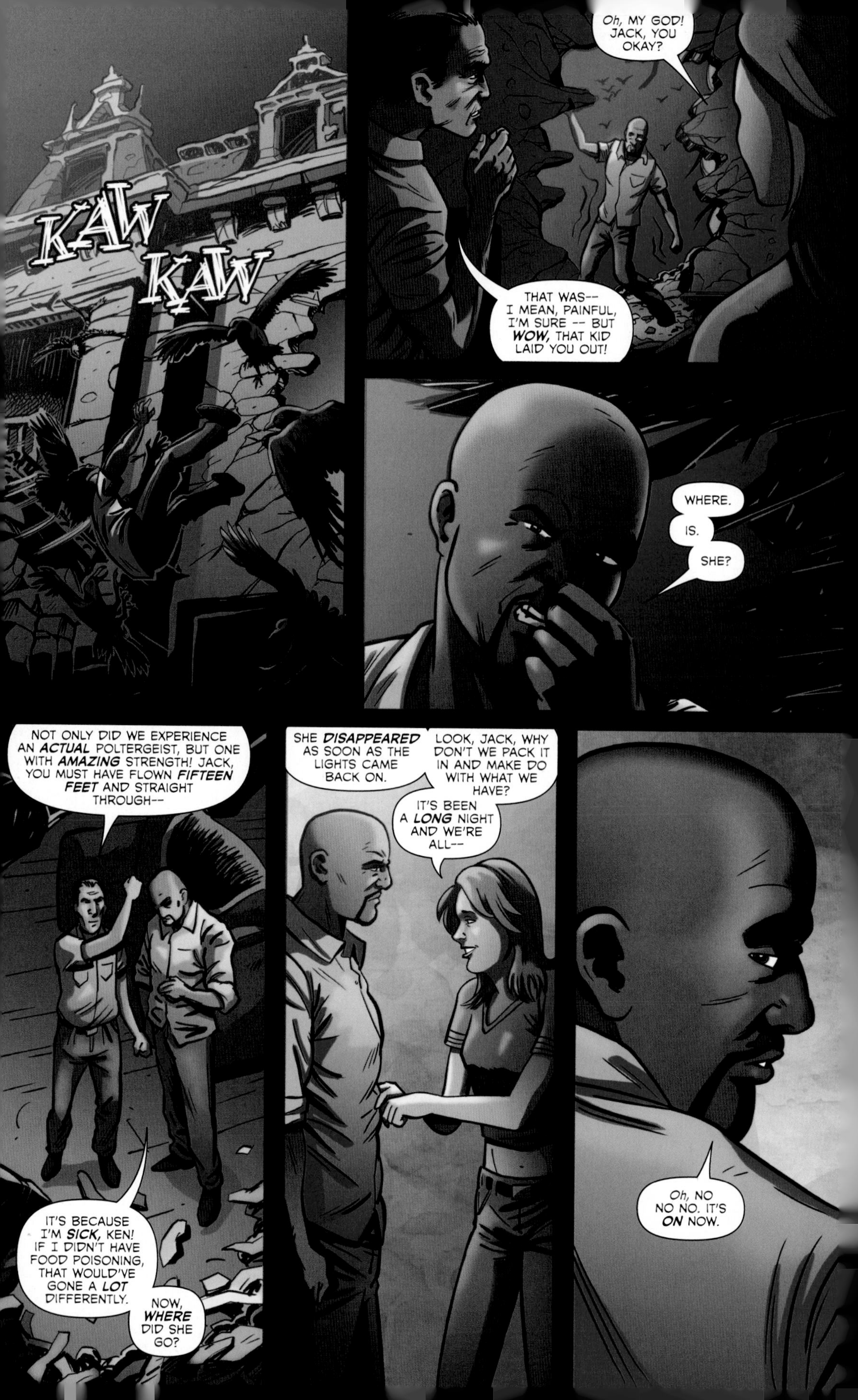
KAW
KAW
Oh, MY GOD! JACK, YOU OKAY?
THAT WAS-- I MEAN, PAINFUL, I'M SURE -- BUT WOW, THAT KID LAID YOU OUT!
WHERE.
IS.
SHE?
NOT ONLY DID WE EXPERIENCE AN ACTUAL POLTERGEIST, BUT ONE WITH AMAZING STRENGTH! JACK, YOU MUST HAVE FLOWN FIFTEEN FEET AND STRAIGHT THROUGH--
IT'S BECAUSE I'M SICK, KEN! IF I DIDN'T HAVE FOOD POISONING, THAT WOULD'VE GONE A LOT DIFFERENTLY.
NOW, WHERE DID SHE GO?
SHE DISAPPEARED AS SOON AS THE LIGHTS CAME BACK ON.
LOOK, JACK, WHY DON'T WE PACK IT IN AND MAKE DO WITH WHAT WE HAVE?
IT'S BEEN A LONG NIGHT AND WE'RE ALL--
Oh, NO NO NO. IT'S ON NOW.

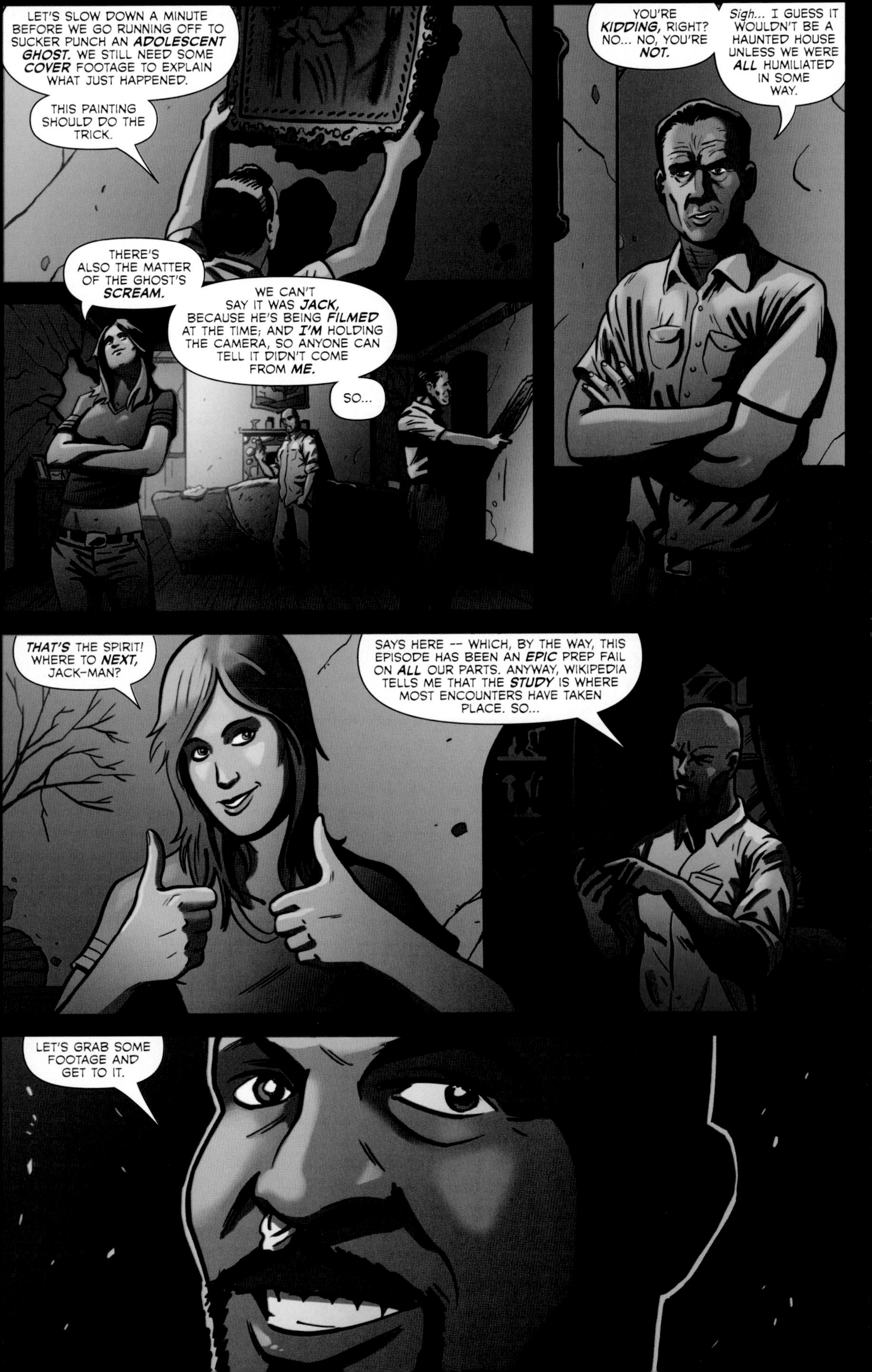
LET'S SLOW DOWN A MINUTE BEFORE WE GO RUNNING OFF TO SUCKER PUNCH AN *ADOLESCENT GHOST.* WE STILL NEED SOME *COVER* FOOTAGE TO EXPLAIN WHAT JUST HAPPENED.
THIS PAINTING SHOULD DO THE TRICK.
THERE'S ALSO THE MATTER OF THE GHOST'S *SCREAM.*
WE CAN'T SAY IT WAS *JACK,* BECAUSE HE'S BEING *FILMED* AT THE TIME; AND *I'M* HOLDING THE CAMERA, SO ANYONE CAN TELL IT DIDN'T COME FROM *ME.*
SO...
YOU'RE *KIDDING,* RIGHT? NO... NO, YOU'RE *NOT.*
Sigh... I GUESS IT WOULDN'T BE A HAUNTED HOUSE UNLESS WE WERE *ALL* HUMILIATED IN SOME WAY.
THAT'S THE SPIRIT! WHERE TO *NEXT,* JACK-MAN?
SAYS HERE -- WHICH, BY THE WAY, THIS EPISODE HAS BEEN AN *EPIC* PREP FAIL ON *ALL* OUR PARTS. ANYWAY, WIKIPEDIA TELLS ME THAT THE *STUDY* IS WHERE MOST ENCOUNTERS HAVE TAKEN PLACE. SO...
LET'S GRAB SOME FOOTAGE AND GET TO IT.

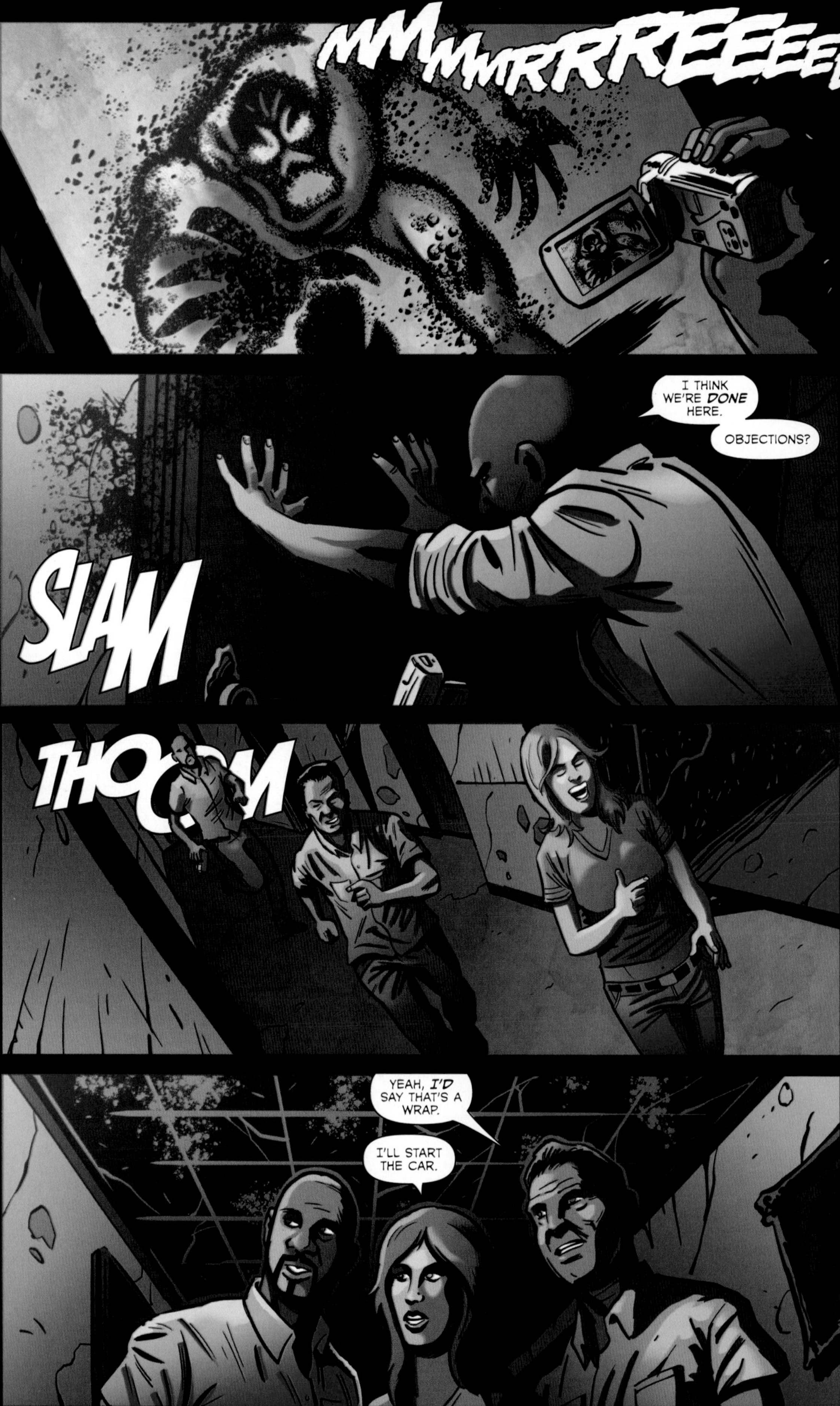
MMMMRRREEEEE
I THINK WE'RE *DONE* HERE.
OBJECTIONS?
SLAM
THOOM
YEAH, *I'D* SAY THAT'S A WRAP.
I'LL START THE CAR.

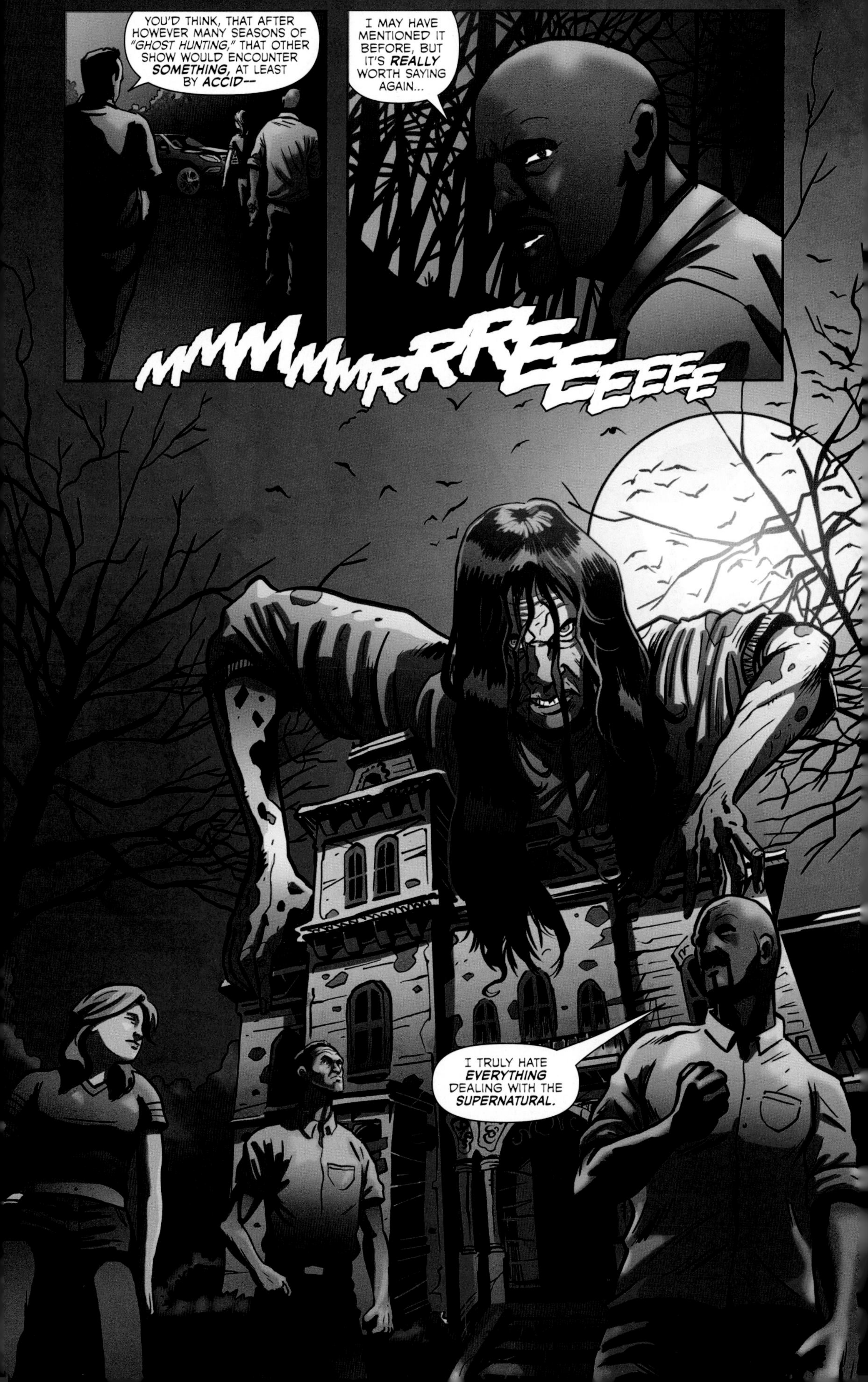
YOU'D THINK, THAT AFTER HOWEVER MANY SEASONS OF "GHOST HUNTING," THAT OTHER SHOW WOULD ENCOUNTER SOMETHING, AT LEAST BY ACCID--
I MAY HAVE MENTIONED IT BEFORE, BUT IT'S REALLY WORTH SAYING AGAIN...
MMMMMMRRREEEEEE
I TRULY HATE EVERYTHING DEALING WITH THE SUPERNATURAL.

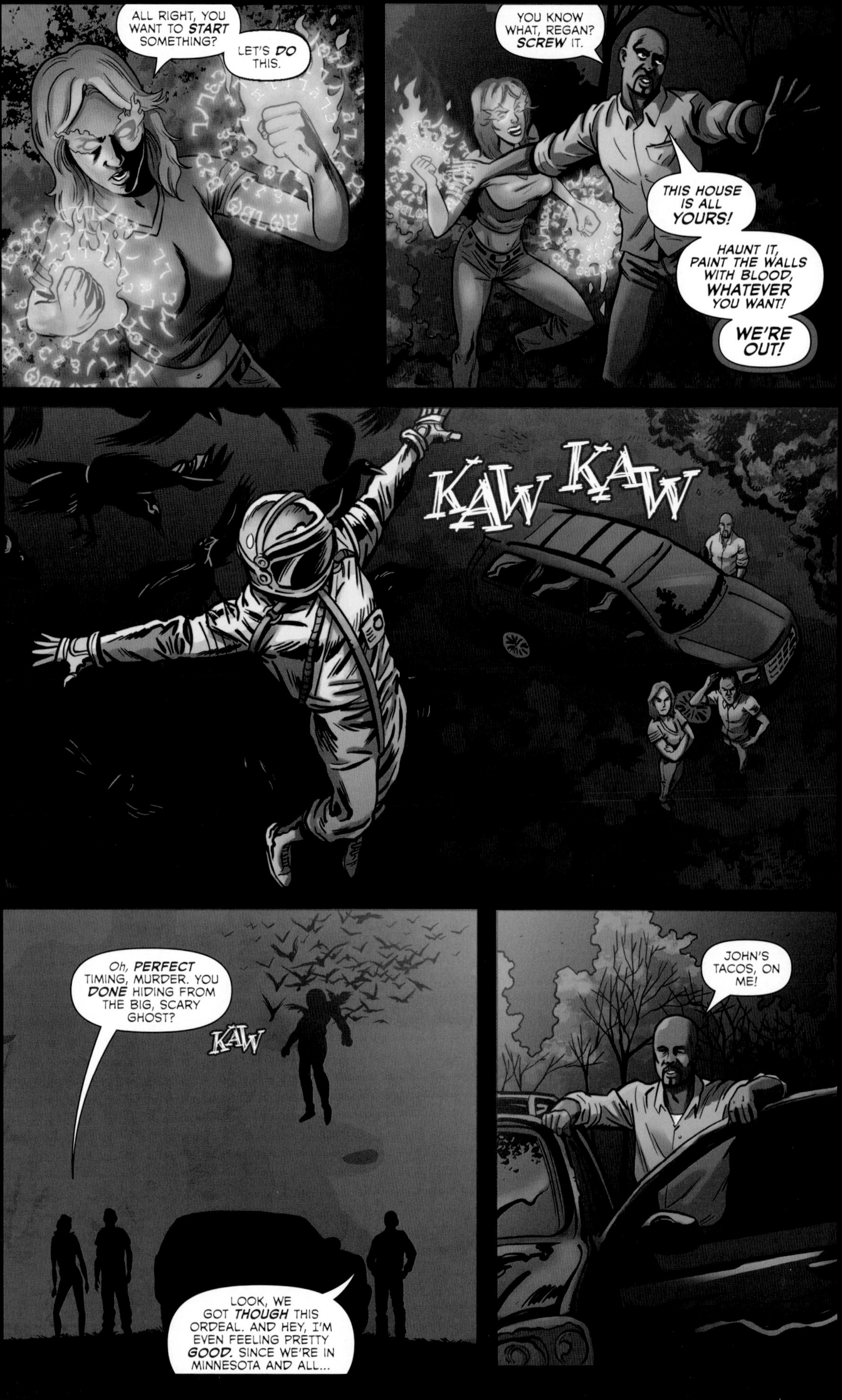
ALL RIGHT, YOU WANT TO START SOMETHING?
LET'S DO THIS.
YOU KNOW WHAT, REGAN? SCREW IT.
THIS HOUSE IS ALL YOURS!
HAUNT IT, PAINT THE WALLS WITH BLOOD, WHATEVER YOU WANT!
WE'RE OUT!
KAW KAW
Oh, PERFECT TIMING, MURDER. YOU DONE HIDING FROM THE BIG, SCARY GHOST?
KAW
LOOK, WE GOT THOUGH THIS ORDEAL. AND HEY, I'M EVEN FEELING PRETTY GOOD. SINCE WE'RE IN MINNESOTA AND ALL...
JOHN'S TACOS, ON ME!

HOAX HUNTERS

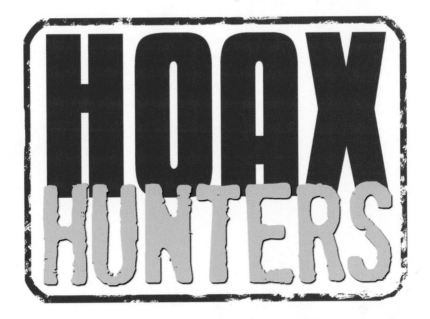

COVER GALLERY

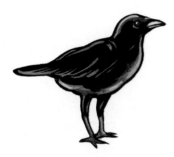

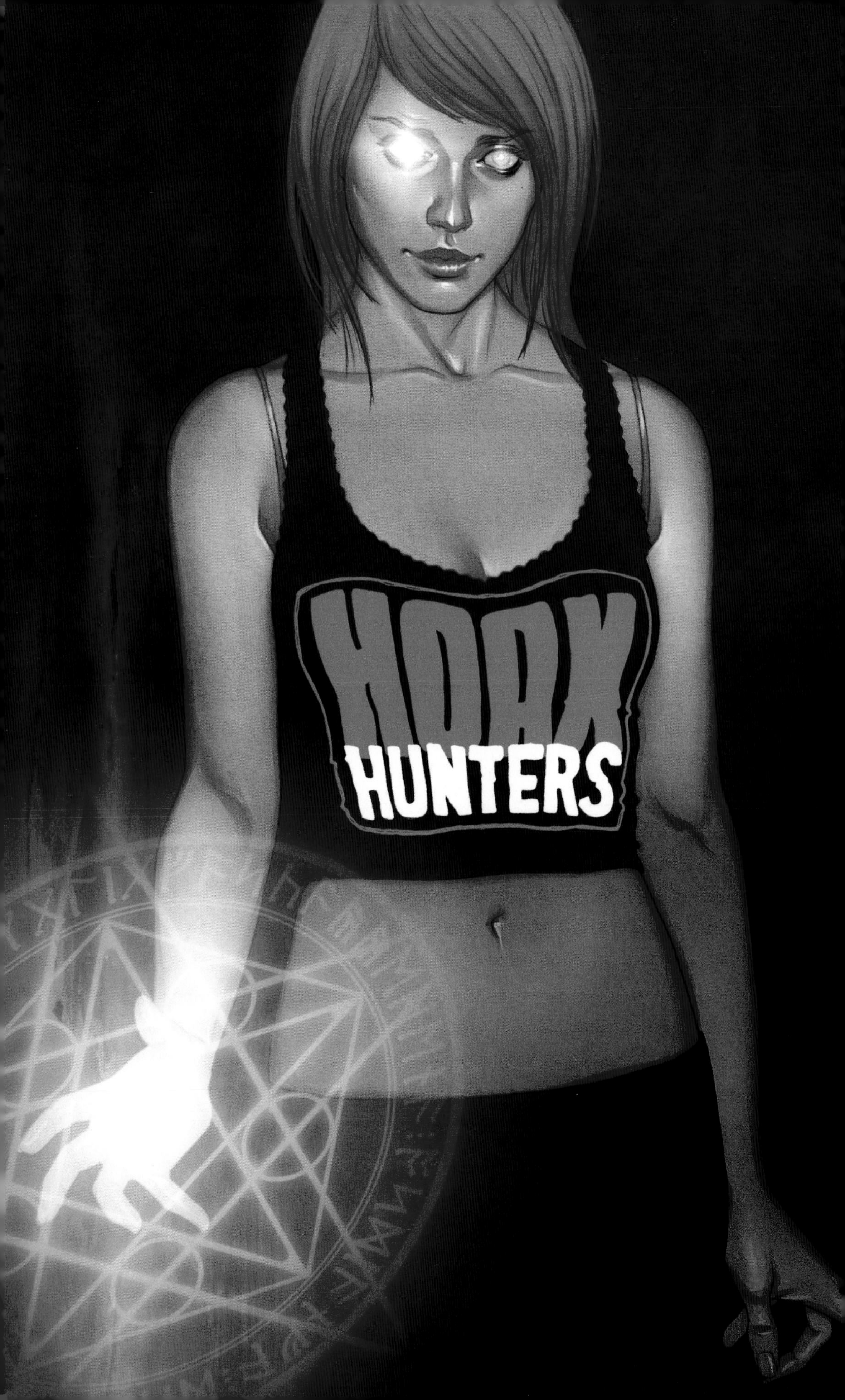
HOAX
HUNTERS

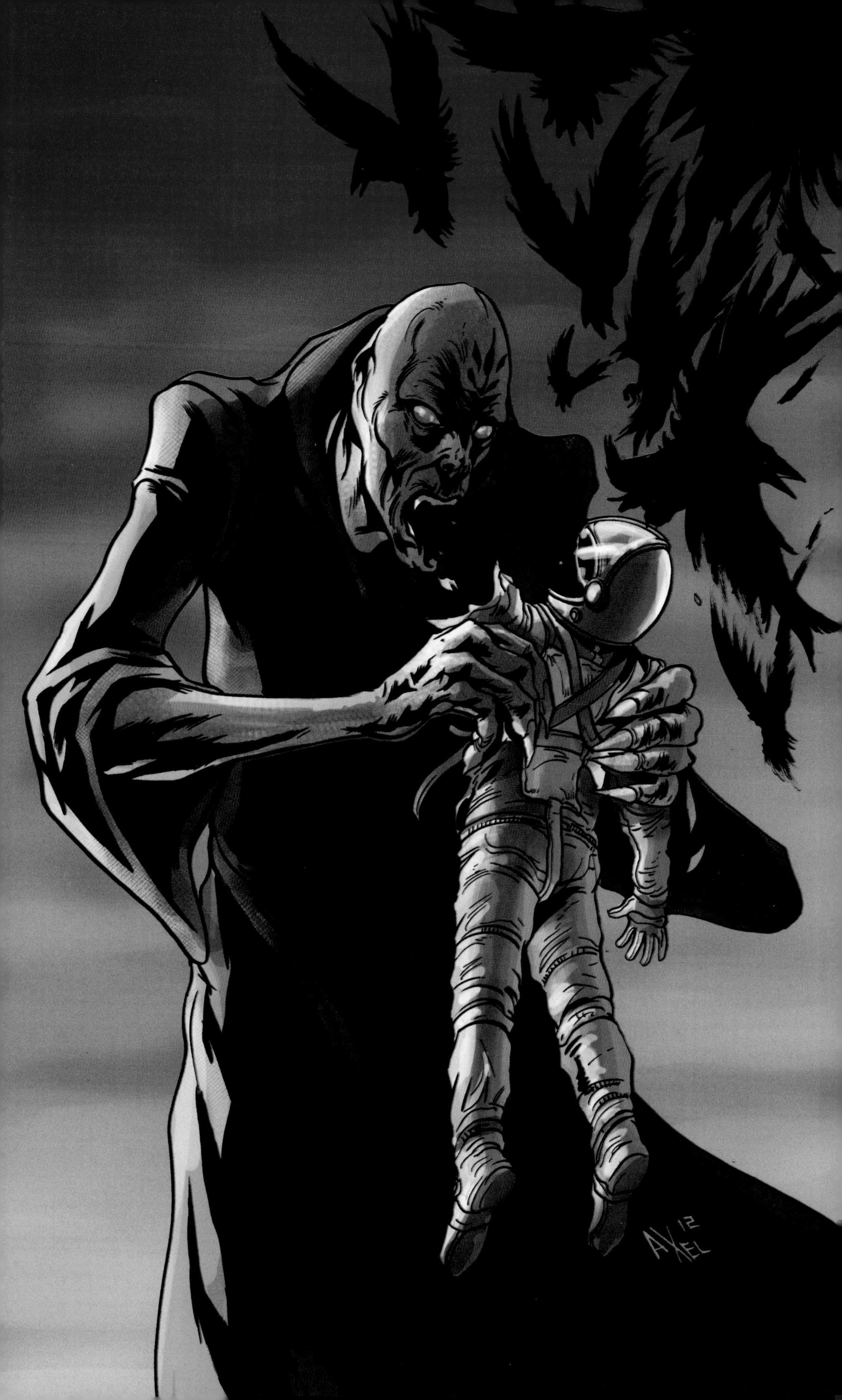
AXEL 12

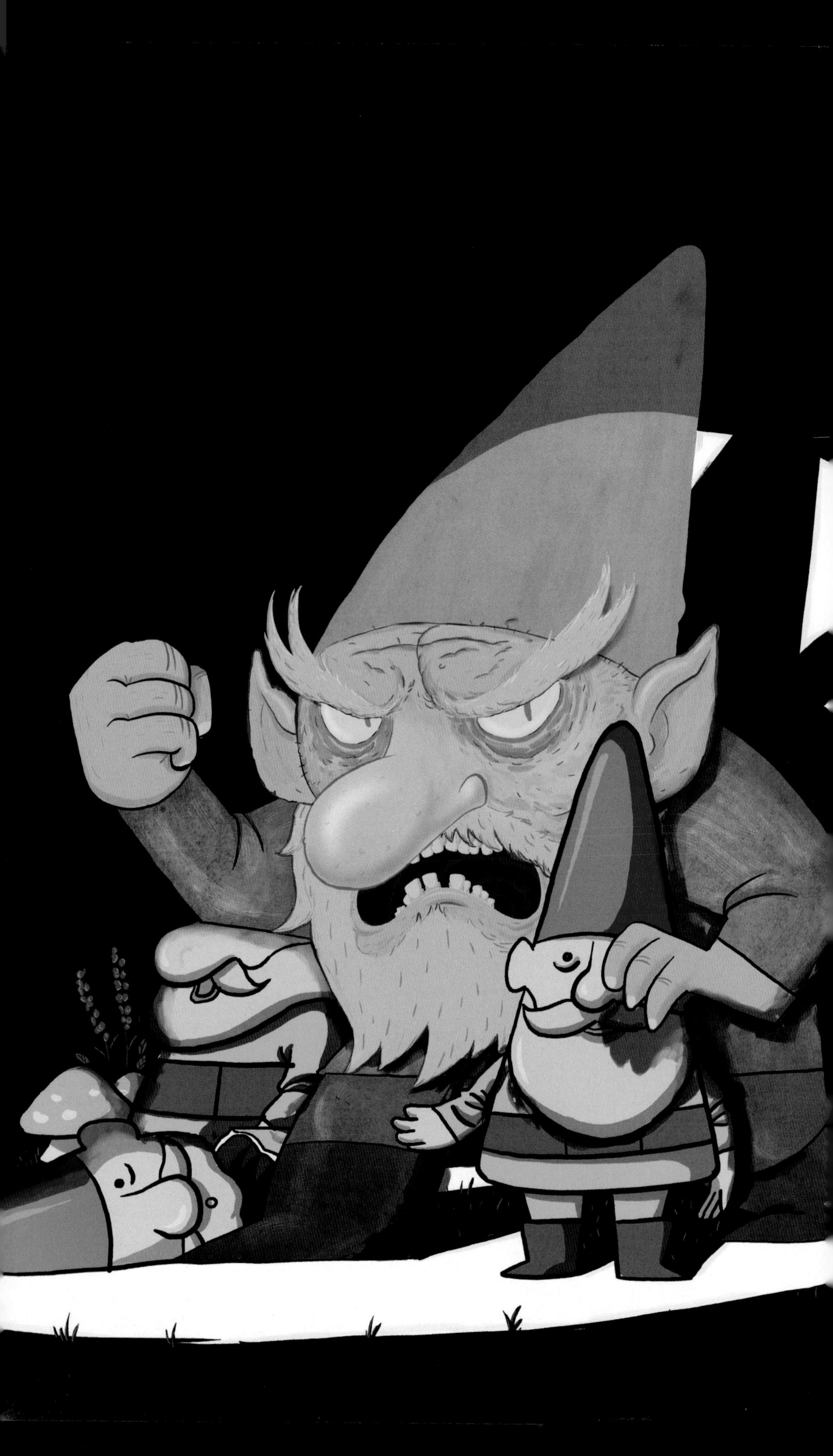

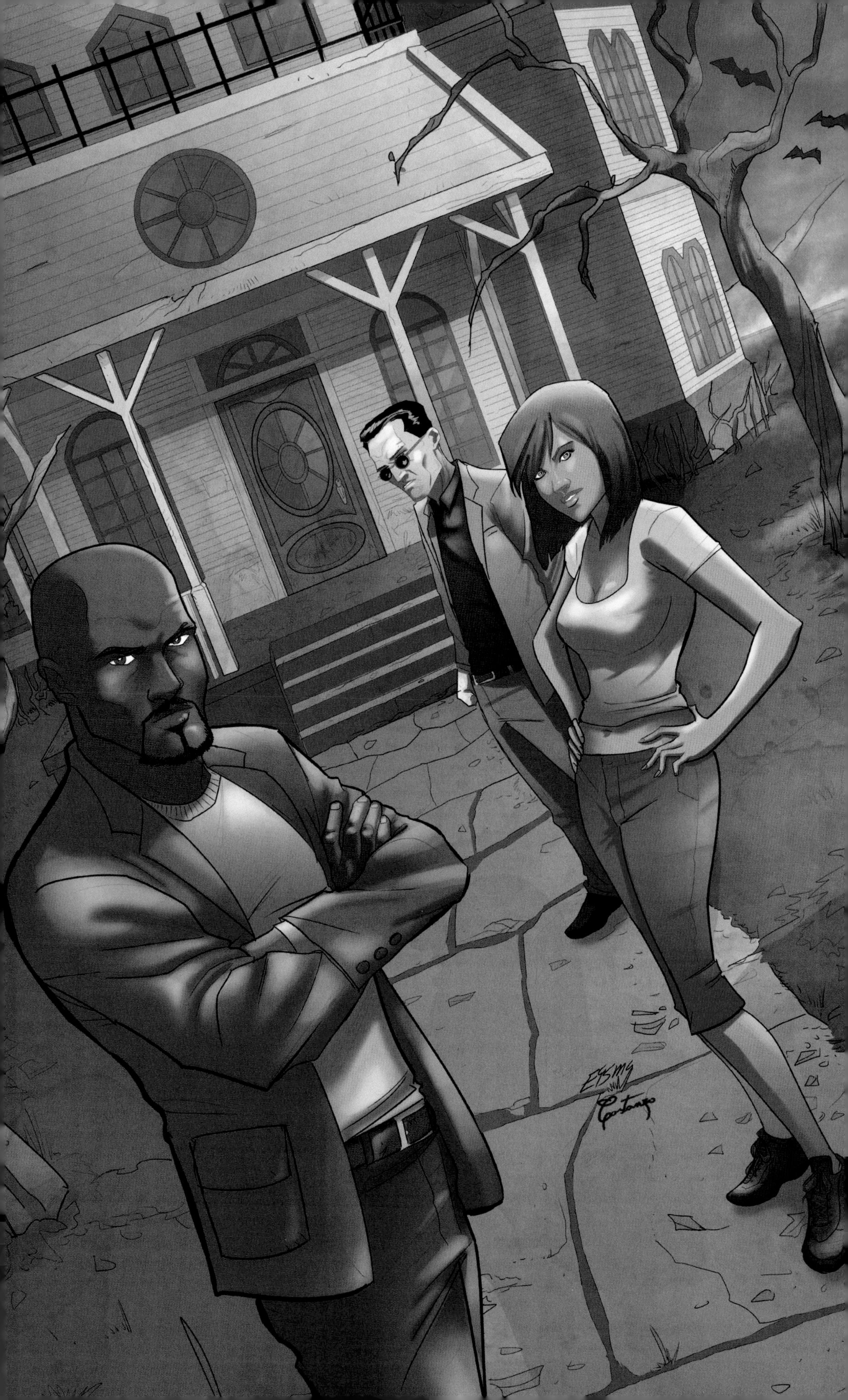

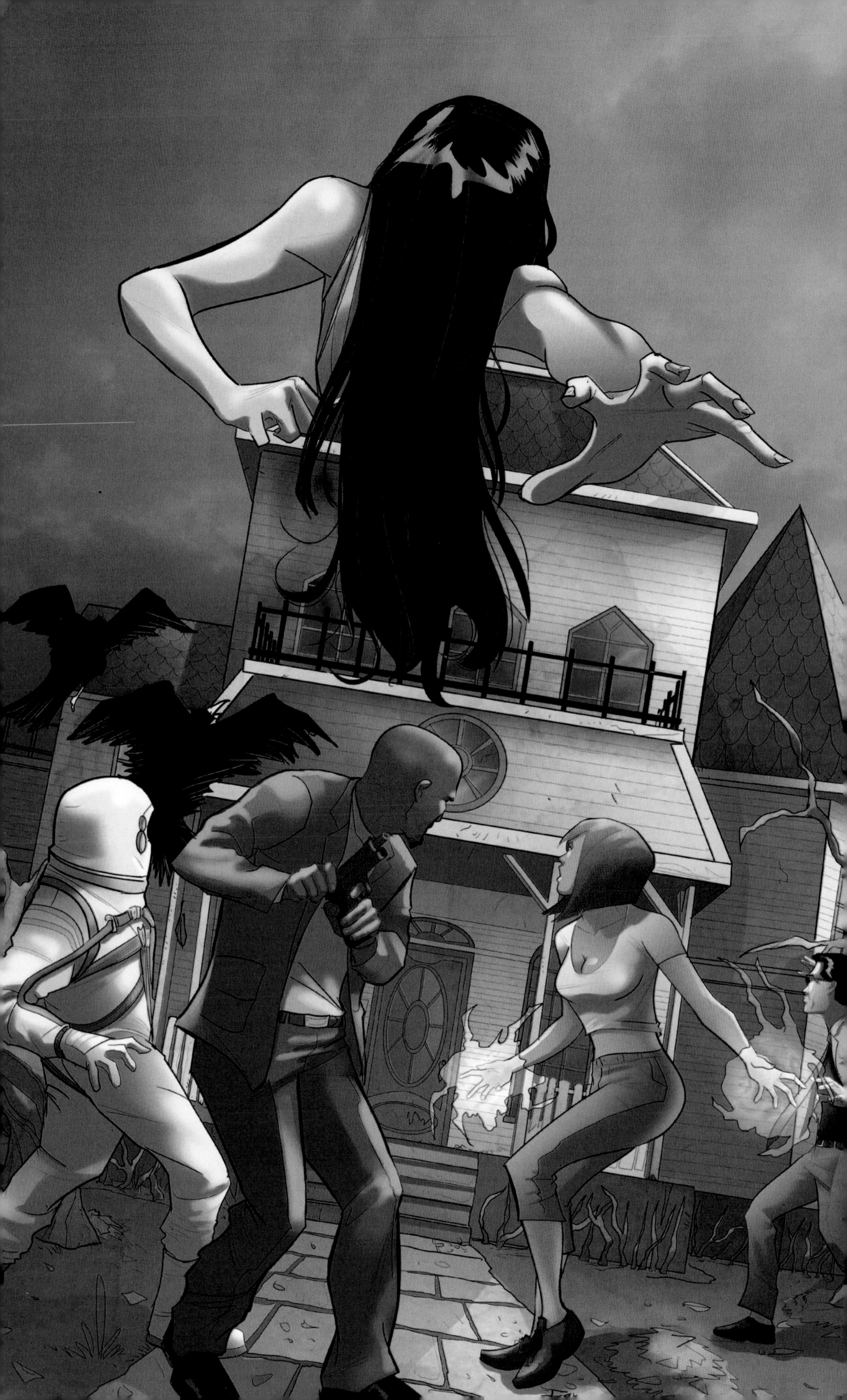

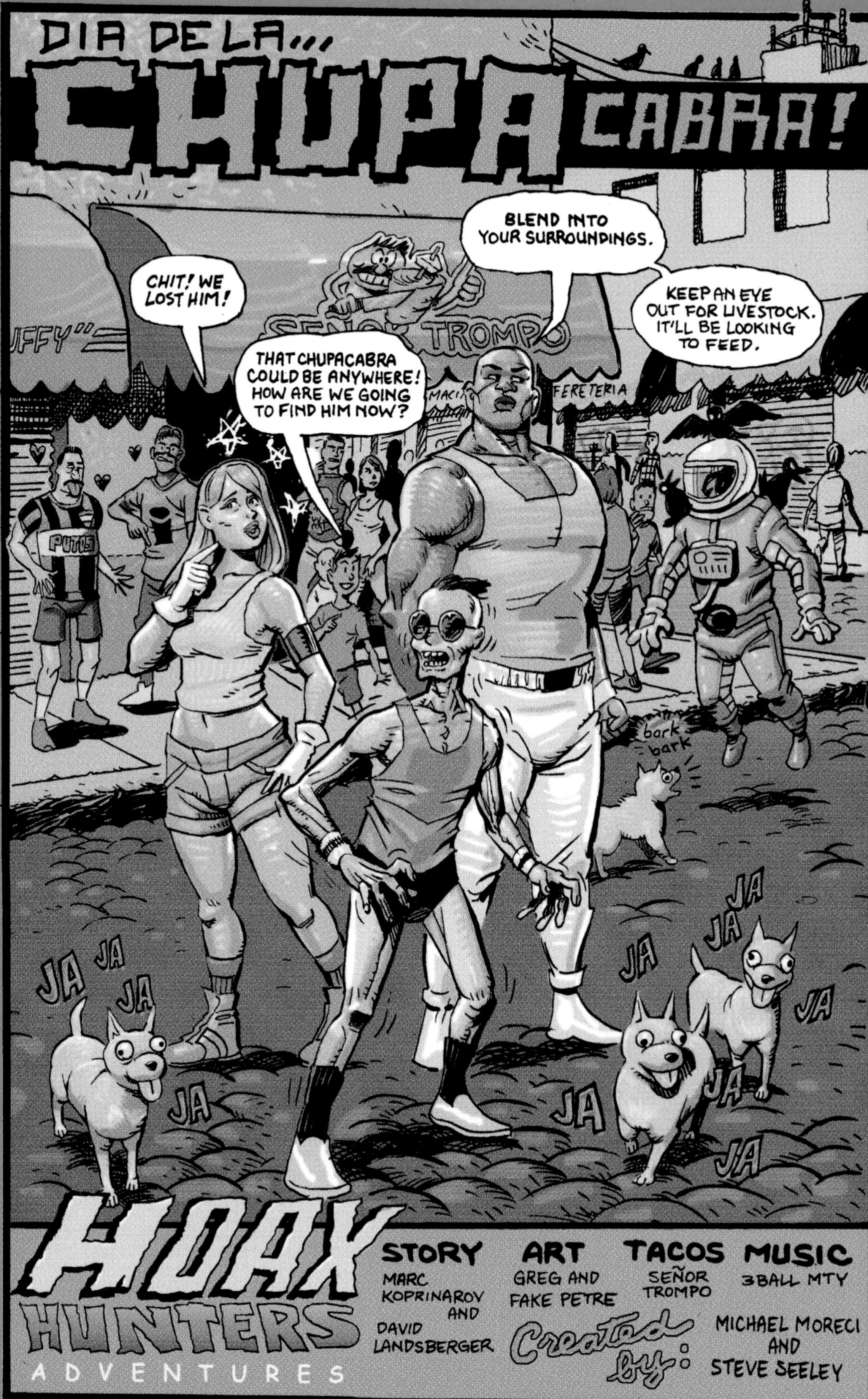
DIA DE LA...
CHUPA CABRA!
"UFFY"
SEÑOR TROMPO
MACI
FERETERIA
PUTOS
CHIT! WE LOST HIM!
THAT CHUPACABRA COULD BE ANYWHERE! HOW ARE WE GOING TO FIND HIM NOW?
BLEND INTO YOUR SURROUNDINGS.
KEEP AN EYE OUT FOR LIVESTOCK. IT'LL BE LOOKING TO FEED.
bark bark
JA JA JA JA
JA JA JA JA JA JA JA JA
HOAX HUNTERS ADVENTURES
STORY MARC KOPRINAROV AND DAVID LANDSBERGER
ART GREG AND FAKE PETRE
TACOS SEÑOR TROMPO
MUSIC 3BALL MTY
Created by: MICHAEL MORECI AND STEVE SEELEY

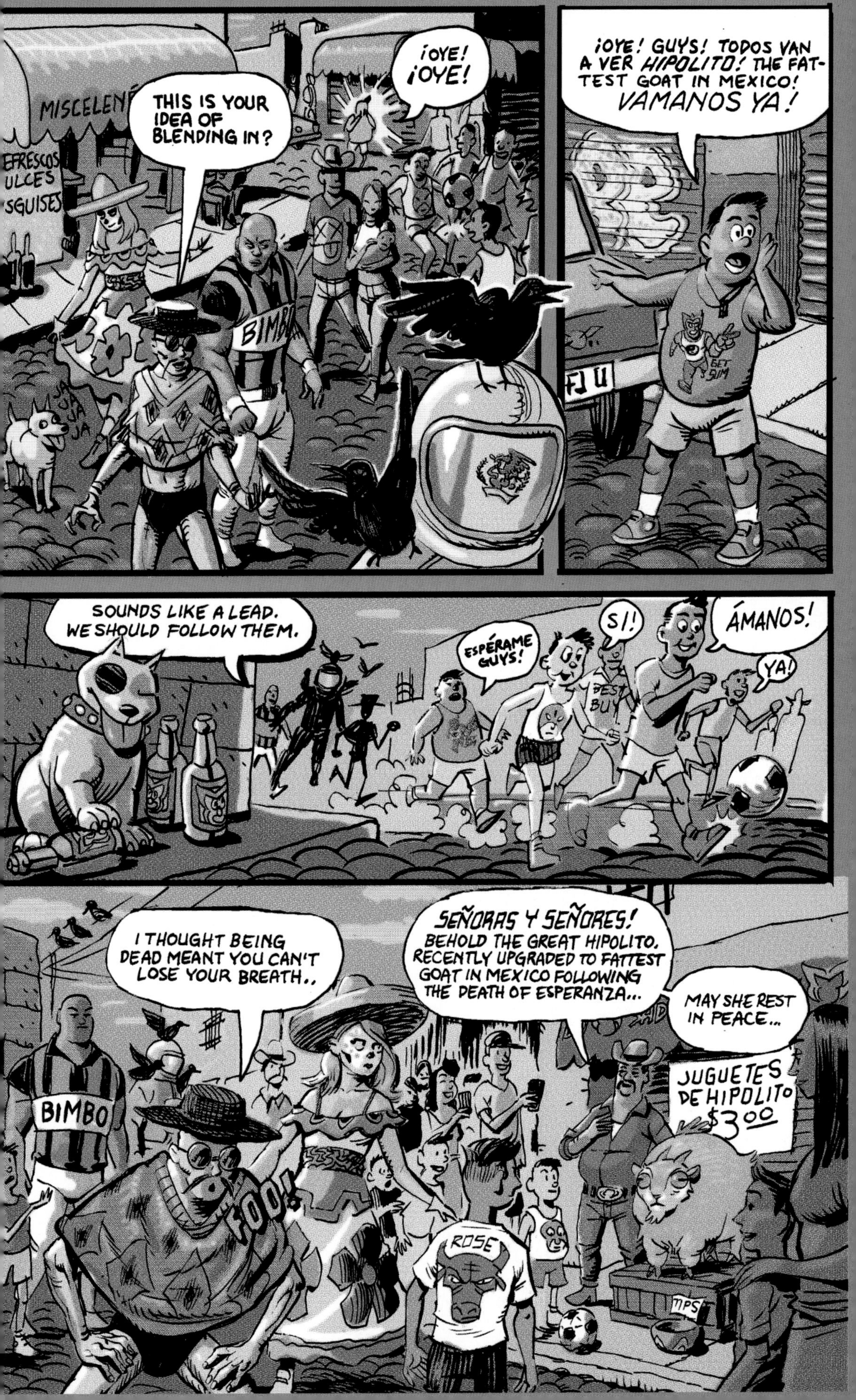
MISCELEN
EFRESCOS
ULCES
SGUISES
¡OYE! ¡OYE!
THIS IS YOUR IDEA OF BLENDING IN?
BIMBO
JA JA JA JA
¡OYE! GUYS! TODOS VAN A VER HIPOLITO! THE FATTEST GOAT IN MEXICO! VAMANOS YA!
GET SLIM
SOUNDS LIKE A LEAD. WE SHOULD FOLLOW THEM.
ESPÉRAME GUYS!
SI!
ÁMANOS!
YA!
BEST BUY
I THOUGHT BEING DEAD MEANT YOU CAN'T LOSE YOUR BREATH..
SEÑORAS Y SEÑORES! BEHOLD THE GREAT HIPOLITO. RECENTLY UPGRADED TO FATTEST GOAT IN MEXICO FOLLOWING THE DEATH OF ESPERANZA...
MAY SHE REST IN PEACE...
JUGUETES DE HIPOLITO $3.00
BIMBO
FOO!
ROSE
TIPS

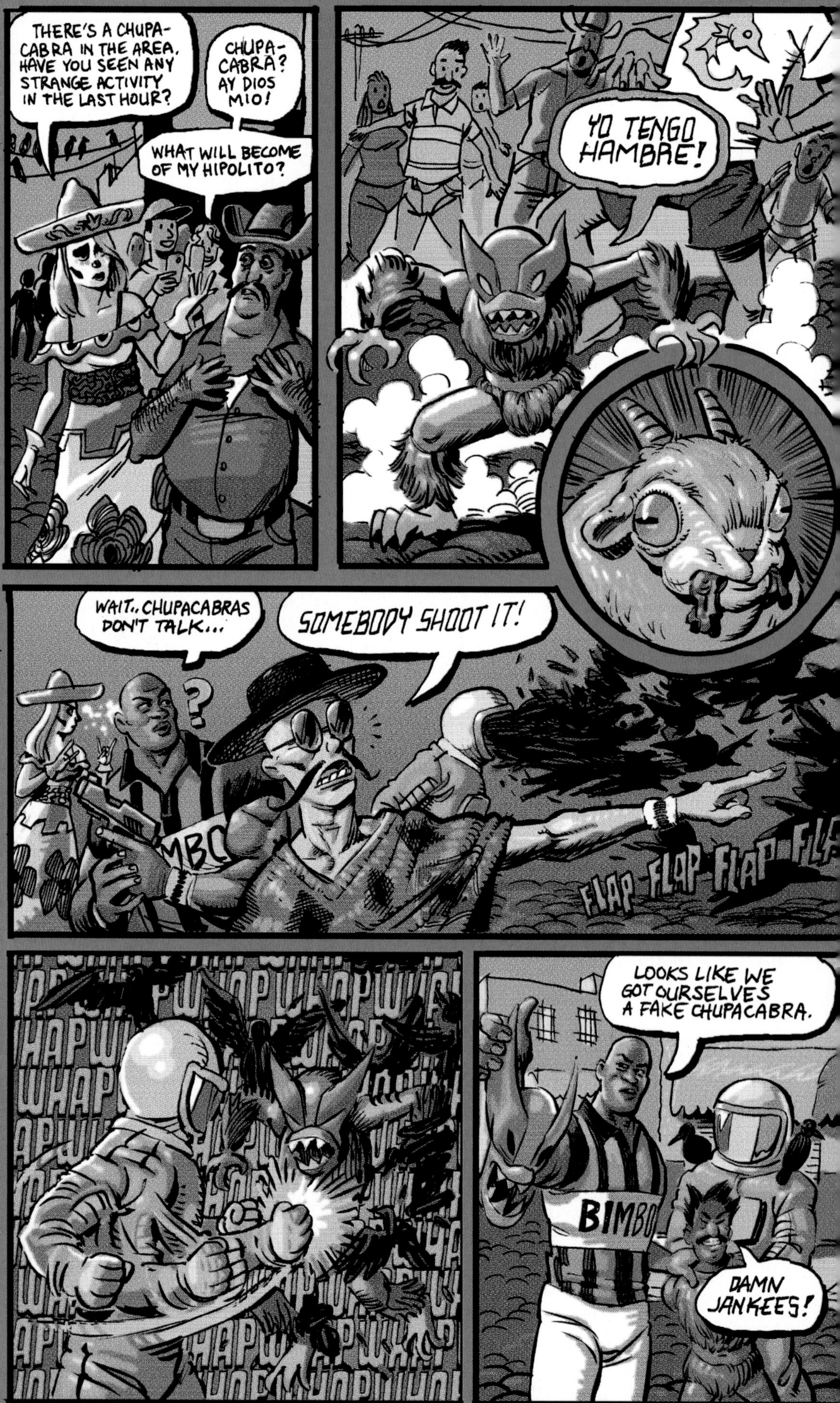
THERE'S A CHUPACABRA IN THE AREA. HAVE YOU SEEN ANY STRANGE ACTIVITY IN THE LAST HOUR?
CHUPACABRA? AY DIOS MIO!
WHAT WILL BECOME OF MY HIPOLITO?
YO TENGO HAMBRE!
WAIT.. CHUPACABRAS DON'T TALK...
SOMEBODY SHOOT IT!
MBC
FLAP FLAP FLAP FLA
LOOKS LIKE WE GOT OURSELVES A FAKE CHUPACABRA.
BIMBO
DAMN JANKEES!

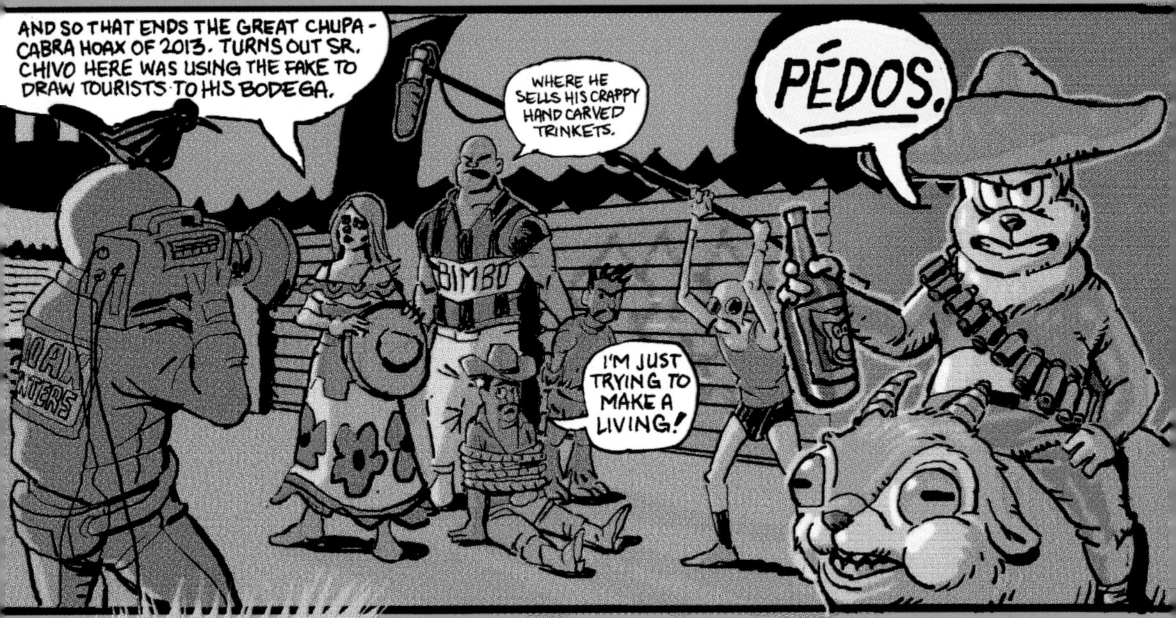
AND SO THAT ENDS THE GREAT CHUPA-CABRA HOAX OF 2013. TURNS OUT SR. CHIVO HERE WAS USING THE FAKE TO DRAW TOURISTS TO HIS BODEGA.
WHERE HE SELLS HIS CRAPPY HAND CARVED TRINKETS.
PÉDOS.
BIMBO
I'M JUST TRYING TO MAKE A LIVING!

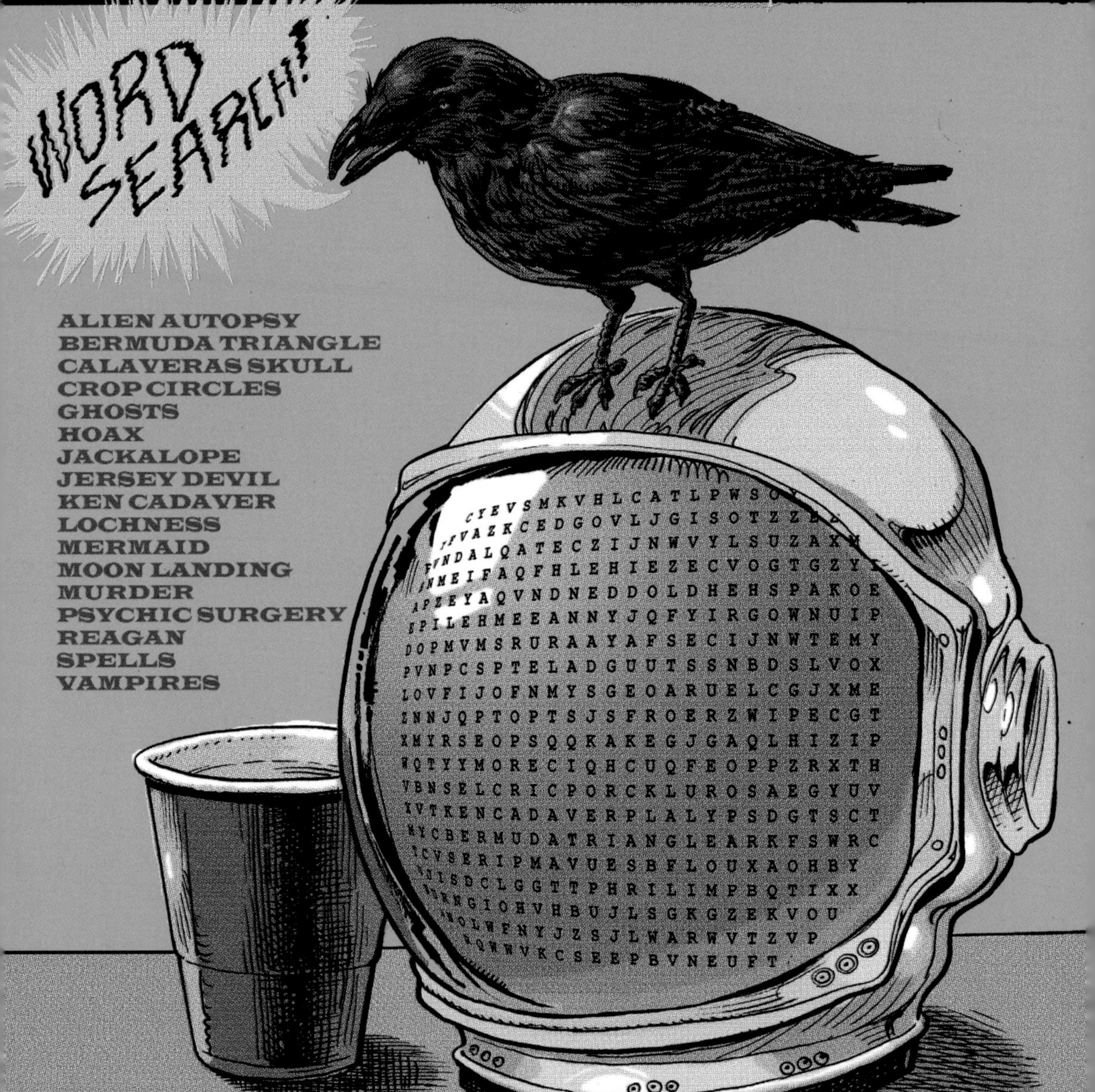
WORD SEARCH!

ALIEN AUTOPSY
BERMUDA TRIANGLE
CALAVERAS SKULL
CROP CIRCLES
GHOSTS
HOAX
JACKALOPE
JERSEY DEVIL
KEN CADAVER
LOCHNESS
MERMAID
MOON LANDING
MURDER
PSYCHIC SURGERY
REAGAN
SPELLS
VAMPIRES

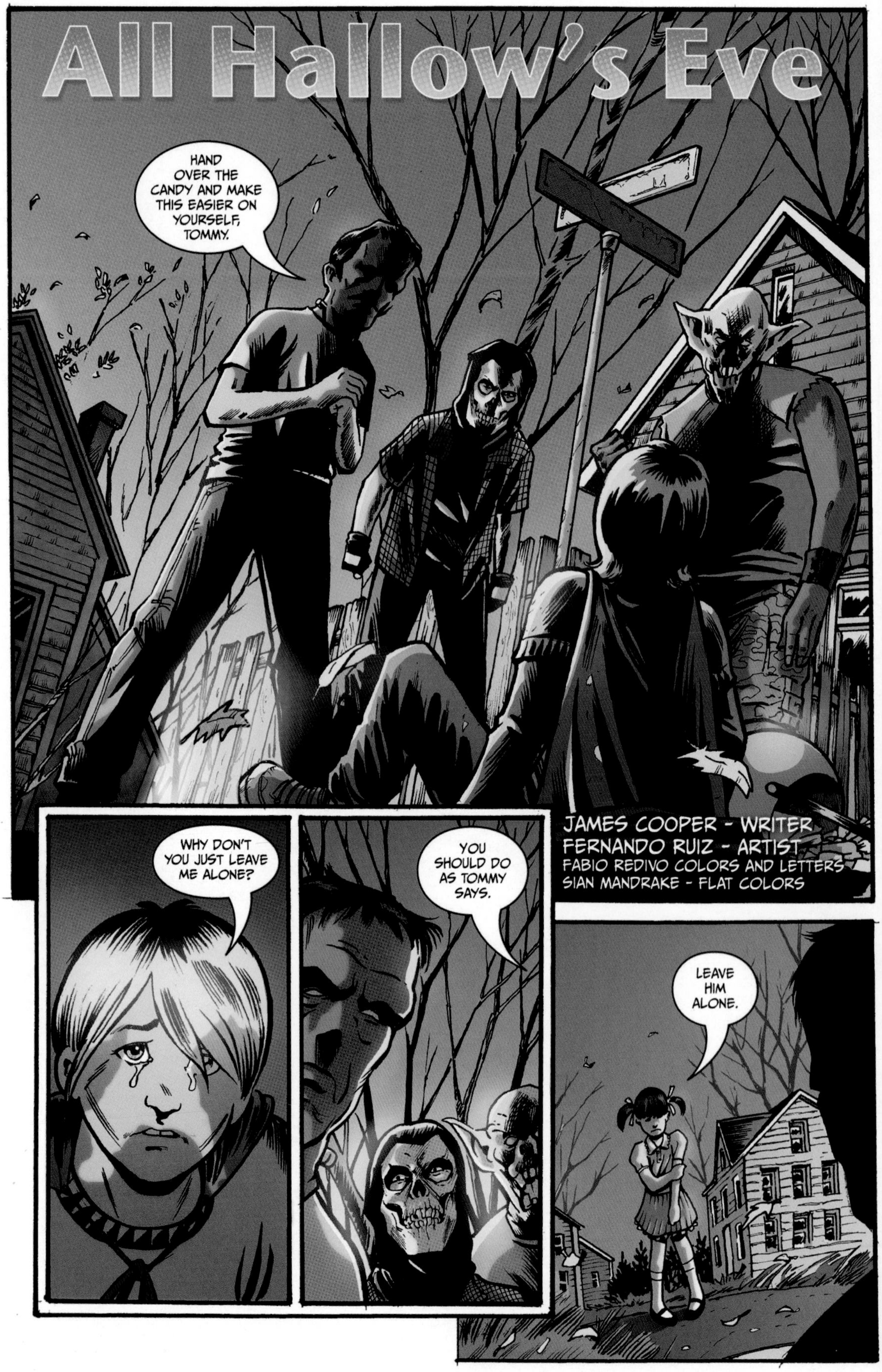

All Hallow's Eve
HAND OVER THE CANDY AND MAKE THIS EASIER ON YOURSELF, TOMMY.
JAMES COOPER - WRITER
FERNANDO RUIZ - ARTIST
FABIO REDIVO COLORS AND LETTERS
SIAN MANDRAKE - FLAT COLORS
WHY DON'T YOU JUST LEAVE ME ALONE?
YOU SHOULD DO AS TOMMY SAYS.
LEAVE HIM ALONE.

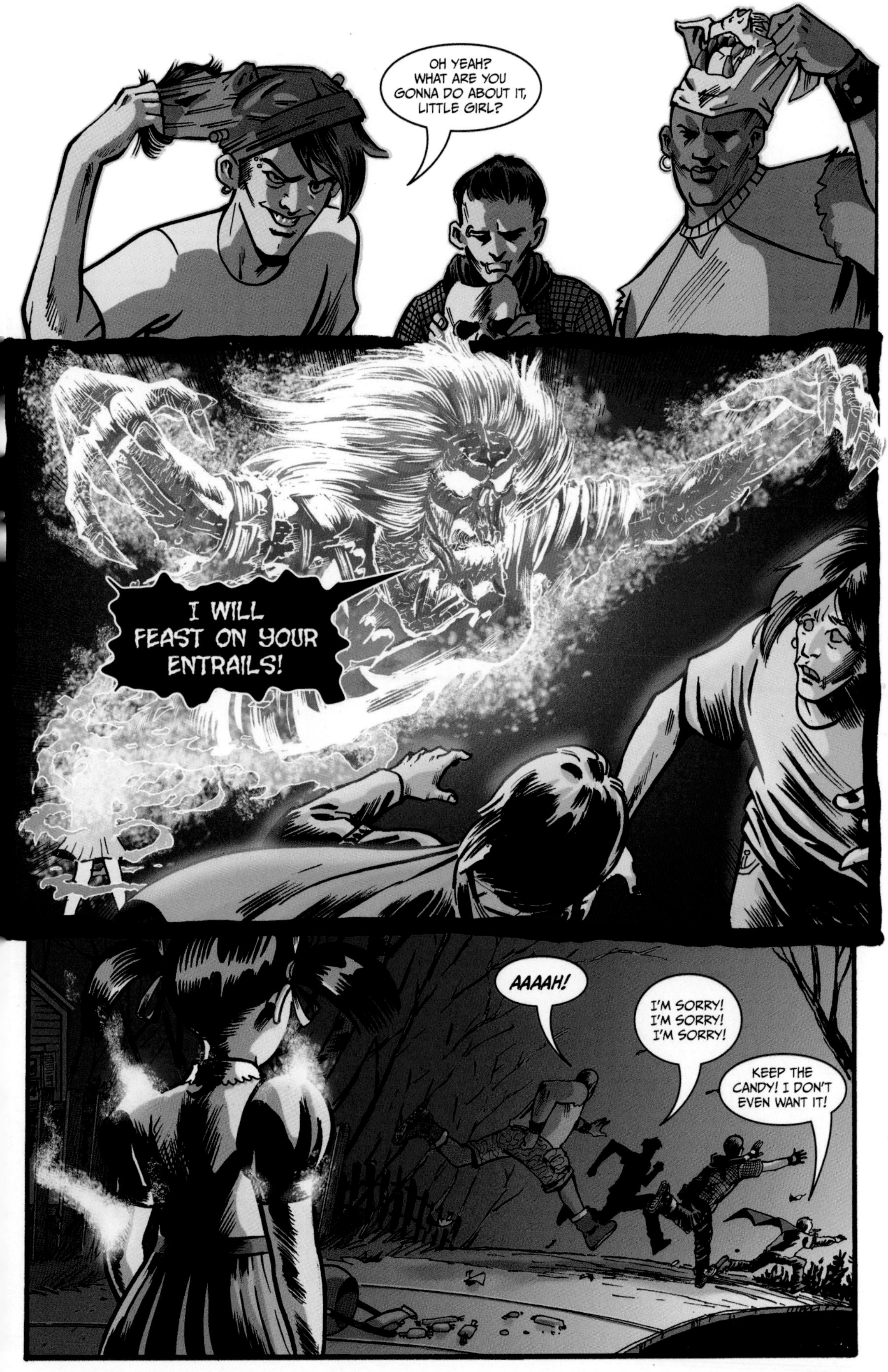
OH YEAH? WHAT ARE YOU GONNA DO ABOUT IT, LITTLE GIRL?
I WILL FEAST ON YOUR ENTRAILS!
AAAAH!
I'M SORRY! I'M SORRY! I'M SORRY!
KEEP THE CANDY! I DON'T EVEN WANT IT!

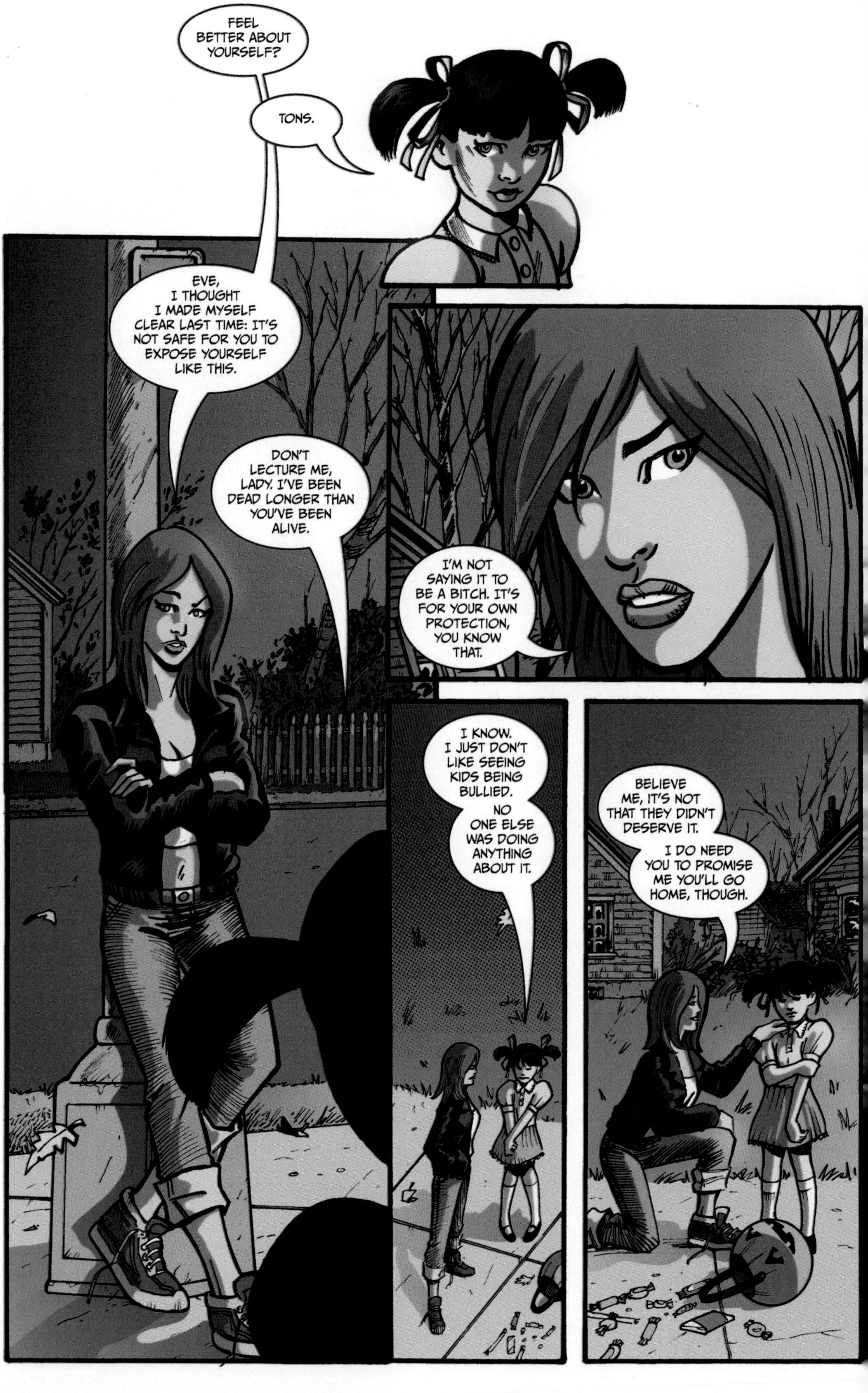
FEEL BETTER ABOUT YOURSELF?
TONS.
EVE, I THOUGHT I MADE MYSELF CLEAR LAST TIME: IT'S NOT SAFE FOR YOU TO EXPOSE YOURSELF LIKE THIS.
DON'T LECTURE ME, LADY. I'VE BEEN DEAD LONGER THAN YOU'VE BEEN ALIVE.
I'M NOT SAYING IT TO BE A BITCH. IT'S FOR YOUR OWN PROTECTION, YOU KNOW THAT.
I KNOW. I JUST DON'T LIKE SEEING KIDS BEING BULLIED.
NO ONE ELSE WAS DOING ANYTHING ABOUT IT.
BELIEVE ME, IT'S NOT THAT THEY DIDN'T DESERVE IT.
I DO NEED YOU TO PROMISE ME YOU'LL GO HOME, THOUGH.

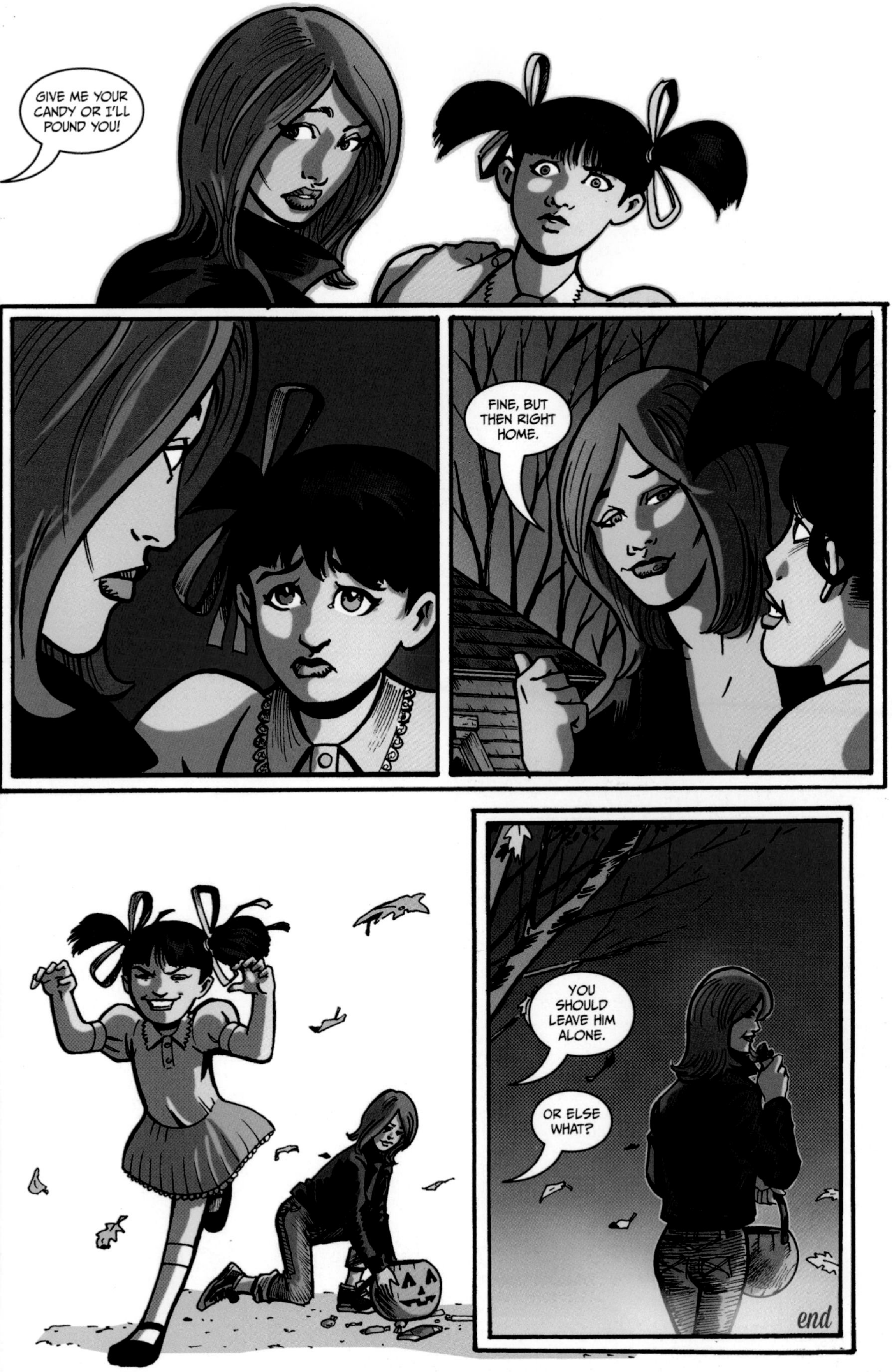
GIVE ME YOUR CANDY OR I'LL POUND YOU!
FINE, BUT THEN RIGHT HOME.
YOU SHOULD LEAVE HIM ALONE.
OR ELSE WHAT?
end

Surveillance File 8134b

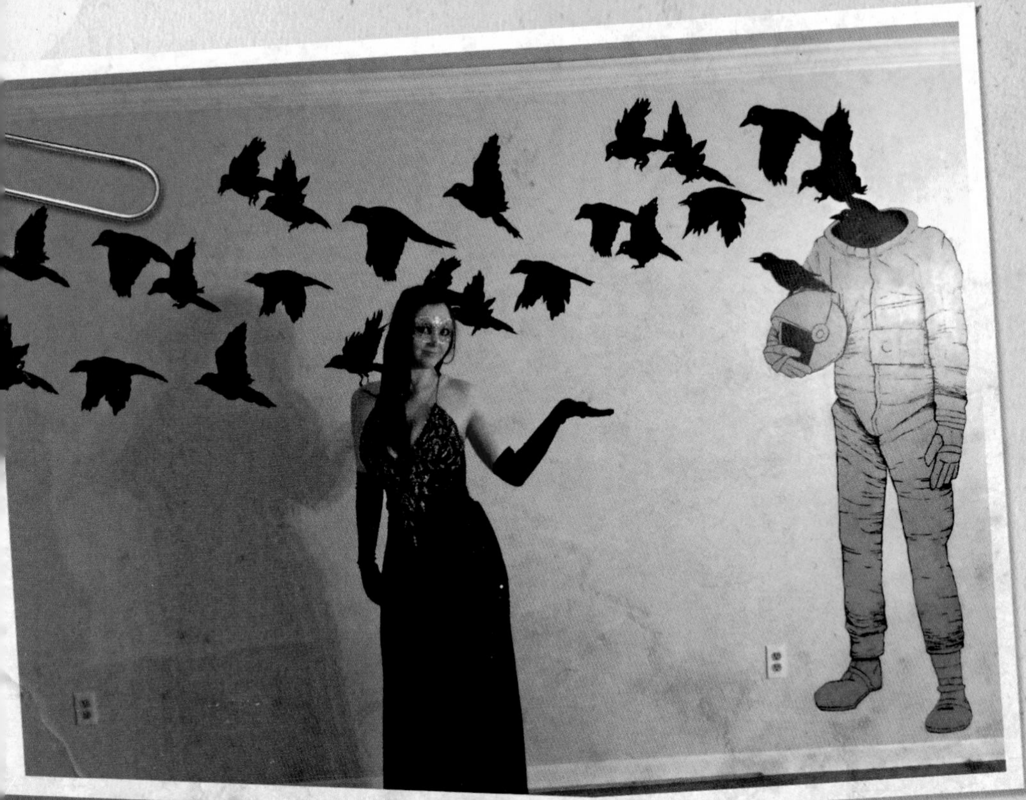

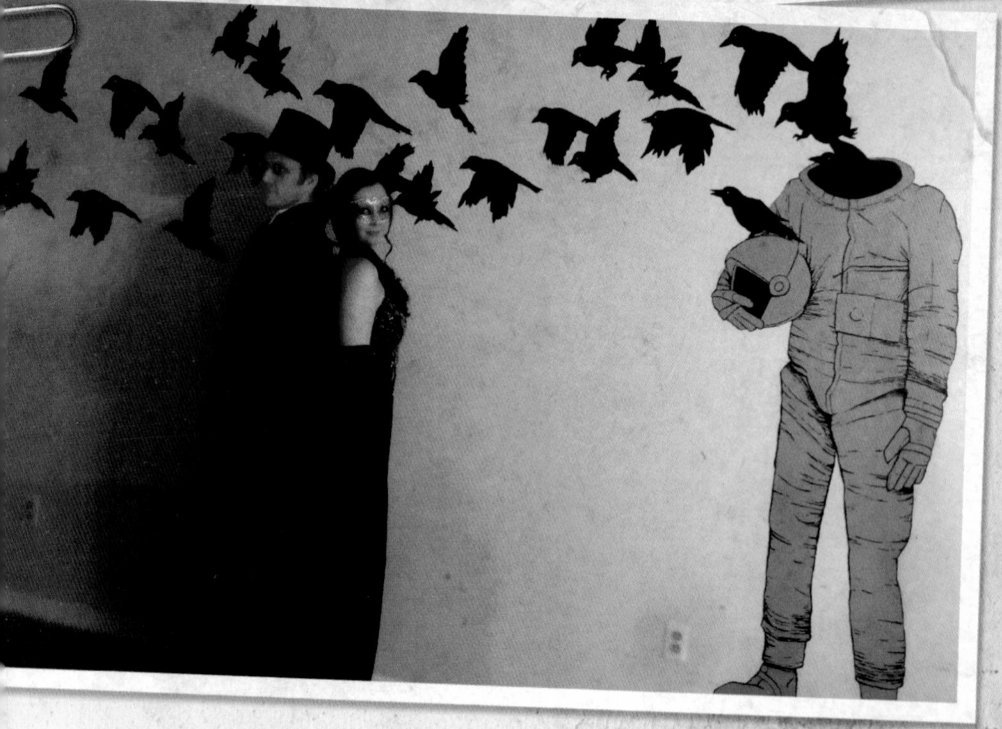

Photographic evidence suggests suspects 'Tony Sullivan' and 'Stephanie Wilson' have extensive knowledge of Operative codename 'Murder'. Accuracy of supposed 'mural' highly [redacted] suspicious.

Possible security breach? Further observation authorized.